Human Rights and Humanity's Rights During Year Three of the French Revolution

Eduardo Baker

Human Rights and Humanity's Rights During Year Three of the French Revolution

palgrave
macmillan

Eduardo Baker
Law
Pontifical Catholic University of Rio de
Rio de Janeiro, Brazil

ISBN 978-3-030-99507-2 ISBN 978-3-030-99508-9 (eBook)
https://doi.org/10.1007/978-3-030-99508-9

This Palgrave Macmillan imprint is published by the registered company Springer Nature Switzerland AG.
The registered company address is: Gewerbestrasse 11, 6330 Cham, Switzerland

Contents

CHAPTER 1

Introduction

How are we to do a political philosophy of law that is firmly anchored in History? How are we to think about law and the dynamics that it puts into motion in such a way as to better fulfill our desire for freedom and equality? These two questions—the first one about reasoning and the second one about what this reasoning entails—are the starting point for this book.

The initial intuition behind this work was to see the French Revolution as an event from which it would be possible to extract a whole framework of reflections, inquiries, and proposals about law within a context where social justice, democratic radicalization, and popular political participation were actively pursued goals. I believed that the way philosophy was practiced in the years between 1789 and 1799 would be a great tool to bring some relevant questions for our contemporary reflections on the different roles of law—be it its roles then or its roles now. This hypothesis did not seem so far-fetched, as the claim that the French Revolution was the birthplace, or at least one of the birthplaces, of contemporary human rights is widespread in legal literature, even if this idea is not often extensively developed.

However, my first readings on the subject pointed to a problem: philosophers of law, as a rule, did not provide readings of the French Revolution that were particularly careful in regard to its history. If we look at some of the main interpretations found within the domain of philosophy of law, we can detect a restricted frame of analysis, perhaps because they are trapped within a narrow historiographical purview.

E. Baker, *Human Rights and Humanity's Rights During Year Three of the French Revolution*,
https://doi.org/10.1007/978-3-030-99508-9_1

The immense richness of the French revolutionary experience thus disappears under the quill of law. Reduced to a few interpretative historiographical commonplaces, the French Revolution appears almost to be a mere allegory, a brief illustration to help think about other things. As a result, it risks becoming a single and monolithic block.

As I will show in the first chapter, even philosophers of law that explicitly set out to think about law as a tool for social change, toward a more just and egalitarian present, may repeat a reductionist reading of the Revolution. Exclusion, abstractionism, and nationalism would be, in this point of view, the trademarks of that French historical process.

But is it not possible to use those years of intense social mobilization to think about another political philosophy of law? The first challenge lies here. If we are to criticize a totalizing view of this historical phenomenon, it is important not to incur the same mistake; otherwise, we would simply be proposing yet another version of the same grand narrative. It is in this sense that this work is not purely historical; I do not aim to tell the historical truth of the French Revolution so that it may be appropriated by philosophy. My intention is to fish out of the stormy sea of the Revolution elements that may help us envisage a political philosophy of law that considers the values that the Revolution itself claimed to defend: freedom, equality, and, as we will see later, reciprocity.

The idea was to choose a precise time frame that would allow me to undertake a deeper analysis of the historical sources. The period chosen was the one-year period between 1792 and 1793 known as the Year 3 of the French Revolution or Year 1 on the Republic. For convenience, I will use simply "Year 3" when referring to the period.

More precisely, I focused on the drafts, proposals, and debates for a new declaration of rights and a new constitution that would mark the veritable end of the monarchical rule, of feudality, and the establishment of the French Republic, after Louis XVI and Marie Antoniette's trial and execution.

For this analysis, I make the assumption that popular participation in political processes is an important component in promoting freedom, equality, and democracy. Also, I believe that the knowledge produced in diverse social conflicts that were obliterated from collective memory may open up lines of interpretation that were abandoned or not yet discerned.

The Year 3 is one of the French revolutionary periods with the widest popular involvement. Not only were people in constant activity but also the reflections developed by some of the most important revolutionary actors were especially concerned with finding ways to change the life of those historically neglected by the French government: Robespierre and his idea of the right to existence, Marat and his radical outcry for equality, and the consolidation of an anti-colonial thought that stood against the violent conquest of other peoples.

This does not mean that other strands of thought were not active parts in the revolutionary debates. For example, the debate on the French expansionist war marked a split inside the Legislative Assembly. The disagreement extended also to other public spaces: inside the Jacobin club, Robespierre, not a congressman at the time, was one of the fiercest opponents of war, antagonizing with a large Jacobin group favorable to the conflict.

The 1792–1793 debate offers us yet a second advantage. By bringing together the debates on both the Declaration and Constitution, we have the opportunity to cover two distinct but complementary issues.

In Florence Gauthier's words, paraphrasing Robespierre, the Declaration was revolutionaries' Constitution.[1] The Declaration had the important role of consolidating the most fundamental issues regarding men and women, a reflection of the rights that could not be negotiated or relativized by the government. In the face of concrete injustices, the rights enunciated by the Declaration were not abstract constructs detached from the real world. Each right inscribed in the Declaration articulated itself with actual struggles of the French people for the liberty of humankind. The Declaration, including its drafts and debates, is, in this sense, a document that is closer to the political philosophy of law.

In contrast, the Constitution, as well as its drafts and debates, highlight a less strictly philosophical dimension, but one that is nonetheless important to help answer the second of our guiding questions. In contemporary terms, it is about the problem of institutionalization, that is, how to give shape to the State, the government, and society itself in order to accomplish the project of freedom and equality outlined in the Declaration.

This is not a minor topic when considering the French Revolution's political philosophy of right. For example, it is in the constitutional drafts that we find the different solutions proposed to the problem of guaranteeing the exercise of sovereignty. It is not mere theorizing on the subject of sovereignty, but a discussion on how to create concrete mechanisms and

[1] Florence Gauthier, *Triomphe et Mort de la révolution des droits de l'homme et du citoyen* (Paris: Syllepse, 2014), 32.

institutions that may accomplish it. The problem of how to secure rights, be it by the people in deliberation or by using the legal form, will permeate the revolutionary process—throughout Year 3 and all the way until at least the Thermidorian period.

This does not mean that I intend to uncover some hidden French Revolution magical formula lost to time. My aim here is to map a theoretical and practical field of possibilities, a sort of historical laboratory devoted to thinking a political philosophy of law that is committed to the French revolutionary values and also to contemporary concerns over social justice and democratic radicalization.

With regard to the 1793 debates, the immense richness of this historical source remains mostly forgotten in the archives. There is little published work about the drafts—and almost none in English. Most of the published work focuses on a specific topic or a limited number of drafts—with the notable exception of Nathalie Ollivier's doctoral thesis.[2]

More recently, some historiographical developments have explored the idea of a philosophy of modern natural law, to use the term coined by Florence Gauthier. Alongside the French historian, other authors, such as Marc Belissa and Yannick Bosc, have been focusing on the place of law and rights within the scope of the French Revolution, highlighting its more strictly revolutionary aspects. In a way, this is the main hermeneutic framework through which we will read these revolutionary phenomena.

Following the footsteps of Mathiez and Soboul, as Gauthier says, these historians argue for a positive contribution of the popular movement, be it rural or urban, to the way the Revolution unfolded, while, at the same time, emphasizing the concerns and yearnings for justice, freedom, and equality of the Revolution itself and the way law was a part of such process.

It is within this tradition that we can find a discussion of the right to existence and a popular economic program, both against physiocratic economic liberalism and political despotism: of a cosmopolitics of freedom against the colonialist defense of the violent control of American and African peoples and against defending wars of conquest; of active sovereignty by the people against strategies of aristocratic representation and passive citizenship; of an egalitarian liberalism rooted in humankind's nature against the alleged natural inequality among men.

[2] Nathalie Ollivier, "Les Projets Constitutionnels de 1793," PhD diss. (Université Panthéon-Assas, 2002).

In Chap. 2, I will focus on the trend mentioned in this introduction, which tends to read the French Revolution as a monolithic bloc. After presenting the ways the Revolution is portrayed in works on human rights by prominent philosophers from various political affiliations such as Habermas, Rawls, Meister, and Baxi, I will focus on two authors. The works of Greek philosopher of law Costas Douzinas and US historian of human rights Samuel Moyn—both representing almost diametrically opposed ideological views on human rights—will be the object of particular scrutiny.

Also in Chap. 2, I will present some of the issues which may arise when interpreting the French Revolution and how they can be traced to a specific kind of historiography that is more hindering than helpful when trying to get to the essence of this event. I will also focus more directly on the relation between law and revolution, and propose a reflection on the historiography of the philosophy of modern natural law.

After a brief presentation of the primary source materials, it will be time to properly plunge into the archive (see Chap. 3) and start reading and analyzing the texts and debates surrounding the 1793 Declaration and Constitution drafting procedures. Chapter 4 will discuss the topic of external relations and their relation to the different approaches to the sovereignty of the peoples during Year 3, as they are reflected in the constitutional drafts and text—for example, regarding the people's role in declaring war.

Chapters 5 and 6 will discuss how the government is organized. Chapter 5 will present the different proposals and reflections on the role assigned to the Executive and other administrative bodies. This also includes the Judiciary since, as we will see, the idea of a separate Judiciary branch was not yet found in the revolutionaries' political thought, as the Judiciary was only a function within the power wielded by Executive bodies. Regarding the subject of the Judiciary or the Executive and its administrative bodies, special care will be given to the place assigned to the people in organizing and controlling these bodies.

The Legislature will be the subject of Chap. 6: how it is formed, how it is controlled, and how the constitutional text can be amended. Likewise, I will focus on the relation between the Legislature, its actions, and the people—highlighting the idea of popular sanction of laws and of citizen's control over the Legislature, both topics which were dear to the revolutionaries.

In Chap. 7, I will discuss the different ideas on the subject of republicanism and citizenship found in the drafts and debates and how they connect to the topics covered up to this point. In a way, concepts of the Republic and of citizenship help coalesce and sum up the questions and concerns raised and discussed so far. External relations, the Executive, the Legislature, and other analyzed subjects inform the revolutionaries' idea of the Republic and of citizenship, in the same way these last two permeate the reflections on the first three.

The order of the chapters follows, if not too rigidly, the usual order adopted by the studied drafts, but it is possible to summarize seven more closely philosophical issues that will accompany us throughout this exploration: a monolithic interpretation of the French Revolution versus a popular and radical historiography; Revolution versus History; the problem of abstractionism; atomization and individualism; nationalism and the Nation-State; sovereignties; and right, law, and "legicentrism."

In the concluding remarks, I will return to the questions raised in the first chapter and contrast them with the reasonings developed in the other chapters. By doing so, I hope to present a possible political philosophy for thinking about law, as well as its promises and accomplishments. The main focus will be on the ways that body of texts can be used to think about a political philosophy of law that stems from the French Revolution while keeping its promise to recognize the central role that the individuals who are historically excluded from political, economic, and social processes are to play in developing law and institutional frameworks committed to extending freedoms and promoting equality.

In sum, a political philosophy of law that does not have History as a mere starting point, but as a space for immersing oneself in the production of knowledge. A historical-political philosophy of law that opens up hermeneutic possibilities against anti-political and totalizing philosophies of history and law.

References

Gauthier, Florence. *Triomphe et Mort de la Révolution des Droits de l'Homme et du Citoyen*. Paris: Éditions Syllepse, 2014.

Ollivier, Nathalie. *Les Projets Constitutionnels de 1793*. PhD Diss. Université Panthéon-Assas, 2002.

CHAPTER 2

Thinking the French Revolution (and Law)

2.1 The French Revolution and the Uses of History

As I've already mentioned in this book's introduction, this work walks a not-so-fine line between History and Philosophy. In the words of Pierre Rosanvallon: "History is both the matter and the form of political philosophy."[1]

We are less interested here in a genealogy of (human) rights dating back to the French Revolution, and more in what we can excavate from that historical moment, in order to help us think of other perspectives for today's discourse on rights. In this sense, it is less important to assess who would be right in the historiographical debate. Instead, the focus should be on which interpretations make the best use of the potential present in the historical sources of the contemporary debate.

This chapter aims to work through the different forms that the law stemming from and in the Revolution has been read, especially in the domains of History and Philosophy.

As a starting point, I will borrow Paula Spieler's approach to human rights conceptions. She establishes a distinction between a hegemonic

[1] Pierre Rosanvallon, *La Démocratie Inachevée: Histoire de la Souveraineté du Peuple en France* (Paris: Gallimard, 2000), 37. Unless otherwise noted, all translations from non-English texts are mine.

E. Baker, *Human Rights and Humanity's Rights During Year Three of the French Revolution*,
https://doi.org/10.1007/978-3-030-99508-9_2

conception of human rights and a critical conception.[2] The first group would include, among others, Jürgen Habermas, John Rawls, Fábio Konder Comparato, and James Griffin. The second group, Upendra Baxi, Robert Meister, and José-Manuel Barreto.

Among Habermas' works, we find four main texts that establish a connection between human rights and the French Revolution: *The Philosophical Discourse of Modernity* (1990), *Between Facts and Norms* (1996), *The Inclusion of the Other* (1998), and a paper titled "The Concept of Human Dignity and the Realistic Utopia of Human Rights" (2010).[3]

With few exceptions, Habermas makes little use of historical or historiographical research. His main source of inspiration in reading the revolutionary phenomenon seems to be authors from the domains of Philosophy, Politics, or Theory of History, such as Kant, Hegel, Brubaker, Schulze, and Koselleck, to name a few.[4] Only in his 1996 book can we find any direct reference to a historian of the Revolution, and the only mentions are of François Furet and Denis Richet. We will discuss further below

[2] Paula Bartolini Spieler, "*Direitos Humanos como Discurso Emancipatório? O Caso das ONGs que Atuam no Brasil*," PhD diss. (Universidade do Estado do Rio de Janeiro, 2014). Paula Spieler, "Direitos humanos como discurso emancipatório? O caso das ONGs que atuam no Brasil," Doctoral diss. (UERJ, 2014).

[3] Chapter 3 of his 1971 *Theorie und Praxis*, with an abridged version published in English in 1974, discusses Hegel's interpretation of the French Revolution and, only indirectly, also the Revolution. Since its focus is not on the Revolution itself, I did not include it in the list. Even so, the critique that follows could be equally applied to this text, if our focus is his reading of the French Revolution and not Hegel's position.

[4] Koselleck's case is especially interesting. In his text *Critique and Crisis*, the one Habermas analyses, Koselleck mentions Cochin and exclusively German historians, such as Adalbert Wahl. Cochin is one of Furet's main "discoveries," as we will see later on. Regarding Wahl, his book on the French Revolution is only available in German: *Geschichte des europäischen Staatensystems im Zeitalter der französischen Revolution und der Freiheitskriege* (1992)—which can be translated as "History of the European State System during the Era of the French Revolution and the Liberation Wars." However, a footnote in Lefebvre's book gives us an indication of which historiographical interpretation is adopted by Wahl, and presumably also by Koselleck and, finally, by Habermas: "Heinrich von Sybel, in *Geschichte der Revolutionszeit* (5 vols., Düsseldorf, 1853–1879), and Albert Sorel, in *L'Europe et la Révolution française* (8 vols., Paris, 1885–1904), agree that the Girondins alone were responsible for the war. (…) Their thesis has been summarized without nuance by Adalbert Wahl in *Geschichte des europäischen Staatensystems im Zeitalter der französischen Revolution und der Freiheitskriege (1789–1815)* (Munich and Berlin, 1912), and has been repeated with no new arguments by H. A. Goetz-Bernstein in *La diplomatie de la Gironde, Jacques-Pierre Brissot* (Paris, 1912)." (Georges Lefebvre, *The French Revolution* (London: Routledge, 2005), 217, note 1).

in more detail the historiographical trend headed by Furet and the problems involved in reading the French Revolution through its lenses.

Habermas seems to read the Revolution as a harmonic event, devoid of internal contradictions or divergent trends, as we can see in this quote from his 1990 text: "the Declaration of the Rights of Man and the Napoleonic Code validated the principle of freedom of will against historically preexisting law as the substantive basis of the state."[5] Such a claim implies two discursive movements. It posits 1789 and the Napoleonic regime as two close phenomena, as if a continuous line existed between the two; otherwise said, the 1789 Declaration leads to Napoleon. It also puts forth the idea that revolutionary law came to reject all past experiences.

This de-historicization connects itself to a certain classical liberal idea about law, which purports to build a connecting continuity beginning from 1789, passing through Kant, and coming all the way to Rawls' principles of justice. The Revolution thus puts us already within an atomization process:

> modern law is especially suited for the social integration of economic societies, which rely on the decentralized decisions of self-interested individuals in morally neutralized spheres of action [...] These laws draw their legitimacy from a legislative procedure based for its part on the principle of popular sovereignty. The paradoxical emergence of legitimacy out of legality must be explained by means of the rights that secure for citizens the exercise of their political autonomy.[6]

This idea of the French Revolution as the birthplace of proceduralism is expanded in Appendix I of *Between Facts and Norms*, in which Habermas articulates Furet's and Tocqueville's thesis in support of his hypothesis, and also adds a further one on the (ethno)nationalist aspect of the Revolution:

> as democratization proceeded along the lines of the French example, it developed into the nation-state. [...] this is what primarily interests us here—it laid the foundation for the ethnic and cultural homogeneity that made it possible, beginning in the late eighteenth century, to forge ahead with the democratization of government, albeit at the cost of excluding and

[5] Jürgen Habermas, *The Philosophical Discourse of Modernity* (Cambridge: Polity Press, 1990), 17.

[6] Jürgen Habermas, *Between Facts and Norms* (Cambridge: MIT Press, 1996), 83.

> oppressing minorities. Nation-state and democracy are twins born of the French Revolution. From a cultural point of view, they both stand under the shadow of nationalism.[7]

This same idea of the French Revolution as the birthplace of (ethno) nationalism is repeated in his 1998 book: "Nationalist movements have almost always modeled themselves on the Republican nation-state that emerged from the French Revolution."[8]

In connection with the alleged French nationalism, the constitutional democracy would have emerged: "only one remaining candidate for an affirmative answer to the question concerning the relevance of the French Revolution."[9] This was the contact point between (ethno)nationalism and popular sovereignty since this constitutional democracy was not legitimized by religious or metaphysical reasons, but through the exercise of citizenship, within the larger framework of a social contract theory.

On the other hand, Habermas acknowledges the role assigned to morality[10] in the eighteenth-century jurisprudence, denoting a tension between those rights that are guaranteed only within a particular political community—the Nation-State, not forgetting the ethnic connotation proposed by Habermas—and its universal validity claim—that goes beyond national borders.[11]

In summary, the French Revolution and its conception of law was distinguished, for Habermas, by their de-historicizing and (ethno)nationalist

[7] Habermas, *Between Facts and Norms*, 493.

[8] Jürgen Habermas, *The inclusion of the other: studies in political theory* (Cambridge: MIT Press, 1998), 212.

[9] Habermas, *Between Facts and Norms*, 465.

[10] On the issue of morals and morality, it is important to note that Habermas uses the expression "morality" in connection with the theoretical development starting in the nineteenth century with Kant's moral theory. This principles-based aprioristic interpretation cannot be directly transposed to the French Revolutionary world of the end of the eighteenth century. When the revolutionaries talk about morality, they are not concerned with the same thing as Habermas or contemporary moral philosophers. Therefore, when using the term "moral" or "morality" in this book, I am using it in the revolutionary sense of these words. Morals and morality in this book do not refer to the Kantian construct or contemporary philosophic parlance. This translation problem will also arise in the concluding chapters, when I discuss the notions of "republic" and "citizenship."

[11] Jürgen Habermas, "The Concept of Human Dignity and the Realistic Utopia of Human Rights," *Metaphilosophy* 41, n. 4 (2010).

character at the same time they acknowledge the role of popular sovereignty, even if it subordinated to the latter.

Nonetheless, following the general tone of the Habermasian hypothesis, the French Revolution expressed a (liberal)[12] ideal where the conditions for real implementation were not present at the time, but they could be recovered and achieved today.[13]

In Rawls—one of the main representatives of the contemporary liberal view on human rights—the French Revolution all but disappears. In *The Law of Peoples*, we cannot find any direct or indirect mention of the Revolution. Neither in *Lectures on the History of Political Philosophy*—where there is only a footnote that sums up Hegel's alleged position on the French Revolution in a single sentence.[14]

In *Political Liberalism*'s introduction, Rawls mentions the Declaration—in fact, he mentions *a* Declaration since he does not specify which of the three different French Revolution declarations he is referring to, most likely the 1789 version—as an example of a list of constitutional principles for guaranteeing freedom, but adds that they are "purely form. By themselves, they are an impoverished form of liberalism, indeed not liberalism at all but libertarianism."[15]

More recently, we have James Griffin's *On Human Rights.* As in the case of Rawls, the Revolution is almost non-existent—both within his text and in the bibliography. Griffin states that the expression "human rights" emerged by the end of the eighteenth century, as in the 1789 Declaration, replacing the term "natural rights."

> the French [Revolution] marked the secularization of the concept by changing its name from 'natural rights' to 'human rights' (les droits de l'homme). In its secular form at the end of the Enlightenment, it was often still thought to be derived from natural law, but natural law by then widely reduced to no more than a moral principle independent of law and convention.[16]

[12] Here understood within Habermas' conception of liberalism and its relation to his idea of a modern project, and not as the French revolutionary idea of liberalism.

[13] Habermas, *Between Facts and Norms*, 471.

[14] John Rawls, *Lectures on the History of Moral Philosophy* (Cambridge: Harvard University Press), 330, note 2.

[15] John Rawls, *Political Liberalism* (New York: Columbia University Press, 1996), iv.

[16] James Griffin, *On Human Rights* (Oxford: Oxford University Press, 2008), 1.

As a transition from the hegemonic to the critical approach to human rights, using Spieler's theoretical scheme, we can point to Konder Comparato's history of human rights. He is the only author, among those mentioned so far, that has delved into the revolutionary historiography—which is understandable, considering his proposal. However, his choice of references highlights the historiographic current he supports: the main contemporary bibliographical reference is Furet and Ozouf's dictionary.

By embracing Furet as, apparently, Habermas and Rawls did, Comparato also embraces the idea of the French Revolution as an effort in de-historicization:

> All the political impetus within the French revolution, on the contrary, leaned towards the future and represented an attempt to radically changing the living conditions in society. The intention was to completely erase the past and begin History anew from ground zero.[17]

In addition, for the Brazilian thinker, the French Revolution had been an effort spearheaded by the bourgeoisie, thus marking the beginning of modern democracy, defined by the "general limitation of governmental powers without any concern for protecting the poor majority against the rich minority."[18]

This victory of the bourgeoisie was exemplified by two class concerns addressed in 1789: protecting private property against abusive expropriation and observing strict legality when exacting taxes. The author even claims that "the 1793 Constitution's declaration of rights, in broad terms, limited itself to emphasize the previous declarations' content."[19]

If we continue toward the subject of revolutionary (alleged) abstractionism, the lack of historiographical background literature gets critical. None of the texts mentioned so far reference any relatively recent work on the Revolution, with the exception of Meister, which mentions Arno Mayer's book on Revolutionary terror, claiming proximity between France and Russia.[20]

[17] Fábio Konder Comparato, *Afirmação Histórica dos Direitos Humanos* (São Paulo: Saraiva, 2005), 64.

[18] Comparato, *Afirmação Histórica*, 64.

[19] Comparato, *Afirmação Histórica*, 75.

[20] Arno Mayer, *The Furies: Violence and Terror in the French and Russian Revolutions* (Princeton: Princeton University Press, 2000). I will not discuss Mayer's book in further

Meister starts by differentiating between two human rights discourses: the modern (starting with the 1789 Declaration); and the contemporary (after the fall of communism in 1989).[21] Meister claims that the difference between them lies in the relation between human rights and ethics or politics.

> The ethically centered approach to human rights that triumphed after the fall of communism in 1989 implicitly superseded the politically centered version of the Rights of Man that had been the focus of struggles for equality and liberty since the French Revolution of 1789.[22]

We can note a tension in regard to Habermas' position, for whom morality was a central feature of 1789's rights discourse lost in the contemporary discourse. In this sense, these authors' positions are opposed. However, the consequences they identify from such different starting points are very similar: the 1789 Declaration was characterized by a rejection of the past.[23]

This idea of two human rights discourses appears also in Upendra Baxi. In *Two Notions of Human Rights*, Baxi contrasts the modern discourse (starting with the French and American Revolutions) with the contemporary discourse (starting with the end of World War II).[24]

According to Baxi, modern discourse makes possible the transformation of the natural law discourse into what we now call a human rights

detail. For a detailed discussion within the United States historiography on the French Revolution, cf. *French Historical Studies* 24, n. 4 (2001).

[21] Meister does not use the terms "modern" or "contemporary," but I have chosen to use them in order to better differentiate and show his proximity with Upendra Baxi's hypothesis, presented below.

[22] Robert Meister, *After Evil: A Politics of Human Rights* (New York: Columbia University Press, 2011), 5.

[23] Meister, *After Evil*, 80.

[24] His conception of the modern discourse, at least from what can be inferred from his references, seems to be based on Leo Strauss' work on natural law and, to a minor degree, an Article by Stephan Marks on the connection between the 1789 and 1948 declarations. Delving into Strauss' extensive book is, however, beyond the focus of this book. For a discussion on the relation between his work on natural law and natural law during the French Revolution, see Florence Gauthier, "Éléments d'une histoire du droit naturel: à propos de Léo Strauss, Michel Villey et et Brian Tierney," published April 14, 2011, https://revolution-francaise.net/2011/04/14/432-elements-histoire-droit-naturel-leo-strauss-michel-villey-brian-tierney, where she claims that Strauss' hypothesis would not be faithful to the modern philosophy of natural law.

discourse.[25] On the other hand, agreeing with Habermas, Baxi identifies the French Revolution as the birthplace of the Nation-State and of (ethno) nationalism.

> Were one to 'date' (I evoke the multiple meanings of that term here!) the birth of human rights with the American and French Revolutions, one may well label the era thus beginning as the era of 'modern human rights'. The term 'modem' here marks the consolidation of a Westphalian international law and order. It also signals a whole variety of ideological 'justifications' for colonization and world domination.[26]

These human rights would be "state-centric *and* Eurocentric*; in contrast, the processes of formulation of contemporary human rights are increasingly inclusive.*"[27]

To better understand Baxi's standpoint, we should check his only reference to a text (more or less) about the French Revolution. It is an article by Stephen Marks in which we find only mentions of authors representing conservative historiographies, such as Furet and Tulard. In regard to political theory, Marks quotes Habermas and Tilly—we have already seen which historiographical trend Habermas follows.

Marks imports Habermas' claim of a (relatively) continuity from 1789 to present-day human rights struggles, as well the idea that the revolutionaries aimed to build a constitutional system.[28] Marks describes the 1789 Declaration as: "never applied and criticized as a hastily thrown together, demagogic text to appease the provinces."[29]

Marks also repeats the idea that human rights during the French Revolution were characterized as individualistic and anti-communitarian. Therefore, the 1789 Declaration strengthened state power.

Besides Baxi, a different approach is found in José-Manuel Barreto's introduction to *Human Rights from a Third World Perspective*. But here, again, the revolutionary bibliography is almost non-existent. The only

[25] Upendra Baxi. "Two Notions of Human Rights," in *The Future of Human Rights* (Oxford: Oxford University Press, 2008), 43.

[26] Baxi. "Two Notions," 42.

[27] Baxi. "Two Notions," 47, emphasis in original.

[28] Stephen Marks, "From the 'Single Confused Page' to the "Decalogue for Five Billion Persons": The Roots of the Universal Declaration of Human Rights in the French Revolution." *Human Rights Quarterly* 20, n. 3 (ago./1998): 464.

[29] Marks. "From the 'Single Confused Page'," 466.

work cited that mentions the French Revolution is Habermas' *The Modern Discourse of Modernity*, already discussed above.[30]

It is already easy to see how the French Revolution serves as a mere rhetorical device when discussing human rights issues, with little or no effort to examine the rich revolutionary literature. When an author makes use of the historiography—since a direct study of the primary texts is inexistent—he always uses Furet or thinkers close to his thought, in other words, a conservative and anti-revolutionary historiography, as we will see in detail throughout this book.

Having these contributions as a backdrop, I will now deepen my analysis by taking a look at two authors who develop slightly further the role of the French Revolution when they think about human rights today. They come from two related but separate fields: the history of human rights and the philosophy of human rights. Representing the historical front, we have Samuel Moyn's *The Last Utopia*. Costas Douzinas brings, in his *Human Rights and Empire*, a philosophical approach to contemporary human rights issues.[31]

Both authors present the same reading of the revolutionary moment, closely connected to the other interpretations already explained above, despite the radical differences in approach and overall purpose between Moyn and Douzinas.[32]

[30] The only direct mention appears in a footnote on the racism, sexism, and classism of representatives of modern philosophical tradition: "Other European philosophers can also be found fractured by a twofold engagement with right. While Kant showed 'enthusiasm' for the French Revolution, he kept silent about the Terror unleashed by Robespierre. Hegel, on his part, denounced the Terror but understood colonialism and colonial genocide as the materialization of the display and advance of the Spirit" (José-Manuel Barreto, introduction to *Human Rights from a Third World Perspective: Critique, History and International Law*, ed. José-Manuel Barreto (Newcastle upon Tyne: Cambridge Scholars Publishing, 2013), 18, note 37). This passage seems to indicate that colonialism was part of the revolutionary endeavor, as Baxi suggested, and identifies the alleged Terror with Robespierre without giving any historical or historiographical basis for such claims.

[31] The first author, a law and history professor at Harvard University and one of the main representatives of historical revisionism in human rights (and this has no negative connotations, as it may seem at first sight, at least to some readers). The second author, a law professor at the Birkbeck Institute and an exponent of the British Critical Legal Studies tradition and was an elected member of Greece's Parliament in 2015.

[32] I have chosen Samuel Moyn and Costas Douzinas because they represent two very distinct ways of thinking about human rights. This disparity helps avoid the trap of confining my research to a single political-theoretical framework. I must point out, however, that the French Revolution does not have a prominent place in contemporary discussion in the the-

Moyn's book aims to identify precisely when human rights as we know them today have emerged. It is not a history of humanism or contemporary law, but about dating the birth of the contemporary human rights discourse, following a predetermined definition of what those human rights would be:

> When people hear the phrase 'human rights' they think of the highest moral precepts and political ideals. And they are right to do so. They have in mind a familiar set of indispensable liberal freedoms, and sometimes more expansive principles of social protection. But they also mean something more. The phrase implies an agenda for improving the world and bringing about a new one in which the dignity of each individual will enjoy secure international protection.[33]

For Moyn, human rights are a discourse that comes after the end of political utopias, as in the final years of the Cold War. With the decline of what he names "elite sympathies for once-romantic anticolonial nationalism,"[34] human rights activism found an appropriate space to emerge and consolidate itself since other transformative political ideologies had already lost their appeal.

The author affirms the need to deconstruct the usual conceptions justifying the need to find the "true" historical origin of human rights. The problem with his proposal, as we will see, is its rejection of the past as a possible inspiration for the present. For example, when discussing the contribution of Christianity, Moyn claims that recognizing its universal calling does not help to show how Christianity would be at the root of the political possibility of human rights today. Moyn points that this claim obscures the implicit notion that there only exists one true universalism, the Christian one.[35] As for identifying the French Revolution as the origin of human rights, Moyn states:

> The overwhelmingly important point, however, is that the rights of the revolutionary era were very much embodied in the politics of the state,

ory or philosophy of human rights. Moyn and Douzinas are two of few examples of authors outside the revolutionary historiography itself that articulate a little bit further this relation.

[33] Samuel Moyn, *The Last Utopia: Human Rights in History* (Cambridge, Massachusetts, London: The Belknap Press of Harvard University Press, 2012), 1.

[34] Moyn, *The Last Utopia*, 173.

[35] Moyn, *The Last Utopia*, 15–16.

crystallizing in a scheme worlds away from the political meaning human rights would have later.[36]

The rights proclaimed in the French Revolution, as in the American Revolution, are then rights under a sovereign nation's constitution. They are the manner through which citizenship is created and justified, not some kind of protection given to humankind as a whole. According to Moyn, all social struggles within the revolutionary period had national citizenship as their aim. In his interpretation, no discourse tried to go beyond French borders, but called for concrete achievements only within the national space. In sum, we can synthesize Moyn's thesis as the claim that the French Revolution's human rights had no cosmopolitan element, only a national character.[37] As is shown in Chap. 2, on the contrary there as an intense debate over the rights of the people, including during the Year 1 debates.[38]

Douzinas reaches a similar conclusion by way of a different reasoning. His starting point, as stated in his *The End of Human Rights*, is diametrically opposed to that of Moyn:

> When the apologists of pragmatism pronounce the end of ideology, of history or utopia, they do not mark the triumph of human rights; on the contrary, they bring human rights to an end. The end of human rights comes when they lose their end.[39]

This claim, made more than a decade before the publication of Moyn's book, pinpoints the end of the utopias to the end of the possibility for

[36] Moyn, *The Last Utopia*, 25.

[37] I shall point out, however, that the role the revolutionary discourse played in the fight against slavery is highlighted by one of Moyn's book reviewers, Robin Blackburn. Blackburn explains the complex character of this relationship and criticizes Moyn for seeing it in a grossly simplified manner—especially when discussing the debate on national interest and emancipation (Robin Blackburn, review of *The Last Utopia: Human Rights in History*, by Samuel Moyn, *New Left Review*, 69 (mai./jun. 2011): 130–131.). The reviewer shows how the relation between seventeenth-century thought, the rights declared during the French Revolution, and the struggle against slavery—by whites and by black slaves directly—is much more complex than Moyn leads us to believe.

[38] For a brief presentation of the topic, see Marc Belissa, "Le 'Droit des Gens' dans le Débat Constitutionnel," in *L'An I et l'Apprentissage de la Démocratie*, ed. Roger Bourderon (Saint-Denis: Éditions PSD, 1995).

[39] Costas Douzinas, *The End of Human Rights* (Oxford: Hart Publishing, 2000), 380.

human rights. This is the exact opposite of Moyn's thesis that sees human rights as a political discourse that only comes after the end of all utopias. Moyn's statement that the international human rights movement is something that starts only in the 1970s coincides with a time period in which human rights, according to Douzinas, were used as "*the ideological gloss of an emerging empire*."[40]

However, Douzinas does not limit himself to criticizing the ideologizing function of human rights as justification for armed conflicts during the 1970s. Rights—and not only human rights—have for him a productive and performative dimension in relation to society and to the individual.[41]

The role of rights in constructing the subject's identity came before its protective function. Before using rights against the oppression perpetrated by state or private actors, rights were a constitutive element of our own subjectivity. Douzinas speaks of rights as bargaining elements in our struggle for recognition and as claims about what morality—or any other superior source of authority, like international law—requires.[42]

This duality in the language of rights, between State power and as a tool of social struggle, was already present in the 1789 French Declaration; Douzinas exemplifies this duality with articles 1 and 3. While the first one stated that "[m]en are born and remain free and equal in rights," article 3 identified the Nation as the only source of sovereignty.

According to Douzinas, when the Declaration[43] talks of the universality of rights, it is actually grounding local and national sovereignty. The

[40] Costas Douzinas, *Human Rights and Empire: The Political Philosophy of Cosmopolitanism* (Milton Park, New York: Routledge-Cavendish, 2007), 7. See also Kirsten Stellars' history of the international human rights movement after the second half of the twentieth century. The author summarizes the relation between human rights and war campaigns as such: "*And as President Bush Sr and Clinton have more recently demonstrated, it can provide a sugar coating for potentially unpalatable foreign interventions. As these examples show, human rights campaigns are almost always triggered by domestic impulses within the most powerful nations, rather than by repression in countries elsewhere. And, by the same token, governments judge these campaigns by their success on the home front*" (Kirsten Stellars, *The Rise and Rise of Human Rights* (London: Sutton Publishing Limited, 2002), xiii).

[41] "*Human rights have both institutional and subjective aspects. As institutional entities, they belong to constitutions, laws, court judgments, international organisations, treaties and conventions. But the prime function of rights is to construct the individual person as a subject (of law). Rights are tools and strategies for defining the meaning and powers of humanity*" (Douzinas, *Human Rights and Empire*, 7).

[42] Douzinas, *Human Rights and Empire*, 7, 10.

[43] Douzinas talks generically about "declarations" but refers almost exclusively to the 1789 final text, and he seems to include the American Bill of Rights in the same analysis. Therefore,

universality of rights of the individuals does not treat men as a whole, but only as a restricted and limited set of people.

By identifying State with Nation, the Declaration strengthens nationalism and the state apparatus, even as it utilizes a cosmopolitan discourse. This is why Douzinas uses the term "national principle of universality."[44] The Nation-State marks a privilege: the protection of its citizens by excluding non-citizens. According to the philosopher, citizenship was the condition for recognizing the subject's humanity. Only rights secured by a domestic legal system provide real protection from political agents.

In other words, even considering that Douzinas recognizes a cosmopolitan calling within the human rights discourse of the French Revolution, the event is tarnished by its original sin. Rights are proclaimed, but only for French citizens.

Moyn and Douzinas do agree on one issue. The French Revolution's legacy, in regard to rights, consists mainly of the emergence of the Nation-State and citizen's rights.

This hypothesis has a few visible problems, as synthesized in a Freudian slip made by Douzinas: "*The French Revolution was retrospectively legitimized by its* Déclaration des droits de l'homme, *the American by the Declaration of Independence and the Bill of Rights.*"[45]

We have here a temporality problem. The 1789 Declaration could not have justified the Revolution since the Revolution itself began only in 1789—unless Douzinas is referring not to the Revolution, but only to its early beginnings (in that case, however, the comparison would not hold). The American case is different since the Bill of Rights comes after the armed conflict for emancipation from the British metropolis. This temporality problem also helps us understand why Moyn and Douzinas believe the French Revolution and the Nation-State to be closely related phenomena.

To better understand this topic, it is important to analyze the interaction between the ideas of Nation and the French concept of *Patrie*—that can be loosely translated as "the homeland." Claude Nicolet, in his study on the Republican idea in France, explains how the meaning of the word

when discussing Douzinas' stance, I use the term "Declaration" to refer solely to the 1789 version, even if his reasoning may be extrapolated to the other documents—something he does explicitly in some points of his text.

[44] Douzinas, *Human Rights and Empire*, 98.

[45] Douzinas, *Human Rights and Empire*, 251, emphasis in original.

"nation" changes within French political history, the Revolution being one of the most important transformative moments. The term starts to be abandoned by the Republicans and substituted by the notion of Homeland.[46] What was then the relation between Nation and Homeland for the revolutionaries?

Marc Belissa, in his presentation at the *4e Rencontres d'Histoire Critique*, starts his talk with this concise statement: "Did the French revolution invent the Nation-State? The answer is easy. No." The idea that the French Revolution was the birthplace of the Nation-State would be connected to the idea that the French Revolution was a bourgeois revolution. The Nation-State would then be the byproduct of a national inspiration, of the desire to build a particular State to a particular geographically limited people, to be defended by a national army.

Instead, the French Revolution associated Nation and Homeland—and *Patrie*—defined by Belissa as "the place where human rights are guaranteed."[47] The Nation-State as an expression of nationalism did not exist during the Revolution, because nationalism did not exist at the time. Nationalism and the Nation-State presuppose an idea of exclusion, as Douzinas pointed out in his claim of the exclusionary aspect of the Revolution. The very notion of nationality, as contemporarily understood, did not exist during the Revolution, but only that of citizenship—defined in a much broader way, as we will see.

The Homeland was seen as the accomplishment of this process of revolution in natural law. In the words of Robespierre, in his 1794 speech on political morality, "the essence of the Republic or of democracy is equality; it follows from that that the love of the Homeland necessarily encompasses the love of equality."[48] In other words, the Homeland is the revolutionary process as such.

[46] Claude Nicolet, *L'Idée Républicaine en France: Essai d'Histoire Critique* (Paris: Gallimard, 1982), 18. The choice of "homeland" is not without its problems. For a discussion of the meaning of the French *patrie*, see Albert Soboul, *Dictionnnaire de la Révolution Française* (Paris: PUF, 1989), 822.

[47] The historian gave a speech in a panel called *L'État-Nation: une histoire récente* during the 2015 edition of the meeting. See Marc Belissa, "Marc Belissa aux 4e Rencontres d'histoire critique—Nation(s)/ mondialisation(s) (nov. 2015)," YouTube, February 12, 2016, video, 17: 13. https://www.youtube.com/watch?v=RZ4E5JDn_dw.

[48] Maximilien de Robespierre, *Œuvres de* Robespierre (Paris: A. Vermorel, F. Cournol, 1867), 297. His discourse receives the title *Sur les principes de morale politique qui doivent guider la Convention nationale dans l'administration intérieure de la République* (On the

For example, article 3 of the 1791 constitution[49] extends French citizenship to foreigners under the following conditions:

> Article 3—Those who were born outside of the kingdom from foreign parents and reside in France become French citizens after five years of continued domicile in the kingdom, if they have in addition acquired real estate or married a French woman, or formed an agricultural or commercial establishment, and have taken the civic oath.

In 1793, the conditions are simplified:

> Article 4—Every man born and living in France of twenty-one years of age; every foreigner of twenty-one years of age, who has been domiciled in France for a year, and lives there by his own labor, or acquires property, or marries a French woman, or adopts a child, or supports an aged man, and finally, every foreigner the Legislative body declares as well deserved of humanity, is admitted to the exercise of the rights of French citizenship.

With the 1795 Constitution, the expansive trend comes to a halt and the minimum time required increases:

> Article 10—A foreigner becomes a French citizen when, after having reached the age of twenty-one years and having declared an intention to settle in France, has resided here for seven consecutive years, provided that he pays a direct tax, and in addition possesses real estate or an agricultural or commercial establishment, or has married a French woman.

It is precisely this internal dynamic within the revolutionary period that escapes Moyn and Douzinas. By reading the Revolution from a narrow historiographical standpoint, both authors end up agreeing, maybe unintentionally, with a historiographical interpretation that reads the French Revolution as a mere bourgeois event, as Belissa explains.

They conclude their interpretations by limiting themselves to an extremely restricted historiographical corpus. In Douzinas' case, the only direct reference is to Keith Baker's text "The Idea of a Declaration of

principles of political morality that shall guide the internal administration of the Republic by the National Convention).

[49] All French Constitutions are available, including the scanned original texts, at the French Constitutional Council website at https://www.conseil-constitutionnel.fr/la-constitution/les-constitutions-de-la-france.

Rights," the same text indicated by Moyn in his bibliographical essay,[50] the latter includes only two other titles: Marcel Gauchet's *La Révolution des Droits de l'Homme* and *La Déclaration des Droits de l'Homme et du Citoyen*, by Stéphane Rials.

Keith Baker and Marcel Gauchet are part of a relatively well defined historiographical current, which has François Furet as its main representative. Both Baker and Gauchet contributed to Furet and Mona Ozouf's *Dictionnaire Critique de la Révolution Française*, among other collaborations with Furet.[51]

At this point of my analysis, it is important to take a small detour through the specialized literature in order to better understand the historiographical line of thought that serves as a starting point for Moyn and Douzinas, and how it is prejudicial to this book's proposal, as well as which other possible readings of the relationship between Law and the French Revolution can be entertained.

2.2 How (Not) to Think About the French Revolution

The historiography of the French Revolution has had a long and prolific history, starting with the Revolution itself. Burke publishes his *Reflections* already in 1790, Paine answers the following year with his *Rights of Man*, and the publication of political and philosophical treatises is widespread during the nineteenth century, with Germaine de Stäel's *Considérations*, published in 1818, as one of the most important works of the century on the French Revolution. During the first half of the nineteenth century, we already have vast published histories of the Revolution, such as the

[50] Douzinas, *Human Rights and Empire*, 98, note 9; Moyn, *The Last Utopia*, 314.

[51] Marcel Gauchet is not a specialist in the French Revolution, but in political history in a broader sense. His intellectual history shows his proximity with Furet, as well as a similar political trajectory (both have cut ties with the so-called Marxist "vulgate"). Keith Baker is a specialist in Condorcet and has written extensively about the French Revolution. As an example of his proximity with Furet, we can mention a work edited by Gary Kates presenting a panorama of revolutionary historiography that put Furet and Baker under the same title: "The revisionist orthodoxy." Gary Kates, ed., *The French Revolution: Recent Debates and New Controversie* (London: Routledge, 1998). For an often-quoted and important contribution by Baker, see Keith Baker, "Transformations of Classical Republicanism in Eighteenth-Century France," *The Journal of Modern History* 73, n. 1 (March 2001): 32–52.

ten-volume work by Adolphe Tiers, *Histoire de la Révolution Française*, the first volume being published in 1823.

For the historian Claude Mazauric, in his *L'Histoire de la Révolution française et la pensée marxiste* from 2009, we can identify three structuring trends within Revolutionary historiography already during the nineteenth century. I shall call them, adapting the nomenclature used by the author, classical liberal, conservative liberal, and radical popular.

The first trend described by Mazauric, the classical liberal, is personified by Germaine de Stäel, in the previously mentioned *Considérations*. The main issue for Stäel is the historical necessity of the French Revolution. Because of the impossibility of accomplishing the needed reforms, the Revolution becomes a necessity. In other words, it could not not have happened.[52]

In Mazauric's interpretation of Germaine de Stäel, the reference to natural law was a way to legitimize the change in the kingdom's political constitution. However, the French Revolution brought two negative aspects: the first is inspired by anglophile liberal ideals and the second one by popular despotism. The confusion between the reformist perspective and popular intrusion led to the "Jacobin dictatorship," and the despotism of the Jacobin paved the way to Napoleonic despotism.[53]

Germaine de Stäel's text then establishes the main paradigms of what Mazauric calls the liberal interpretation of the French Revolution.

Regardless of the specific chronology adopted, this interpretation's main purpose is to identify two distinct moments: a legitimate and creative moment and a regressive and absurd backlash. The key interpretive lens is a supposed blind commitment to equality and an ill-conceived idea of freedom when the need for freedom would already lead by itself to equality.[54]

This idea of two revolutions gave birth to a long historiographical school that tries to oppose the 1789–1790's "good revolution" to the 1793–1794 "bad revolution"—"a fatal deviation from the principles of '89."[55] This is the same interpretation adopted by the first Furet in his work together with Denis Richet, *La Révolution Française*. This book's

[52] Germaine de Staël, *Considerations on the Principal Events of the French Revolution* (Indianapolis: Liberty Fund, 2008), 111.

[53] Staël, *Considerations*, 198.

[54] Claude Mazauric, *L'Histoire de la Révolution française et la pensée marxiste* (Paris: Presses Universitaires de France, 2009), 127.

[55] Alice Gérard, *A Revolução Francesa: mitos e interpretações* (São Paulo: Perspectiva, 1999), 33.

impact marked the beginning of a transformation within Revolutionary historiography,[56] but that does not mean that the text invented that revisionist hypothesis.

Vovelle, in his review of the historiography, written just before the bicentennial,[57] identifies the beginning of what he calls a "great attack" by the Anglo-Saxon school, more precisely through Alfred Cobban's text, *The Myth of the French Revolution*.[58] Cobban's two fundamental hypotheses are that the Revolution did not destroy feudalism since it no longer existed at the time, and it would be wrong to think that the 1789 Revolution was bourgeois and anti-feudal because the Revolution itself started as an aristocratic revolution.[59]

With Furet we have the *dérapage* theory. The thinker claims that the Revolution lost its ways because of popular intervention. This impetus created a momentum that led to the 1793–1794 Terror. The "good revolution," that of the Enlightenment, bourgeois elite and the nobility, had been diverted when the popular movement entered the scene.[60]

Against the liberal interpretation inaugurated by Stäel, Mazauric lists two equally hostile responses, one from the right and one from the left. The historian identifies as the first representative of the left-leaning historiography Jacques-Charles Bailleul's text from 1818 commenting on

[56] With regard to the reception of this work, especially in France, cf. Julien Louvrier, "Penser la controverse: la réception du livre de François Furet et Denis Richet, *La Révolution Française*," *Annales Historiques de la Révolution Française* 351 (January–March 2008).

[57] Michel Vovelle, "L'historiographie de la Révolution Française à la veille du bicentenaire," *Estudos Avançados* 1, n. 1 (December 1987).

[58] Initially a conference held at University College, London, on May 6, 1954, the text was published the following year and later incorporated into *Aspects of the French Revolution*. Alfred Cobban, *Aspects of the French Revolution* (New York: Jonathan Cape, 1968).

[59] Some years later, Cobban published a summarized reworking of his fundamental hypothesis: Alfred Cobban, *The Social Interpretation of the French Revolution* (Cambridge: Cambridge University Press, 1964).

[60] In Louvrier's summary: "*Furet et Richet redonnent à l'interprétation libérale de l'histoire révolutionnaire un nouveau souffle. Mais plus encore s'exprime ici la remise en cause de la vision jusqu'alors dominante dans l'historiographie: la lecture d'inspiration marxiste d'une révolution une et indivisible, point de passage obligé de la transition historique du féodalisme au capitalisme, rendue nécessaire par le développement des forces productives entravées par les contraintes de la société d'Ancien Régime. François Furet et Denis Richet refusent cette « révolution bourgeoise à soutien populaire » et favorisent la thèse d'une révolution déjà largement aboutie dans l'esprit des élites, sinon dans les faits, avant même la réunion des États généraux à Versailles au printemps 1789*" (Louvrier, "Penser la controverse," 159).

Germaine's *Considérations*.[61] I will examine this historiographical current throughout the rest of the book. For now, the conservative-liberal interpretation will be my focus.[62]

According to Mazauric's interpretation of this trend, the Revolution dislocated the theocentric order established throughout history, contradicting the divine will. It manifested an alleged individualistic perversion acting against the truth of God. The transformative rationalism against the truth inherent in the nature of things. The Revolution's logic of equality would lead to a society marked by constant disputes between individuals, wrongly mixing the market order with societal order.[63]

Some of the elements within this interpretation are better exemplified through Edmund Burke's *Reflections on the Revolution in France*.[64] Burke's position is initially, that is, before writing his *Reflections*, laudatory. In a letter to the Earl of Charlemont, James Caulfield, from August 9, 1789, Burke describes the French Revolution as a "wonderful spectacle exhibited in a neighboring and rival country (...) watching the French struggle for liberty not knowing whether to blame or applaud."[65]

However, Burke quickly changes his opinion. In November 1790, *Reflections on the Revolution in France was* published in England, comparing the 1688 Glorious Revolution to the French Revolution as it unfolded.

The main issue in the French case was its recourse to abstraction. While the Glorious Revolution was made by the English people according to their moral and political history, the French people were trying to transform their society by using the empty (according to Burke) category of the rights of man.

According to Burke, social change must observe the traditions of the people trying to execute it. The English Revolution of 1688 was thus a

[61] Jacques-Charles Bailleul, *Examen critique de l'ouvrage posthume de Mme la baronne de Stäel, ayant pour titre. Considérations sur les principaux événements de la Révolution française* (Paris: Ant. Bailleul, 1818). Bailleul was a representative at the Convention during the 1793 debates, but his was a minor role. See the May 22, 1793, session (AP, t. LXVI, 190ff).

[62] The adjective "conservative" does not carry a negative connotation. It serves to indicate that, for these thinkers, it is necessary to preserve some aspects of the French society, which was under the risk—according to their interpretation—of disappearing or being corrupted by the revolutionary movement. They are, in a general sense, critics to the French Revolution.

[63] Mazauric, *L'Histoire de la Révolution française*, 127–128.

[64] For a more thorough work on how Burke came to the ideas presented in his *Reflections*, see William Palmer, "Edmund Burke and the French Revolution: Notes on the Genesis of the Reflections," *Colby Quarterly* 20, n. 4 (December 1984).

[65] Burke in Palmer, "Edmund Burke and the French Revolution," 184.

natural development of the English way of life. There could be no revolution starting from the outside. The revolutionary principles must ground themselves in the concrete materiality of existing moral, religious, and political life.

France had made a mistake of trying to revolutionize itself through abstract principles disconnected from its concrete reality:

> Government is not made in virtue of natural rights, which may and do exist in total independence of it, and exist in much greater clearness, and in a much greater degree of abstract perfection: but their abstract perfection is their practical defect.[66]

The source of this problem was for him the idea of natural rights, as presented by the French revolutionaries. They had tried to develop an a priori political science, while the true science of government is a practical art, one that transcends the life of any one person. Therefore, it does not matter how long someone reflects on forms of government or experiences them during their lifetime. Only a gradual accumulation through consolidated social institutions enables actual social change. This idea is reiterated in more recent anti-revolutionary historiographies.

But we must be careful not to confound Burke with those following the interpretative path he opened. It is this sense that we can interpret Gerárd's claim that Burke, even if he was against the French Revolution, was not a reactionary. He was a conservative and liberal, but not a reactionary. For example, in his discussion of the American insurrection, he defends the uprising by appealing to the tradition of English liberties.[67]

At this point, I can go back to Furet's second phase, inaugurated by the publication of *Interpreting the French Revolution* in 1978, and distinguished by his use of Tocqueville and Augustin Cochin, the latter being less known before Furet's book.

Furet starts his work with the chapter "The French revolution is over," where he revisits and modifies some of his previous thesis. One of Furet's fundamental hypotheses is inspired by Tocqueville: the idea of continuity. According to Furet, the French Revolution did not impose any kind of deep transformation in French society, as previously thought, but served mostly as a catalyst for already ongoing social processes.

[66] Edmund Burke, *Reflections on the Revolution in France* (London, New York: Temple Press Letchworth J. M. Dent & Sons Ltd., 1910), 57.

[67] Gérard, *A Revolução Francesa*, 20.

> The problem explored by Tocqueville is that of the domination of communities and civil society by administrative power as a consequence of a centralized state; this tight grip held by the administration over the social body is not only the permanent trait that links the 'new' regime to the 'old' one, from Bonaparte to Louis XIV. It is also that which explains, through a series of mediations, the penetration of the 'democratic' (i.e., egalitarian) ideology in old French society: in other words, the 'Revolution' is, in regard to its constitutive aspect, from their point of view (an administrative State reigning over a society with an egalitarian ideology), largely an achievement of the monarchy, before being concluded by the Jacobins and the Empire. And that which we call the 'French Revolution', this cataloged and dated event, aggrandized as a new dawn, is only the acceleration of a previous political and social revolution. By destroying not the aristocracy, but the aristocratic principle within the society, the Revolution suppressed the legitimacy of social resistance against the central State.[68]

Servitude no longer existed as a prevailing institution and most issues (such as taxes and other related duties) were not decided by a lord or noble, but by the province's intendant or by people elected by the peasants themselves. In Tocqueville's words, "we would be gravely mistaken in believing that the Old Regime was a time of servitude and dependence. There was more freedom then than now, but it was a kind of irregular freedom."[69]

For Furet and Tocqueville, administrative centralization was already an ongoing project by the French monarchy, and not a revolutionary invention. This centralizing process accompanied the rationalization of the governmental apparatus. The political and judicial power wielded by the noble and feudal lords was already being preempted and replaced by proper state-like administrative mechanisms. In this sense, it was not actually a geographical centralization of political power, but its concentration in the State under construction.

From Cochin, Furet borrows the idea of democratic sociability emanating from the Masonic lodges and *sociétés de pensée*. Under Rousseau's inspiration, the idea of a general will became a catalyst in a totalizing and concentrative process.

[68] François Furet, *Penser la Révolution française* (Paris: Gallimard, 1978), 33.

[69] Alexis de Tocqueville, *O Antigo Regime e a Revolução* (São Paulo: WWF Martins Fontes, 2009), 130.

> The myth of the active and actual will of all, imposing itself upon each and everyone, is nothing but a legal fiction, with no real value. What we understand as the will of all is the will of some, formed, imposed, reigning under certain conditions determined by the force of things and the nature of the regime.[70]

It is through this new interpretive lens that Furet justifies his famous hypothesis of the French Revolution as the source of all kinds of totalitarianism: "By way of the general will, the king-people henceforth coincides mythically with power; disbelief is the source of totalitarianism."[71]

By making such a claim, Furet abandons the *dérapage* hypothesis to give way to the drift hypothesis. The Terror was not an accident along the way, brought about by the inadequate intervention of the popular movement. The year 1793 was already implicit in 1789. Furet leaves no room for doubt: it drifts not toward direct democracy, but toward despotism and absolutism, even if under a different guise.[72] This is Furet in his most radical phase.

Regarding his method, Furet was responsible for reigniting political history, a field somewhat stagnant in France since the supremacy of the *École des Annales*.[73] The proposal, however, ends up hypertrophying the political. For Furet, a social approach is synonymous with economicism and social reductionism. Furet's apology of the political is part of his distrust toward the social, whose primacy is necessarily negative. Furet ends up by creating a false, almost absolute, separation between the social and the political, even if he denies it. For the author, the Revolution only created new political and governmental principles, but not new social and economic relations.

The challenge we face when thinking about the Revolution through the lens of political philosophy is not to repeat Furet's mistake. In order to accomplish such a task, I will make use of the third historiographical trend, which I have called the radical popular historiography, to be explored throughout the remainder of this book.[74]

[70] Auguste Cochin, *La Révolution et la Libre Pensée* (Paris: Pion-Nourrit et Cie, 1924), 130.

[71] Furet, *Penser la Révolution française*, 281–282.

[72] Furet, *Penser la Révolution française*, 129.

[73] Vovelle, "L'historiographie de la Révolution Française," 66.

[74] It is hard to name this current. While a more direct approach would be to follow the ideas presented so far and use the term "radical liberal," some of its proponents are clearly not under the liberal umbrella, especially the Marxist-inspired historians. The term "liberal-

2.3 An Introduction to the French Revolution's Philosophy of Right

Reflecting on the 1789 debates, Marcel Gauchet, in his *La Révolution des Droits de l'Homme*, speaks of a "symbolic battle over legitimacy."[75] The constituent debates did not serve as a medium for the representatives to distance themselves from the dynamics and mobilizations that took over France at the time, but as a way to discuss important legal issues among a group of men in a precarious position, confronted by strong opposition and with the ghost of regal power lurking behind them.

The issue at play was—albeit not exclusively—the symbolic principle of authority. Thus, the Declaration was a boost to what the author calls the fictitious appropriation of legitimacy, which put itself as the symbol of the coming of a new world and new society. From the start, it was not about declaring rights, but about the new constitution (not in a legal sense) of the French people.

The Declaration was also a part of the deconstruction of the society of the three estates by "reducing the political body to its original components, the independent individuals, making them truly stand out in their own needs."[76]

That does not mean that the whole process was engineered by the representatives. The Declaration was not some calculated scheme aiming at precise ends, but the "provisional outcome of deliberation rushed by the

democratic" might also not be adequate since it would imply that the other approaches had no concern for the democratic question—something their proponents would surely deny. For lack of a better term, I chose the expression "radical popular historiography," thus avoiding the term "Jacobin historiography" used by the first two currents to classify any historians not fitting to those two prior trends. This is important, since some historians, such as Guérin, explicitly deny the Jacobin heritage while highlighting two concerns of this historiographical trend: recognizing the positive and productive role played by popular movements; and the attempt to strengthen the liberating radicality of the revolutionary movement. For example, to illustrate the contrast between the first two trends and this last one, the reader can compare Keith Baker's "Transformations of Classical Republicanism" with Yannick Bosc's "La Constitution de l'An III: un républicanisme classique?," last modified September 6, 2008, http://revolution-francaise.net/2008/09/06/258-constitution-an-iii-republicanisme-classique.

[75] Marcel Gauchet, *La Révolution des Droits de l'Homme* (Paris: Éditions Gallimard, 1989), vi.

[76] Gauchet, *La Révolution des Droits de l'Homme*, ix.

urgent circumstances [that] made history throughout the centuries, inscribed in the bronze tablets of the law."[77]

One of the characteristics of this new model was the empire of law. An empire of the law, grounded on a strict set of individual rights, engendered a certain notion of collective legitimacy that combined the old with the new: the sovereign people and the permanence of the king; the priority of the Legislature and a reduced need for an Executive power—that is, a reduction of its sphere of influence and attributions. This supreme Legislature poses the problem of how to think about the relationship between the people and their representatives and the dichotomy between the oligarchic and popular regimes that came to traverse the whole Revolution.[78]

This idea of an empire of the law also comes up in other studies on the law of the French Revolution. According to Lucien Jaume, in his analysis of the 1789 and 1793 declarations,[79] the originality of the French contribution lies precisely in this "legiscentrism"—the term is used by Jaume to express the centrality of the written law during the Revolution.

Another invention of 1789 was determining the citizen through negation, clear of all its individuality—similar to Gauchet's idea of the reduction of the political body. The citizen is the nation's primary element and it is from the nation that it derives its civil rights, but not necessarily its political rights. The equality before the law creates a division between man and citizen. However, the Declaration would not have precisely defined this distinction.

For Jaume, the legal regulation of citizenship has increased continuously, putting man in a subsidiary position, at the same time law was progressively considered an expression of the general will. By identifying the sovereign with the people itself, the law was a declaration by the people about itself and it would be contradictory to claim that the sovereign or the people would bring harm to itself.

But we cannot help notice that Jaume seems to sideline the fact that the explicit aim of the Declaration and its writers was the preservation of the natural and imprescriptible rights of men. Jaume's "legiscentrism" hypothesis, in regard to the Revolution's political philosophy, claims that only the law can serve as a guarantee for rights and that France has only inserted an

[77] Gauchet, *La Révolution des Droits de l'Homme*, 10.

[78] Gauchet, *La Révolution des Droits de l'Homme*, xiii–xv.

[79] Lucien Jaume, *Les Déclarations des Droits de l'Homme* (Paris: GM Flammarion, 1989).

element of judgment with the creation of the constitutional review in 1971.

This hypothesis errs by refusing to acknowledge the revolutionary dynamics that, from the beginning, problematized the relationship between law and citizenship. The revolutionaries did not espouse a static conception of law. The law may even be an important guarantee for rights, but that was not its only role and even law itself was not unchanging. I will come back to some of these issues later on, but, as an example, I can point to the fact that the constitutional review had already been proposed in France since at least 1791.[80]

Gauchet understands this empire of the law as having one objective. In addition to the preservation of integrity and independence, the rights of men used liberty and equality as catalysts of an "integral redefinition of the bonds between beings, inscribed within the priority attributed to the individual that activated such rights."[81] This explains the importance of social assistance, on one hand, and, according to the author, the relationship between rights and duties, on the other.

Gauchet suggests that three elements are key in reading the revolution of the rights of men: the individual, the law, and the nation. The decomposition of society into its atoms, the individuals, was the result of the religious revolutions of the sixteenth century that removed the church and the king as mandatory intermediaries when communicating with God—which did not mean that the monarch was dissociated from the divine.

In the pre-revolutionary period, "the Kingdom is, in this sense, symbolically identified with the king. The king concentrates the nation in himself."[82] For Gauchet, the symbolic transformation brought forth by the Revolution had already appeared in Sieyès' famous 1789 text: "the representative body is always, for the nature of its activity, in the place of the nation itself."[83] The Jacobin moment, claims Gauchet, affected the identification between the nation and the people, leading to an indefiniteness between power and society.[84]

The Revolution's mistake, according to Gauchet, was designing itself as a revolution of ends, instead of a revolution of means. The declaration of

[80] Rosanvallon, *La Démocratie Inachevée*, 71; AP, t. LXIII, 589.

[81] Gauchet, *La Révolution des Droits de l'Homme*, xx.

[82] Gauchet, *La Révolution des Droits de l'Homme*, 24.

[83] Emmanuel-Joseph Sieyès, *Qu'est-ce que le tiers état?* (n.p., 1789) 128, https://gallica.bnf.fr/ark:/12148/bpt6k47521t.

[84] Gauchet, *La Révolution des Droits de l'Homme*, 40.

rights, in its universalizing perspective, contributed to a fascination for power and to a philosophy of authority. The problem was not the function of rights and of the Declaration, but that the idea that authority and power, in their totality, reside with the nation.

This idea is close to Moyn and Douzinas' criticism that human rights as expressed during the French Revolution were subordinated to a logic of national politics, losing their ability to serve as a resistance against the state apparatus itself.

We cannot, however, confound the theoretical discourse about the constitution of politics with the social practices of the revolutionary period. A strong political engagement is found both inside the primary assemblies and other spaces where sociability and politics, that is, the political, were being manufactured, and through the popular societies.[85] This recognition highlights the importance of not reducing the political philosophy of the revolutionary moment only to its written and formal expressions.

The declarations of rights did not inspire a blind kind of fascination by authority but served as practical instruments in the revolutionary struggle for transformation. In his new history of the Revolution, Jean-Clément Martin asserts that there was a profoundly pragmatic aspect in the Declaration. The debate among the deputies about the basis for the social bond was not an expression of their alienation from practical life. The Declaration's articles were, in fact, hardly abstract. Each topic was closely connected with some concrete aspect of the social life of that particular historical moment.[86] The idea that the Declaration had a disruptive potential appears, for example, in the 1789 debates about the need, or not, for a declaration of duties. According to Grégoire:

> we cannot present a declaration of rights without also presenting one on duties. It is essential to write a declaration of duties so that men can stay within the limits of their rights.[87]

[85] The literature on this topic is immense. As a mere example, on the popular societies in Paris, see Raymonde Monnier, "Les Sociétés Populaires dans le Département de Paris sous la Révolution," *Annales Historiques de la Révolution Française* 278 (1989). For a discussion of the political engagement of the peasantry, see Florence Gauthier, *La Voie Paysanne dans la Révolution Française* (Paris: F. Maspero, 1977).

[86] Jean-Clément Martin, *Nouvelle Histoire de la Révolution française* (Paris: Perrin, 2012), 174–175.

[87] AP, t. VIII, 340–341.

During the same speech, Grégoire adds that if this is not done, men would be destined to "neglect, fail to recognize, forget [their duties]." The issue also appears in another 1789 draft for a declaration that also reiterates the need for a declaration of duties.

Thoret speaks of a *devoir du citoyen* that could be read, according to Jaume, as an expression of legiscentrism. In article 21 of his declaration draft, Thoret states: "The whole is more than the parts. Private interests, be they from private persons, or be they from public entities, shall yield to the nation's interests."[88]

In this sense, Gauchet's idea that the Declaration was an instrument for the concentration of political power seems closer to the revolutionary current that defended the need for a declaration of duties. The debate on duties is connected with the broader discussion on the relationship between the Declaration and the Constitution.

In an August 1, 1789 speech, La Luzerne and Malouet already denounced the danger of abusing a declaration of rights when taken as an integral part of the constitutional text. What was needed instead was to bind the declared rights to stricter regulations written in the constitution itself, as a way to avoid "the danger of declaring the general principles of natural law in an absolute manner, without the modifications applied by positive law."[89]

The clash between the proponents of a declaration of duties and those against it persisted throughout the history of the Revolution's declarations. Only in 1795 did the first group win, with the approval of the *Déclaration des droits et devoirs de l'homme et du citoyen*—for the first time, the word "duties" appeared in the document's title.

In 1795, social rights were restricted, the idea that men "are born and remain free and equal in rights" (from the 1789 and 1793 texts) disappears from the text and some moral impositions appear more directly when compared to the previous declarations, as in article 4: "No one is a good citizen, if he is not a good son, a good parent, a good brother, a good friend, a good spouse."

We can find a different reading of the 1789 text, for example, in Claude Lefort's text *Human Rights and Politics*, published in 1979. He follows an interpretive perspective similar to the one presented in this book, recognizing the positive and productive social weight of the 1789 Declaration.

[88] Jacques Thoret, *Projet de Déclaration des Droits de l'Homme* (N.p.: Versaiiles, 1789), 4.
[89] AP, t. VIII, 322.

Lefort is addressing a certain common reading of human rights during the 1970s, including within the French left, that reduced the rights of men to the rights of the individual. The question raised by Lefort was: starting with the relationship between political emancipation and human emancipation, as presented by Max in his On t*he Jewish Question*, would it be possible to recognize some kind of continuity between the democratic-bourgeois revolution (in Lefort's own words) and the totalitarian revolution? It is easy to see how his position opposes the reading proposed by Gauchet and, more broadly, the Furetian thesis.[90]

Lefort highlights that political emancipation is a necessary moment toward human emancipation: "Since this moment is conceived by the bourgeoisie as the moment of human emancipation's fulfillment, [that] makes it the moment of 'political illusion' p*ar excellence*."[91] We have a double illusion here. On the one hand, the political illusion that the elements of civil life are independent of each other. On the other hand, that human rights would be enough to sustain them.

Totalitarianism would not be the next step, but the negation of this first stage, since it implies the destruction of civil society through the exacerbated enlargement of the political sphere. Totalitarianism would deny the independence of the elements that the illusion of political emancipation had established.

This does not mean that the atomized individual identified by Gauchet is not present. Lefort makes it clear that Marx's reading supports this hypothesis, but Marx and Gauchet are wrong to see only this in the revolutionary text. If the revolutionary proposal had limited itself to the atomization of the citizens, maybe the hypothesis about the empire of law and the submission of citizens to the will of a central authority would be adequate. Lefort, however, shows us that we cannot reduce the declarations to their individualistic dimension.

If the rights of man hide the mechanisms that allow their own exercise, they also "give us the support necessary for law awareness."[92] The interpretation of the law opens the possibility of fighting for social transformation.

[90] Furet's "first phase" book on revolutionary history had been published in 1965 and his drifting hypothesis was presented a year before Lefort's text.

[91] Claude Lefort, "Direitos do homem e política," in *A Invenção Democrática: Os Limites do Totalitarismo* (São Paulo: Brasiliense, 1987), 45.

[92] Lefort, "Direitos do Homem e Política," 57.

It is in this sense that we can look at the revolutionary uprisings. Even if popular uprisings were not an invention of the Revolution,[93] the new legislation, far from suppressing them, served as fuel for more protests.[94] There were six peasant revolts between June 1789 and fall 1792, which are interpreted by Gauthier as a response to the Assembly's inability to consider the peasants' demands, including problems such as subsistence, payment of taxes, and seignorial rights, since the Girondin majority dominated the Convention and the August decrees were not enforced.[95]

The peasants had fixated on the beginning of the August 4 Declaration ("The Assembly completely destroys the feudal regime") and did not accept the remaining seignorial fees. This resistance could take the shape of peaceful resistance, by simply not paying said fees, or through more aggressive acts, like the destruction of seignorial property.[96]

Their interpretation appears as a consequence of the social experience accumulated during the elaboration of the *Cahiers*. Part of the peasantry seemed to believe that the act of inscribing their wishes and desires for reform in their *cahiers* could, by itself, end feudalism.[97] Nonetheless, we cannot forget how the revolutionary government responded at the time.

Martial law was declared in response to the "agrarian problems" on February 23, 1790, in addition to the Le Chapelier laws of June 14 and July 20, 1791, regarding the right to assembly and collective petitioning. That (a part of) the government opposed the popular movement does not erase the fact that these struggles were being driven by legislation approved by that same government just moments before.[98]

[93] See Guy Lemarchand, "Troubles populaires au XVIIIe siècle et conscience de classe: une préface à la Révolution française," *Annales historiques de la Révolution française* 279 (January–March 1990).

[94] On the 1789 rural uprising, see Georges Lefebvre, *La Grande peur de 1789* (Paris: Armand Colin, 1932).

[95] Florence Gauthier, "Très brève histoire de la Révolution française, révolution des droits de l'homme et du citoyen," last modified December 2, 2005, access February 9, 2016, http://revolution-francaise.net/2005/12/02/10-tres-breve-histoire-de-la-revolution-francaise-revolution-des-droits-de-l-homme-et-du-citoyen.

[96] Gauthier, *Triomphe et Mort de la Révolution des Droits*, 79.

[97] De Dabuisson in Lefebvre, *La Grande Peur*, 51.

[98] On this specific piece of legislation, it is worth quoting Robespierre's speech during the February 22, 1790, session: "*Les nations n'ont qu'un moment pour devenir libres, c'est celui où tous les anciens pouvoir sont suspendus ne proclamons pas une nouvelle loi martiale contre un peuple qui défend ses droits, qui recouvre sa liberté*" (AM, III: 438). In other words, the possible paths for the revolutionary movement were many and varied. We cannot reduce the

Going back to Gauchet's thesis, the general rule of coexistence and freedom—of not doing that which hinders the rights of others—presented a practical problem in its enforcement. Even if there is no disagreement when abstractly conceiving the issue, the proposal offers no solution to how this conflict could be decided. The need for a third external agent to mediate this clash was evident, but the question of which agent this could be is less so. According to Gauchet, it was the law. The law was the instrument with which those limits were devised, and it was also responsible for determining when a violation had occurred. This revolutionary solution redirected the general regime of freedom to a supremacy of positive law.

For Gauchet, this happens, in part, because of abstract categories such as "public order" and "public utility." This theoretical language created the need for a specific praxis to fulfill it. As it was written, the sphere of protection for individuals remained undefined in relation to the public sphere. In order to ensure the source of the law as something external to its practical achievement, that is, the search for a strong kind of legitimation, and in the lack of an identifiable institutional arbiter that could be responsible for the protection and implementation of these rights, the only solution was to declare them with no concern for their enforceability. The result is the apparent transfer of the power to judge acts of the government to the people, when in fact we have the legislator as the sole judge over his own actions.[99]

Even the right to resistance, according to Gauchet, did not strengthen the position against arbitrary violence by the State. On the contrary, it reinforced the idea that the State can make use of the law and violence to suppress any (alleged) improper use of force by the citizens since the right to resistance would have been tempered by article 7: "Any citizen called or seized under the terms of the law must obey at once; he is considered guilty if he resists".

Jaume follows a similar interpretation.

> It is because the constituent power was not clearly recognized by the people from the beginning (besides Sieyès' warning), that it returned in the form of insurrection. Insurrection appears as the expression, and even the guarantee, of sovereignty, as presented by the people.[100]

Revolution's political philosophy to the final text of its Declarations, its Constitution, and its hundreds of laws.

[99] Gauchet, *La Révolution des Droits de l'Homme*, 148.

[100] Jaume, *Les Déclarations des Droits de l'Homme*, 52.

We can analyze the relationship between insurrection and the Republic, still in its formation, by way of the role played by the popular movement during the first months of the Revolution. On June 17, the National Assembly had sworn not to dissolve until a new constitution for the kingdom had been established. After Louis XVI's relative capitulation, in his "Declaration of Intent" and the June 27 request for the remaining members to join the Assembly, thousands of mercenaries waited a few kilometers from Versailles for an order from the court to end the third estate adventure.

The insurrection of the Parisian people—the fall of the Bastille being its best-known symbol—guaranteed that the Assembly remained united and that the revolutionary process could continue. After the fall, the *Grande Peur*[101] ignited the French countryside. News about the peasants' revolts reached the Assembly daily, having a twofold effect: they gave the Assembly the legitimacy needed to continue its work and pressured the Assembly to do so in a certain direction. This double effect is responsible for the August 1789 decrees abolishing feudalism.

These decrees and the Declaration, however, were not ratified by the king until a new insurrection—when seven thousand Parisian women marched to Versailles—compelled Louis XVI to do so. These examples demonstrate that Gauchet's idea that the hermeneutic openness of the Declaration led to the subversion of power by individuals' prerogatives does not tell the whole story.

By now, we can start to see how Douzinas' hypothesis that the law of the French Revolution was based on exclusion leaves behind an important part of revolutionary thinking.

As we have already seen, legiscentrism was one of Jaume and Gauchet's main theses. The problem of abstraction appears in Gauchet and in the historiographical current I have called conservative liberal, having Burke as its main representative. To justify their positions, they adopt a certain notion of how the revolutionaries understood natural law. Their reading, however, is not the only possible one.

[101] Cf. Lefebvre, *La Grande Peur*.

2.4 Back to Natural Law

The fundamental thesis in Edelstein's book *The Terror of Natural Rights*[102] centers on the interpretation of natural rights and republicanism developed in France at the end of the eighteenth century. The author considers the centrality of a question already raised above, that of the relation between nature and society. For Edelstein, Mably was one of the first thinkers to articulate natural law and republicanism without having the former superimpose itself onto the latter.[103]

For Edelstein, the influence of natural law on republicanism did not change it in a significant manner. However, a new tension emerged: that of the relationship between natural law and the state of nature, on one side and between positive law and civil society, on the other. For Locke, natural law continued to exist within the civil society and Mably agrees with this interpretation; we have already seen how this conception is directly articulated in some of the 1789 drafts, but this was in fact only one of many revolutionary readings.

Nevertheless, Edelstein states that this interpretation reduces the importance of contractualism and, at the same time, that it considers natural law as the sole measure of positive law since the latter would be an improvement over the former. The distinction between the political state and the state of nature becomes fuzzier, as institutions are more important than the social contract or a constitution, and therefore the greater crime would be to violate natural law.[104]

[102] Dan Edelstein, *The Terror of Natural Right: Republicanism, the Cult of Nature, & the French Revolution* (Chicago, London: The University of Chicago Press, 2009).

[103] Edelstein's hypothesis is preceded by a long discussion on French republicanism and the relation between the state of nature and the Golden Age, as portrayed by authors such as Montaigne, Fénelon, and Montesquieu. It is not my place to delve into this discussion. As a side-note, I point out that Edelstein's argument is based on the alleged Jacobin attempt to reproduce an old model of republicanism, and the author quotes Robespierre's mentions of ancient Rome and Greece. Gauthier, however, makes it clear that this position can be traced back to Furet, who had denounced the alleged anachronism of Robespierre as he tried to simply transpose classical antiquity to eighteenth-century France. However, Robespierre did not make such an attempt. Rome is not something to be imitated. The *Incorruptible* highlights the opposition between the theory of modern natural law and Antiquity. Slavery disgraced Antiquity as poverty disgraced his contemporary France, so came the need for a popular political economy. Furthermore, the old division between citizens and non-citizens was completely contrary to modern natural law, as well as the old wars of conquest based on the love for the homeland (Gauthier, *Triomphe et Mort*, 181–182).

[104] Edelstein, *The Terror of Natural Right*, 74.

As he continues his joint history of natural law and republicanism in France, the author, however, identifies the physiocrats as the final development of the idea of a natural republic. In the usual model for the passage into civil society from the state of nature, the latter would be abandoned because of its incapacity in dealing with emerging issues. From the family to more complex societies, the structure is the same: a "tutelary authority" responsible for guaranteeing the right to property. In physiocratic thought, the state of nature and civil society coincide, thus dismissing the need for a social contract.[105]

Edelstein claims that this physiocratic republicanism served as the basis for Jacobin natural republicanism. His thesis helps us identify some misconceptions to try to avoid. Even considering that there is some kind of temporal continuity between Mably and the physiocrats and that they dealt with similar topics, this does not imply a continuous line of thought linking them. The drafts presented during the debates show the plurality of philosophical approaches within the same revolutionary time frame.

There is no philosophical continuity between Mably and the physiocrats. On the contrary, they held opposing views in regard to society and the law.[106] Physiocracy was not the basis, as a general framework, for Jacobin thinking. Mably and Robespierre were preoccupied with conceiving an egalitarian political economy, while the physiocrats believed that laissez-faire would lead to the best possible economic arrangement.[107] While Mably and Robespierre were worried about guaranteeing people's participation in the political process, the physiocratic philosophy, if we take Quesnay as its greatest representative, openly defended despotism as the best social regulatory solution, as a way to ensure laissez-faire.[108]

Edelstein aims to present the philosophical basis of the alleged revolutionary terror and, while doing so, he ends up paying little attention to the

[105] Edelstein, *The Terror of Natural Right*, 102–104.

[106] See Florence Gauthier, "Political Economy in the Eighteenth Century: Popular or Despotic? The Physiocrats Against the Right to Existence," *Economic Thought* 4, n. 1 (2015).

[107] See Florence Gauthier, "De Mably à Robespierre: un programme économique égalitaire 1775–1793," *Annales Historiques de la Révolution Française* 261, n. 1 (1985).

[108] See David McNally, "'Guard Dogs of the Monarch': Legal Despotism and the Natural Order," in *Political Economy and the Rise of Capitalism: A Reinterpretation* (Berkeley; Los Angeles; Londres: University of California Press, 1988). One of Quesnay's texts in which we can see a clear defense of despotism, affirming that a despotic government can be a simple realization of natural rights is François Quesnay, "Despotisme de la Chine," in *Œuvres économiques et philosophiques de F. Quesnay*, ed. Joseph Baer (Frankfurt: Joseph Baer et cie. Libraires-Éditeurs; Paris: Jules Perelman et cie, 1888), 563–660.

theoretical and practical disputes that define the frontiers between the different schools of thought.[109] We should not forget that the word "Terror" was first used within the revolutionary context in the expression *terreur des droits de l'homme*. It was used to name and highlight natural and imprescriptible rights themselves, not to designate some governmental practice of eliminating political opponents.[110]

That does not mean that natural rights did not play a part in governmental practices during the Revolution. But it does mean that we should not reduce natural law philosophy to its instrumental role during the purges. As we will see later on, natural rights were a justification for doing precisely the opposite: preserving life and guaranteeing liberties.

Gross, in his history of Jacobin egalitarianism, highlights the transition from the abolition of privileges and the guarantee of equality before the law in 1789 to the reduction of real inequalities and the distribution of goods and properties, especially between 1793 and 1794. At the same time, the Revolution radicalized itself, and a new radical theory of revolutionary violence emerged, as well as the idea of instituting a new man and the new society, brought inseparably together through a Republican identity. That does not mean, however, that all these elements are one and the same. It is important to distinguish between them:

> There is, for example, a marked difference, which is more than semantic, between price controls brought about by bread riots or the violent rhetoric of subsistence and a consciously elaborated and coherently executed programme of food rationing.[111]

If a "punitive egalitarianism," in Gross' words, did exist, an egalitarianism based on distributive justice was also present, as in the proposals for progressive taxation and the defense of the right to subsistence, under the guise of a right to existence.[112] This discussion over revolutionary egali-

[109] The problem of the alleged Terror is beyond the scope of this work. For a good introduction to this topic, see Michel Alpaugh, *Non-violence and the French Revolution: Political Demonstrations in Paris, 1787–1795* (Cambridge: Cambridge University Press, 2015).

[110] See Yannick Bosc, "Introduction," in *Le terreur des droits de l'homme: le républicanisme de Thomas Paine et moment thermidorien* (Paris: Kimé, 2016).

[111] Jean-Pierre Gross, *Fair Shares for All: Jacobin Egalitarianism in Practice* (Cambridge: Cambridge University Press, 1997), 8.

[112] Gross, *Fair Shares for All*, 3–5. Regarding the passage from the right to subsistence to the right to existence, see Cynthia Bouthon, "Les mouvements de subsistance et le problème

tarianism is present in the Revolution since its beginning, even though individual liberties gained prominence in 1789, following the model of the Anglo-American *Bills*, and we should be attentive to its political and economic implications.

The 1789 Declaration presented a top-down model of physiocratic inspiration. The imperfect society was to be directed toward a moral ideal—for regulating, for example, market forces. Gross highlights the change between 1789 and 1793. In 1789, we had a mix of individual and collective rights and the mitigated protection of "sacred and inviolable" property. In 1793, property was still under the Declaration's protection, but attributes such as "sacred" and "inviolable" were removed from the text. Social, economic, and political rights gained importance, as did universal suffrage, the right to subsistence, and the right to work.[113]

In 1793, we had a declaration that understood individual liberties and social rights to be necessarily entangled, even if such entanglement is, in practice, uncomfortable. In this arrangement, Jacobin thinking assigns a special role to fraternity as the uniting bond between liberty and equality, without which the government could not adequately function, and politics could not happen.

This pairing serves as the basis for the theory of modern natural law presented by Florence Gauthier. According to the historian, however, a relative primacy of freedom is observed. The philosophy of modern natural law was founded in a certain comprehension of humankind, and liberty was the element giving unity to the human race. This liberalism of natural law, as Gauthier puts it, fundamentally meant not submitting oneself to the power of any other men, but it is not reducible just to this negative dimension. The unity of humankind also includes the counterpart of liberty, that is, equality: "the social connection is, therefore, strongly expressed in the reciprocity between liberty and equality."[114]

Liberty and equality as natural and imprescriptible rights are the basis for popular sovereignty, the right of men to form a political society. For this to happen, these two rights are complemented by the societal dimension of freedom, that is, citizenship as the corollary of popular sovereignty. The fact that citizenship is a derived right does not remove it from the

de l'économie morale sous l'ancien régime et la Révolution française," *Annales Historiques de la Révolution Française* 319 (January–March 2000).

[113] Gross, *Fair Shares for All*, 42–44.

[114] Gauthier, *Triomphe et Mort*, 29.

roster of natural rights. Sociability is a positive form of the fulfillment of freedom, now within a politically established society.

Gauthier states that the relationship between freedom, equality, and citizenship means a reconciliation between nature and society. Otherwise said, it is the formation of the political as a defense and fulfillment of natural rights through the citizens' participation in drafting the law they will come to obey.[115]

This interpretation helps us read the 1789 declarations and serves as a hermeneutical guide to 1793. The problem of the passage from the state of nature to the social state appears, explicitly and implicitly, in many legislative proposals. The main point of disagreement is the debate over the permanence, or not, of natural rights within the social state.

This question is one way of analyzing the division between the advocates of the philosophy of modern natural law, as presented by Gauthier, and their opponents. For the first group, natural rights are not reducible to individual rights. Natural rights are human qualities linked to humankind itself. The individual-universal right implies its reciprocity, equality, and this reciprocity does not express itself as an individual right, but as a social connection or as a way to form social connections. This intersubjective dimension is evident in the discussion over the right to resistance.[116]

The right to resist oppression is based precisely on the permanence of natural rights within the social state. The idea that we give up our natural rights when forming the political society acts, in the revolutionaries' speeches, as a justification for restricting rights and delegitimizing active resistance. This conservative trend can be identified with Moyn's reading of law during the Revolution, but it is not the only possible interpretation.

The reconciliation between nature and society points to the interconnectedness of both realities and the preservation of natural and imprescriptible rights as effectively opposable to abuse and oppression—to paraphrase Condorcet's understanding of the requirement of intelligibility when writing a Declaration.

It is in this sense that we should interpret Gauthier's assertion that, following Robespierre, the Declaration would be the Constitution.

[115] Gauthier, *Triomphe et Mort*, 43.
[116] Gauthier, *Triomphe et Mort*, 43.

> The declaration of rights is the constitution. Natural law should be declared to constantly remind us of the ethics that subordinate politics. Natural law is, therefore, the common criterion that allows each one to exercise its own faculty of judgment over political matters.[117]

The philosophy of natural law denies the autonomy of politics in relation to ethics, but here we should be attentive. The liberal trend in historiography, in its classical or conservative variation, sees the ethical discourse as one of the main sources for revolutionary excesses. In the end, ethics, as well as the popular movement intromission, are then to blame for the Terror.[118]

For the philosophy of modern natural law, however, ethics have another role, and they allow us to re-read some juridical institutions, as we can see in the debates over property and the right to existence. In 1789, property appeared in all drafts for a new declaration, with a large variety of proposals. The final version, adopted by the National Assembly on August 26, adopts a strictly private definition of property, but it does not include terms such as "unlimited right" or "free disposal"—not uncommon in the drafts—using instead the term "natural right."

Gauthier interprets that provision in relation to the idea of property circulating at the time. Freedom was the property of an individual. The same was valid for personal freedom (property over oneself) and for freedom in society or citizenship (the citizens' property as citizens)—as we can deduct from articles 3 and 6 of the Declaration.

This ethical understanding of property as a natural right allows for criticism of economic freedom. Gauthier mentions Montesquieu, Rousseau, and Mably as representatives of this critical trend. Mably, for example, criticizes the despotic aspect of economic power that could be seen in the physiocratic economic policies of Turgot.[119]

[117] Gauthier, *Triomphe et Mort*, 32.

[118] For example, on the relationship Furet established between virtue and Terror: "*La fête de l'Être suprême et la Grande Terreur sont investies de la même finalité: assurer le règne de la vertu*" (Furet, *Penser la Révolution Française*, 115).

[119] Gauthier mentions Mably's text *Du Commerce de Grains*. Gabriel Bonnot de Mably, "Du commerce de grains," in *Collection complète des Œuvres de l'abbé de Mably*, t. 13 (Paris: Ch. Desbriere, 1794–1795), 242–298.

In a more general sense, Mably, in a letter to John Adams,[120] criticizes the "commercial elites" and denounces the concentrated economic power: "our European manners which, probably, are, at this period, too common in America, will enable money (or, in other words, the rich) to usurp and to maintain an absolute dominion throughout the several states."[121]

As we can see, the criticism of economic despotism had already created, before the declaration, an understanding of the contradiction between the universal property of freedom and the private property of material goods. The contradiction between economic freedom and political freedom. Between economic freedom and the philosophy of natural rights. This tension was explored and highlighted by the popular movement that resisted the new economic policies and proposed, sometimes through direct action, another project for society and for economic policies based on the right to existence. Gauthier highlights the struggle over the recognition of the right to existence as the focal point of this new political theory.

According to the historian, the declaration was the center of social struggles between 1792 and 1795, demarcating the separation between two divergent visions on natural law. In this dispute, Robespierre was one of the main theoreticians of the right to existence during the Revolution, exposing the contradiction between economic power and political freedom. For example, on the subject of censitary suffrage, as we have already seen, he had denounced its anti-social and anti-constitutional character.[122]

Gauthier also calls our attention to another important point, that of fraternity as the basis to a cosmopolitics of freedom. In his 1793 speech on the constitution,[123] Robespierre affirms: "the declaration of rights is the constitution of all peoples. Other laws are changeable by their nature and are subordinated to it."[124]

Robespierre's positions contradict Moyn and Douzinas' hypothesis that revolutionary law was characterized by its exclusivist nationalism. In his 1793 draft for a declaration, presented to the Convention on April 25,

[120] Gabriel Bonnot de Mably, "Concerning the Dangers to which the American Confederation stands exposed; the Circumstances which will give rise to Troubles and Divisions; and the Necessity of augmenting the Power of the Continental Congress," in *Remarks concerning the Government and Laws of the United States of America: in Four Letters addressed to Mr. Adams* (Dublin: Moncrieffe, 1785), 183–262.

[121] Mably, "Concerning the Dangers," 258–259.

[122] Gauthier, *Triomphe et Mort*, 88.

[123] Maximilien de Robespierre, "Sur la constitution (Convention, séance du 10 mai 1793)," in *Œuvres de Robespierre*, 276–293.

[124] Robespierre, "Sur la constitution," 292.

Robespierre describes the revolutionary process as the process where the rights of men are reconquered beyond the frontiers of the French state. It is not about the freedom of the French people, but the collective property of all peoples over their own sovereignty.

The discussion over revolutionary cosmopolitanism helps us understand the difference between the following two approaches: one that tries to read the Revolution through the lens of modern natural law philosophy, as Gauthier does, and one that tries to identify the Revolution's error, as Edelstein does. For the latter, the theory of natural law and the Golden Age would serve only to demonize the native inhabitants of the American continent—the savage was an enemy, that is, Edelstein's *hostis humani generis*.[125]

For Gauthier, conversely, the philosophy of modern natural law that developed in the eighteenth century is connected to the idea of freedom as an attribute of the person, not of things, as derivable from the principle of the unity of humankind—following Bartholomé de las Casas and the Salamanca School's response to the "discovery" and violent conquest of the Americas. All human beings are equal since they are all born free.[126]

From an internal point of view, the guarantee of popular sovereignty manifests itself in two main forms: in restricting the power of magistrates (short terms, only one magistracy per person, separating the making of laws and their execution, etc.); and in submitting public agents to strong responsibilities and the "real dependence, not on the individuals, but on the sovereign."[127]

The discussion over how to regulate law and where it originates was an important discussion topic in 1793, as this book will show.

Appendix

Historical Documents

Parliamentary Notes, Newspapers and Legal Texts

Archives parlementaires de 1787 à 1869 (First series). Paris: Paul Dupont, 1867–2021. [cited as 'AP', followed by tome number, page, and the document's date, when available]

[125] Edelstein, *The Terror of Natural Right*, 29, 54, and 110.
[126] Florence Gauthier, "Les Lumières et le Droit Naturel," Revista HMiC 1 (2003): 112.
[127] Gauthier, *Triomphe et Mort*, 108.

Ancién moniteur (Réimpression de l'), *Seule Histoire Authentique et Inaltérée de la Révolution Française depuis la Réunion des États-Généraux jusqu'au Consulat (Mai 1789–Novembre 1799)*, 31 t. Paris: Henri Plon Imprimeur-Éditeur, 1862–1863. [cited as 'AM', followed by tome number, page, and the document's date, when available]

References

Alpaugh, Michel. *Non-Violence and the French Revolution: Political Demonstrations in Paris, 1787–1795.* Cambridge: Cambridge University Press, 2015.

Baker, Keith. "Transformations Of Classical Republicanism In Eighteenth-Century France." *The Journal of Modern History* 73, n. 1 (March 2011): 32–52.

Bailleul, Jacques-Charles. *Examen Critique de l'Ouvrage Posthume de Mme la Baronne de Stäel, ayant pour Titre. Considérations sur les Principaux Evénemens de la Révolution Française.* Paris: Ant. Bailleul, 1818.

Barreto, José-Manuel (ed.). *Human Rights from a Third World Perspective: Critique, History and International Law.* Newcastle upon Tyne: Cambridge Scholars Publishing, 2013.

Baxi, Upendra. *The Future of Human Rights.* Oxford: Oxford University Press, 2008.

Belissa, Marc. Le 'Droit des Gens' dans le Débat Constitutionnel. In *L'An I et L'Apprentissage de la Démocratie*, 97–106. Saint-Denis: Éditions PSD, 1995.

Belissa, Marc. "Marc Belissa aux 4e Rencontres d'histoire critique—Nation(s)/mondialisation(s) (Nov. 2015)." *YouTube.* February 12, 2016. Video, 17: 13. https://www.youtube.com/watch?v=RZ4E5JDn_dw.

Bosc, Yannick. "La Constitution de l'An III: Un Républicanisme Classique?" Révolution Française.net. Published September 6, 2008. http://revolution-francaise.net/2008/09/06/258-constitution-an-iii-republicanisme-classique.

Bosc, Yannick. *Le Terreur des Droits de l'Homme: le Républicanisme de Thomas Paine et Moment Thermidorien.* Paris: Kimé, 2016.

Bouthon, Cynthia. "Les Mouvements de Subsistance et le Problème de l'Économie Morale sous l'Ancien Régime et la Révolution Française." *Annales Historiques de la Révolution Française* 319 (January–March 2000): 71–100.

Burke, Edmund. *Reflections on the Revolution in France.* Londres, Nova Iorque: Temple Press Letchworth J. M. Dent & Sons Ltd., 1910.

Cobban, Alfred. *Aspects of the French Revolution.* New York: Jonathan Cape Ltd., 1968.

Cobban, Alfred. *The Social Interpretation of the French Revolution.* Cambridge: Cambridge University Press, 1964.

Cochin, Auguste. *La Révolution et la Libre Pensée.* Paris: Pion-Nourrit et Cie, 1924.

Comparato, Fábio Konder. *Afirmação Histórica dos Direitos Humanos*. São Paulo: Saraiva, 2005.

Douzinas, Costas. *Human Rights and Empire: The Political Philosophy of Cosmopolitanism*. Milton Park, NY: Routledge-Cavendish, 2007.

Douzinas, Costas. *The End of Human Rights*. Oxford: Hart Publishing, 2000.

Edelstein, Dan. *The Terror of Natural Right: Republicanism, the Cult of Nature, & the French Revolution*. Chicago, Londres: The University Of Chicago Press, 2009.

Furet, François. *Penser la Révolution Française*. Paris: Gallimard, 1978.

Gauchet, Marcel. *La Révolution des Droits de l'Homme*. Paris: Éditions Gallimard, 1989.

Gauthier, Florence. "De Mably a Robespierre: Un Programme Economique Egalitaire 1775–1793." *Annales Historiques de la Révolution Française* 261, n. 1 (1985): 265–289.

Gauthier, Florence. "Éléments d'une Histoire du Droit Naturel: A Propos de Léo Strauss, Michel Villey et Brian Tierney." Révolution Française.net. Published April 14, 2011. https://revolution-francaise.net/2011/04/14/432-elements-histoire-droit-naturel-leo-strauss-michel-villey-brian-tierney.

Gauthier, Florence. *La Voie Paysanne dans la Révolution Française*. Paris: F. Maspero, 1977.

Gauthier, Florence. "Les Lumières et le Droit Naturel." *Revista HMiC* 1 (2003): 109–119.

Gauthier, Florence. "Political Economy in the Eighteenth Century: Popular or Despotic? The Physiocrats Against the Right to Existence." *Economic Thought* 4, n. 1 (2015): 47–66.

Gauthier, Florence. "Très Brève Histoire de la Révolution Française, Révolution des Droits de l'Homme et du Citoyen." Published December 2, 2005. http://revolution-francaise.net/2005/12/02/10-tres-breve-histoire-de-la-revolution-francaise-revolution-des-droits-de-l-homme-et-du-citoyen.

Gauthier, Florence. *Triomphe et Mort de la Révolution des Droits de l'Homme et du Citoyen*. Paris: Éditions Syllepse, 2014.

Gérard, Alice. *A Revolução Francesa: Mitos e Interpretações*. São Paulo: Perspectiva, 1999.

Griffin, James. *On Human Rights*. Oxford: Oxford University Press, 2008.

Gross, Jean-Pierre. *Fair Shares for All: Jacobin Egalitarianism in Practice*. Cambridge: Cambridge University Press, 1997.

Habermas, Jürgen. *Between Facts and Norms*. Cambridge: MIT Press, 1996.

Habermas, Jürgen. *The Philosophical Discourse of Modernity*. Cambridge: Polity Press (Blackwell Publishing), 1990.

Habermas, Jürgen. "The Concept of Human Dignity and the Realistic Utopia of Human Rights." *Metaphilosophy* 41, n. 4 (2010): 465–480.

Habermas, Jürgen. *The Inclusion of the Other: Studies in Political Theory.* Cambridge: MIT Press, 1998.

Jaume, Lucien. les *Déclarations des Droits de l'Homme.* Paris: Gm Flammarion, 1989.

Kates, Gary (ed.). *The French Revolution: Recent Debates and New Controversies.* London: Routledge, 1998.

Lefebvre, Georges. *Le Grande Peur de 1789.* Paris: Armand Colin, 1932.

Lefebvre, Georges. *The French Revolution.* London: Routledge, 2005.

Lefort, Claude. "Direitos do Homem e Política." In a *Invenção Democrática: Os Limites do Totalitarismo.* 37–69. São Paulo: Brasiliense, 1987.

Lemarchand, Guy. "Troubles Populaires au XVIIIe Siècle et Conscience de Classe: une Préface a la Révolution Française." *Annales Historiques de la Révolution Française* 279 (1990): January–March 32–48.

Louvrier, Julien. "Penser la Controverse: la Réception du Livre de François Furet et Denis Richet, la *Révolution Française.*" *Annales Historiques de la Révolution Française* 351 (January–March 2008): 151–176.

Mably, Gabriel Bonnot de. "Du Commerce de Grains." In *Collection Complète des Œuvres de l'Abbé de Mably.* t. 13, 242–298. Paris: Ch. Desbriere, 1794–1795.

Mably, Gabriel Bonnot de. "Concerning the Dangers to which the American Confederation Stands Exposed; The Circumstances which Will Give Rise to Troubles and Divisions; and the Necessity of Augmenting the Power of the Continental Congress." In *Remarks Concerning the Government and Laws of the United States of America: In Four Letters Addressed to Mr. Adams,* 183–262. Dublin: Moncrieffe, 1785.

Marks, Stephen. "From the 'Single Confused Page' to the 'Decalogue for Five Billion Persons': The Roots of the Universal Declaration of Human Rights in the French Revolution." *Human Rights Quarterly* 20, n. 3 (August 1998), 459–514.

Martin, Jean-Clément. *Nouvelle Histoire de la Révolution Française.* Paris: Perrin, 2012.

Mazauric, Claude. *L'Histoire de la Révolution Française et la Pensée Marxiste.* Paris: Presses Universitaires de France, 2009.

McNally, David. "'Guard Dogs of the Monarch': Legal Despotism and the Natural Order." In *Political Economy and the Rise of Capitalism: a Reinterpretation,* 121–129. Berkeley; Los Angeles; Londres: University of California Press, 1988.

Meister, Robert. *After Evil: A Politics of Human Rights.* New York: Columbia University Press, 2011.

Monnier, Raymonde. "Les Sociétés Populaires dans le Département de Paris sous la Révolution." *Annales Historiques de la Révolution Française* 278 (1989): 356–373.

Moyn, Samuel. *The Last Utopia: Human Rights in History.* Cambridge, Massachusetts, London: The Belknap Press of Harvard University Press, 2012.

Nicolet, Claude. *L'Idée Républicaine en France: Essai d'histoire Critique.* Paris: Gallimard, 1982.

Palmer, William. "Edmund Burke and the French Revolution: Notes on the Genesis of the Reflections." *Colby Quaterly*. 20, n. 4 (December 1984): 181–190.

Quesnay, François. "Despotisme de la Chine." In: *Œuvres Economiques et Philosophiques de F. Quesnay*, edited by Joseph Baer (Frankfurt: Joseph Baer et cie. Libraires-Éditeurs; Paris: Jules Perelman et cie, 1888), 563–660.

Rawls, John. *Lectures on the History of Moral Philosophy*. Cambridge: Harvard University Press, 2000.

Robespierre, Maximillien de. *Œuvres de Robespierre*. Paris: A. Vermorel, F. Cournol, 1867.

Rosanvallon, Pierre. *La Démocratie Inachevée: Histoire de la Souveraineté du Peuple en France*. Paris: Gallimard, 2000.

Sieyès, Emmanuel-Joseph. *Qu'est-Ce Que le Tiers Etat?*. N.p, 1789. https://gallica.bnf.fr/ark:/12148/bpt6k47521t.

Soboul, Albert (ed.). *Dictionnaire Historique de la Révolution Française*. Paris: Presses Universitaires de France (Quadrige), 2005.

Spieler, Paula Bartolini. "*Direitos Humanos Como Discurso Emancipatório? O Caso das Ongs que Atuam no Brasil.*" Phd Diss. Universidade do Estado do Rio de Janeiro, 2014.

Staël, Germaine de (Madame la Baronne). *Considerations on the Principal Events of the French Revolution*. Indianapolis: Liberty Fund, 2008.

Stellars, Kirsten. *The Rise and Rise of Human Rights*. London: Sutton Publishing Limited, 2002.

Thoret, Jacques. *Projet de déclaration des droits de l'homme et du citoyen*. Versailles: n.p., 1789.

Tocqueville, Alexis de. *O Antigo Regime e a Revolução*. São Paulo: WWF Martins Fontes, 2009.

Vovelle, Michel. "L'historiographie de la Révolution Française a la Veille du Bicentenaire." *Estudos Avançados* 1, n. 1 (December 1987): 61–72.

CHAPTER 3

Excursus: Introducing the Archive

In total, 206 texts from 137 authors were analyzed—including 21 anonymous contributions and 4 collective writings (the drafts written by the Constitution Committee, the Committee of Public Safety, the Committee of General Security, and the approved final text). This number does not include the speeches given during the constituent debates. Even if we consider that some of these speeches also have separate written versions, I have favored the records of the parliamentarian interventions and, as such, these were not added to the sum above. However, I have included them when analyzing the topics which will be discussed in the following chapters.[1]

[1] Among the documents mentioned during the conventional debates, the only one I have chosen not to include in my analysis is William Godwin's *Enquiry Concerning Political Justice and Its Influence on Morals and Happiness*, which was sent by letter to the Convention on January 26, 1792 (AP, t. LXIII, 498–499). Even though it was sent as a contribution to the debates, Godwin's work, which was inspired by the revolutionary moment, does not discuss the political events happening in France at the time (the word "France" only appears 27 times in the whole text), nor does it present any institutional proposals for solving France's then current deadlock (the National Convention is only mentioned in passing when introducing a section about ways of discussing a constitution; see William Godwin, Enquiry concerning political justice, v. 2 (London: G.G.J. and J. Robinson, 1793), 658). Godwin's book is a treaty of political philosophy reaching almost a thousand pages and it is considered one of the foundational texts of anarchist thought (George Woodcock, Anarchism: A History of Libertarian Ideas and Movements (Cleveland: Original Meridian, 1962), 60ff.). In light of its nature, it would not make sense to include it with the rest of the constitutional drafts.

E. Baker, *Human Rights and Humanity's Rights During Year Three of the French Revolution*,
https://doi.org/10.1007/978-3-030-99508-9_3

After selecting the texts, the first challenge is identifying the number of proper drafts. The few works on this topic do present a number for how many of these could be properly considered drafts for a declaration of rights or for a constitution. For example, Galy states that there are 25 actual drafts, but he includes some drafts that are limited to just a few articles.[2] Pertué counts about 15 complete drafts.[3]

As we know, Lanjuinais mentions the existence of about 300 projects,[4] but we do not know if he's referring to drafts written as complete legal documents (as in Pertué count), to all legal texts sent to the Convention (even if the text itself is just a few articles long, as in Galy's count), or if Lanjuinais refers to the total volume of documents sent with the express purpose of adding to the constituent debates, even if the texts were themselves, as we will see in some cases, closer to political philosophy essays than proper constitutional drafts.

In my methodology, it seems relevant to distinguish between drafts for the declaration of rights and constitutional drafts. In the first group, I have located 44 texts. However, it is important to mention that not all of these drafts for a declaration are legal texts in the contemporary sense. The very idea of a "Declaration" was itself the object of discussion. Some defended the need for some kind of explanatory text instead of the mere enunciation of articles—this was Bohan's position, for example. That is why I have included in my account all texts titled "Declaration" even if the wording of some of them seems unusual for a legal text. I have also included some contributions that were limited to correcting other drafts.

If we wish to choose a narrower selection of declarations, this number would be reduced to 41 drafts: Anonymous A, Anonymous C, Anonymous I, Bancal, Barailon, Barère, Beaulieu, Beffroy de Reigny,[5] Boissel, Boissy

[2] François Galy, *La Notion de Constitution dans les Projets de 1793* (Paris: Editions Albert Mechelinck, 1932), 38.

[3] Michel Pertué, "Les Projets Constitutionnels de 1793," in *Révolution et République: L'Exception Française*, dir. Michel Vovelle (Paris: Kimé, 1994), 176.

[4] AP, t. LXIII, 193.

[5] Louis-Abel Beffroy de Reigny, *La Constitution de la Lune, Rêve Politique et Moral, par Le Cousin-Jacques* (Archives Nationales, Series Lb41, n. 706). Beffroy de Reigny's text deserves an explanatory note. Titled *La Constitution de la Lune, rêve politique et moral* ("The Moon's Constitution, a political and moral dream"), the draft sent by the playwright, also known as *le Cousin Jacques*, is presented as a constitutional draft for a fictitious kingdom on the moon. But his intention is clearly to intervene in the constituent debates. Even if the text is not directly applicable to the French circumstances—the author himself states that the Moon would be in a unique situation, since it did not have any borders with other nations, it had a

d'Anglas, Bonguyod, Bonnemain, Bourgois, Cappin, Carnot, Chabot, Chevret, the Committee of Public Safety, the Committee of General Security, Coupe, Cusset, Daunou, Debrey, Durand-Maillane, Harmand, Isnard, Ladey, Lanthenas, Momoro, Montgilbert, Mont-Réal, Pénières, Pepin, Ragonneau, Robespierre, Romme, Ruault, Schreiber, Thorillon, and Varlet. Other partial texts are: Anonymous F, Anonymous H, and Bacon. Blaviel and Grégoire limit their texts to a declaration of the rights of peoples and not a declaration of the rights of men. If we include these, we would have a total of 46 drafts for a new declaration of rights.

The total amount of constitutional drafts, however, depends on a central dilemma unfolded during the 1792 and 1793 debates of the National Convention, that is, the discussion over what a constitution should include. It is this lack of definition that explains the discrepancy between Pertué's and Galy's number of constitutional drafts. As we have stated in the first chapter, this book aims precisely to explore the forgotten possibilities within the lost revolutionary memory. In this sense, it seems more compatible with such an approach to accept a broader definition of the term "constitution." Again, every time an author calls their text a constitution or a constitutional draft, I have considered it as such, excepting the cases where evidently only a proposal for a section or title within a larger constitutional text is presented.

With these considerations in mind, we arrive at the number of 38 drafts: Anonymous A, Anonymous D, Anonymous E, Anonymous P, Bacon, Bancal, Barailon, Beaulieu, Beffroy de Reigny, Boissel, Boissy d'Anglas, Bonnemain, Bourgois, Capin, Chabot, Constitution Committee, Committee of Public Safety, Cusset, Daunou, Debry, Ducastellier, Dupont, Durand-Maillane, George Edwards, Gleizal, Lambert, Lesuer, Lefebure, Montgilbert, Montréal, Pénières, Poultier, Pressavin, Ragonneau, Rouzet, Ruault, Saint-Just, and Thorillon.

The partial drafts or mere proposals for changing drafts that had already been presented amount to 32 texts—covering a variety of topics such as, and not limited to, the imperative mandate, establishing censors and changing how the French territory was to be divided. These are:

homogenous people and a stable climate—it is not difficult to identify the sections where the author is dealing with topics that are relevant to the Year 3 debates. Furthermore, the draft is followed by a text titled *Profession de foi du Cousin-Jacques sur la Révolution française* ("Confession of Cousin-Jacques on the French revolution") where the playwright expresses his concerns and ideas over the then present state of the Revolution.

Anonymous C, Anonymous G, Anonymous H, Anonymous I, Barlow, Bonguyod, Borel, Brunel, Calès, Constantini, Defrance, Delacroix, Desacy, Dunouy, Duplantier, Hazard, Kersaint, Lafont, Lanjuinais, Lanthenas, Masuyer, Robert Merry, Oudot, Philippeaux, Picqué, Prunelle, Raffron, Rubigny, Sade, Thibaudeau, Thirion, and Varlet. Cloots presents a draft for the organization of humankind's Executive power, including the organization of the Judiciary. If we include Cloots' text and the two categories mentioned above, we have 71 drafts.

Before analyzing these texts, I shall briefly discuss two preliminary topics. Firstly, the historical context in which these drafts were presented and discussed. In other words, examining which reading of the historical events, especially those concerning the National Convention, shapes our interpretations. Secondly, the structure of the presented drafts and the proper hermeneutical approach to deal with them.

The first question is why drafts were presented by two different committees. The Constitution Committee is created on October 11, 1792, and has as its members: Sieyès, Paine, Brissot, Pétion, Vergniaud, Gensonné, Barère, Danton and Condorcet—as well as six deputy members (Barbaroux, Hérault de Séchelles, Lanthenas, Debry, Fauchet, and Lavicomterie). On September 29 of that same year, Cambon had demanded the creation of a Constitution Committee to elaborate a constitutional draft,[6] after the decision, made just eight days before, that a new constitution—to be ratified by the people—was needed.[7] This committee's final work is generally known as the Condorcet project.[8] The following month, a report by Barère is published. The text invites "all friends of freedom and equality"[9] to send their contributions to the French constitutional debate.

[6] AP, t. LII, 232.

[7] AP, t. LII, 72.

[8] For example, see Rosanvallon, *La Démocratie Inachavée*, 76.

[9] Complete quotation: "*La Convention nationale, après avoir entendu le rapport de son comité de constitution, invite tous les amis de la liberté et de l'égalité à lui présenter, en quelque langue que ce soit, les plans, les vues et les moyens qu'ils croiont propres à donner une bonne constitution à la république française*" (Barère, Bertrand (Barére De Vieuzac), *Rapport Fait au Nom du* Comité de Constitution *sur l'Invitation a Faire aux Amis de la Liberté et la République Française* (October 19, 1792) (Archives Nationales, Series AD/XVIIIC/256, n. 1), 2–3).

The project is presented on February 15, 1793,[10] and just two days later the Convention calls all of its members to present their own projects[11]—which seems to indicate the initial rejection of the text presented by the Constitution Committee. An Analysis Committee (also known as the *Comité des six*) is created on April 4 to receive and process all drafts sent to the Convention. Its members are: Debry, Mercier, Dufriche-Valazé, Lanjuinais, Romme, and Barère.[12] This committee even presents its own draft for the declaration of rights, which is read by Romme during the conventional sessions.[13]

After some months of debating, and little time before the uprisings that would lead to the arrest of 29 Girondin representatives on May 29, 1793, five new members were added to the Committee of Public Safety, after a proposal by Barère, with the purpose of presenting to the Convention "as soon as possible, a Constitutional plan consisting only of the articles that should be made non-derogable by the Legislative Assemblies."[14] On May 30, Hérault de Séchelles, Ramel-Nogaret, Couthon, Saint-Just, and Mathieu join the Committee of Public Safety.[15] We should keep in mind that on May 29, the Convention had just approved a new declaration of rights.[16]

On June 10, Hérault de Séchelles presents the Committee of Public Safety's draft[17] and the debates continue until June 23. The final version is approved the following day, June 24, 1793.[18] However, a reading of only these two drafts is not enough to give us a good grasp of the complex network of constituent proposals and perspectives that were put forth during Year 3.

[10] AP, t. LVIII, 601.

[11] AP, t. LVIII, 620.

[12] Cf. AP, LXI:180. The initial work done by the Constitution Committee is rejected by the Jacobins. They form their own commission outside the institutional space of the Convention. Their members were Jean-Bon Saint-André, Robespierre, Saint-Just, Rober, Thuriot, Bentabolle, Billaud-Varenne, and Antointe, and their deputies were Collot d'Herbois, Dubois-Crancé, Cloots, and Couthon (Ulrich Coste, *Le Pouvoir Législatif dans la Constitution de 1793* (Paris: Librairie générale de droit & de la jurisprudence, 1909), 14). However, unfortunately, I could not find any material written by this commission or any record of its discussions.

[13] AP t. LXVII, 267–269.

[14] AP, t. LXVI, 580.

[15] AP, t. LXVI, 610.

[16] AP, t. LXVI, 579–580.

[17] AP, t. LXVI, 256–264.

[18] AP, t. LXVII, 143.

The first topic in my examination of the drafts, as an introduction to the other points, is the way they are organized by the different authors. Even before I examine the structures themselves, it is worth pointing out the great diversity of ideas regarding what is considered constitutional and what is not. Ollivier lists 43 constitutional topics among the 135 authors identified by her.[19] Not one topic is present in all authors. Only two themes are nearly universal, being found in 134 of the 135 authors: the terms *peuple* and *nation*—people and nation. They are followed in frequency by the terms: constitutional referendum, national sovereignty, and popular sovereignty (present in 132 authors); and representative system (found in 125 authors).[20] Besides these six most common terms, the average presence for the remaining ones is only 33.2 drafts. Even if we include the top six, distorting the average a little, the final frequency would still be low, only 46.9.

One of the reasons for such disparity is that many drafts do not aim to cover the whole spectrum of constitutional matters. For example, Varlet's contribution deals only with the imperative mandate.[21] Sade's speech is solely about how legislation is to be sanctioned,[22] Prunelle presents just a proposal on how to organize a court of censors,[23] and Anonymous C's draft is limited to a proposal concerning the organization of the Judiciary and some articles on external relations.[24]

If we limit ourselves to the constitutional projects that are closer to a complete constitution, there is still considerable diversity. I will focus on four different examples:[25] Anonymous D, Daunou, the Constitution

[19] There is a small difference between the *corpus* selected by me and by Ollivier. The researcher had identified 17 anonymous projects, while I have selected 21 of those. Furthermore, I include, for example, texts by the Bishoprics of Basel and Borel not selected by Ollivier. Also, Ollivier includes some of the speeches made in the Convention as separate texts, while I count all debates relating to the constitution or the declaration.

[20] Nathalie Ollivier, "Les Projets Constitutionnels de 1793", 533–540.

[21] Jean-François Varlet, *Projet d'un Mandat Spécial et Impératif aux Mandataires du Peuple à la Convention Nationale* (AP, t. LIV (December 9, 1792)), 719–722.

[22] Donatien Alphonse François Sade (Comte de), *Idée sur le Mode de la Sanction des Loix* (Archives Nationales, Series Lb41, n. 2400).

[23] Léonard Joseph Prunelle, *Observations et Projet de Décret sur l'Établissement d'un Tribunal de la Conscience du Peuple* (Archives Nationales, Series AD/XVIIIC/261, n. 13).

[24] Anonymous C, *Plan d'une Constitution Libre et Heureuse selon Justice, Raison et Sagesse, Trouvé Chez M. Laporte* (Archives Nationales, Series AD/XVIIIC/219, n. 14).

[25] In this debate over textual structures, I have left out the declaration drafts. There is one main reason for doing so. Differently from the constitutions, the declarations do not have a

Committee (whose draft was presented before the May 31–June 2 uprisings) and the Committee of Public Safety (whose draft was presented after this event).

Anonymous D's draft, titled *La France heureuse ou tout le monde content* ("The Happy France or everybody is pleased"), can be divided into eight main chapters: Legislative power;[26] laws; Executive power (including regional administrative powers); citizens' echelons or ranks; mores; right of property protection; freedom of the press; and luxury.

Daunou's draft is also divided into eight chapters: constitutional grounds (territorial division, and civil and political status of people); primary assemblies; statutes and decrees; the Legislative Assembly; the Executive council; administrative bodies; the administration of justice; and principles of French laws.

The differences between the two proposals are clear. Anonymous D aims to establish a constitutional text with the main goal of integrating social organization with political organization; that is why he or she presents class echelons for citizens and dedicates an important part of the text to social mores. Furthermore, some additional questions would have to be addressed so that the constitution could guarantee an ideal social functioning, so the draft also includes other topics, such as property protection, freedom of the press, and luxury.[27]

It is important to present what may seem like an excessively peculiar structure, to avoid a common mistake found in the few research works that study the 1793 drafts. In a widely cited work on the topic, Galy's doctoral dissertation, the author points to these kinds of textual structures as an argument to diminish their historical or intellectual importance. For example, when discussing Ducastellier's proposal on how to divide the French territory, Galy says the idea "is crazy" and that the text is the work

chapter-based structure or anything similar to that. The closest thing would be the order in which each text lists different topics or the topics chosen in each draft. For example, we can find liberty, equality, and property in almost all declaration projects, but not all, since Anonymous A only discusses property and Beffroy de Reigny does not include property in his declaration. There is therefore a great diversity, making such an analysis of little to no use.

[26]The author actually usually uses the term *puissance* instead of *pouvoir*, so "potency" could seem as a possible translation, but it would change the meaning of the expression. As Montesquieu used *puissance* to refer to the three branches of government, I chose to translate the term using the current expression.

[27]Luxury is related to regulation of the economy, more precisely to the different limitations to property proposed by the popular political economy, in Gauthier's words.

of a madman. As for Anarchasis Cloots and Chabot, the author declares that "one is a madman and the other a fanatical."[28] Some dismissals are less severe, as the claim that Harmand's contribution does not deal with a real constitutional issue,[29] but the bias is, in any case, blatant.

My challenge here is to read all the drafts with a focus on the texts themselves and take the proposals seriously, even if in today's standards they may seem ridiculous (like Anonymous D's tribunes) or merely regulatory (as the many extensive detailing of the inner workings of primary assemblies). Stating this rule of interpretation may seem unnecessary, but we will see throughout this book that many readings of the 1793 drafts do not follow this methodological rule.

Daunou's text, on the other hand, seems to present us with a more familiar constitutional project for today's readers. Even if his constitutional grounds are inscribed outside the constitutional text itself, we still find the modern three powers: the Legislative, the Executive, and the Judiciary. But the resemblance can be deceitful. When the revolutionaries talk about the Legislature, the Executive, and Judiciary they do not necessarily mean the same thing as us. For example, when analyzing the different proposals for a censorship committee or court, Galy says that such institutions could be read as Judiciary bodies. They would be a primitive form of judicial review or constitutional control. However, Galy himself recognizes that these institutions deal mainly with mores.[30] Governmental bodies responsible for shaping and preserving the republican mores and censoring those that lack the proper zeal do not exercise a Judiciary role in the modern sense of the term.

From the revolutionaries' point of view, the framing depends on what we understand as the Judiciary and, as we will see in Chap. 4, this question has many different answers during the French Revolution's Year 3. The Judiciary can be an extension of the Executive, an independent power by itself (a rare choice among the drafts), or something in between. This plasticity is also present when discussing the Legislative power in light of questions such as the existence, or not, of representation and, if it exists, what its content should be. Such apparently theoretical distinctions mean that the term "Legislative body" can have divergent meanings when expressed by different revolutionary figures.

[28] Galy, *La Notion de Constitution dans les Projets de 1793*, 76, 61, and 39 (respectively).
[29] Galy, *La Notion de Constitution dans les Projets de 1793*, 56.
[30] Galy, *La Notion de Constitution dans les Projets de 1793*, 136–137.

Lastly, we can focus on the Constitution Committee's and the Committee of Public Safety's drafts—also referred as Condorcet's and Hérault de Séchelles' drafts. They carry a similar overall structure: they start by declaring France to be an indivisible and unitary republic—reiterating the declaration of September 25, 1792—and they present its territorial division and establish the conditions for acquiring French citizenship, followed by a regulation of the primary assemblies. They are both preceded by a declaration of rights, but each having different titles. For the Constitution Committee, we have a *Déclaration des droits naturels, civils et politiques des hommes* and the Committee of Public Safety presents a *Déclaration des droits de l'homme*.[31]

The first difference between these texts is that the Committee of Public Safety's draft has a chapter called "On the sovereignty of the people" before the chapter on the primary assemblies, in which it is declared that the people exercise their sovereignty in those gatherings.[32] On the other hand, the Constitution Committee only uses the term "sovereignty of the people" at the end of its text, when dealing with the relation between France and the foreign nations—more precisely when limiting the French army's actions when occupying another country, a subject we will discuss more in depth in the following chapter.

Also, both drafts offer a treatment of what they call the national Executive and the Legislative body, but in reverse order. The Constitution Committee's draft begins with the Executive, while the Committee of Public Safety's text starts with the Legislature. In both cases, after these two sections, we are introduced to the institutions responsible for correcting the people's representatives: the people's censorship and the grand national jury, exercised respectively by the Constitution and the Public Safety committees. This concern will appear in many different drafts under different names. Censorship or censors is the preferred term (Kersaint, Lanthenas, Barailon, Dupont, among others, use the term), but this is not unanimous. Anonymous E uses the term "custodians" (*gardiens*) and Ruault proposes a revisory body.

The similarities and differences in the structure of these two projects—that I believe we can take to be the two main 1793 drafts since they serve

[31] We will go back to this distinction, its implications, and philosophical foundations later on.

[32] Comité de Salut Public, *Projet de Constitution du Peuple Français* (AP, t. LXVI (June 10, 1793), IV, Article 1.

as the basis for the constituent debates—help us identify a variety of concerns that are common to many different proposals. This helps orient how we should approach the drafts (as it is made clear in the titles of this book's chapters) and it also prevents us from conflating a similarity of subjects into a similarity of proposals.

These difficulties have led me to some necessarily arbitrary choices since the revolutionary categories of thought are far removed from our current ones—as the debate over the Executive (power) will show us. Also, there is no homogeneity among the drafts themselves—as the discussion over the Judiciary, and not Judiciary power, can help us understand. My tentative categorization is therefore more a reflection of methodological choices and of a specific approach than of a pre-existing structure found in the texts.

Appendix

Historical References for the 1792–1793 Debates

Explanatory Notes

1. Whenever possible, the drafts are cited by article or chapter and article, not by page.
2. I reference the anonymous texts' authors as "Anonymous A" to "Anonymous U" to more easily reference them in the main text of this book.
3. Since this is an abridged version of the original thesis, not all of the texts listed below are mentioned throughout the main text. I chose to include them in the references for fellow researchers interested in the topic.
4. The final and approved text of the Declaration and Constitution of the Year 1 of the Republic are cited as *Declaration* and *Constitution*. The other primary texts are listed below.

Parliamentary Notes, Newspapers, and Legal Texts

Archives parlementaires de 1787 à 1869 (First series). Paris: Paul Dupont, 1867–2021. [cited as "AP," followed by tome number, page, and the document's date, when available]

Drafts

Anonymous C. *Plan d'une Constitution Libre et Heureuse selon Justice, Raison et Sagesse, Trouvé Chez M. Laporte*. Archives Nationales, Series AD/XVIIIC/219, n. 14.

Barère, Bertrand (Barére de Vieuzac). *Rapport Fait au Nom du Comité de Constitution sur l'Invitation a Faire aux Amis de la Liberté et la République Française* (October 19, 1792). Archives Nationales, Series AD/XVIIIC/256, n. 1.

Beffroy de Reigny, Louis-Abel. *La Constitution de la Lune, Rêve Politique et Moral, par le Cousin-Jacques*. Archives Nationales, Series Lb41, n. 706.

Comité de Salut Public. *Projet de Constitution du Peuple Français*. AP, t. LXVI (June 10, 1793) 260–264.

Prunelle, Léonard Joseph. *Observations et Projet de Décret sur l'Établissement d'un Tribunal de la Conscience du Peuple*. Archives Nationales, Series AD/XVIIIC/261, n. 13.

Sade, Donatien Alphonse François (Comte de). *Idée sur le Mode de la Sanction des Loix*. Archives Nationales, Series Lb41, n. 2400.

Varlet, Jean-FrançPos. *Projet d'un Mandat Spécial et Impératif aux Mandataires du Peuple à la Convention Nationale*. AP, t. LIV (December 9, 1792) 719–722.

References

Coste, Ulrich. *Le Pouvoir Législatif Dans la Constitution de 1793*. Paris: Librairie Générale de Droit & de la Jurisprudence, 1909.

Galy, François. *La Notion de Constitution dans les Projets de 1793*. Paris: Editions Albert Mechelinck, 1932.

Ollivier, Nathalie. "Les Projets Constitutionnels de 1793." PhD Diss. Université Panthéon-Assas, 2002.

Rosanvallon, Pierre. *La Démocratie Inachevée: Histoire de la Souveraineté du Peuple en France*. Paris: Gallimard, 2000.

Vovelle, Michel (Dir.). *Révolution et République: L'Exception Française*. Paris: Kimé, 1994.

Woodcock, George. *Anarchism: A History of Libertarian Ideas and Movements*. Cleveland: Original Meridian, 1962.

CHAPTER 4

External Relations and Sovereignties

Personne n'aime les missionnaires armés
Robespierre

4.1 War and External Relations

Before discussing the National Convention's establishment on September 20, 1792, it is important to note three previous events to help us situate the constitutional debate. The event that most closely connected to this debate was the August 09 and 10, 1792, insurrection spurred by the Brunswick Manifesto, issued the preceding month, which would lead to the king's downfall. However, one broader background issue is particularly important when interpreting the constitutional discussions within the revolutionary period: the external war—an important but not determining issue when analyzing ideas put forth in relation to dealing and institutionalizing the subject of external relations.

Our starting point to understanding why the war was declared is the king's escape attempt on June 20, 1791. In the episode known as the Flight to Varennes, the monarch tried to flee his Parisian surveilled life with a plan intermediated by the Marquis of Bouillé, but the king is recognized in Sainte-Menehould and captured in Varennes, being back in Paris by June 25. His plan to regroup troops loyal to the House of

E. Baker, *Human Rights and Humanity's Rights During Year Three of the French Revolution*,
https://doi.org/10.1007/978-3-030-99508-9_4

Bourbon and to establish a constitutional monarchy with a strong Executive centered around himself was frustrated.[1]

The king's capture is instrumental to his acceptance of the Constitution of 1791 and the later establishment of the Convention, but with regard to warfare, the main focus is on the international repercussions of this event. Until that moment, most European powers had not yet acted to counter the continuing French revolutionary experience.

Leopold II, the Holy Roman Emperor, had the intention of bringing the European courts together to save the French royal family, but their first act together would be subtler: a declaration signed on August 27 by Leopold II and Frederick William II of Prussia. Between August 25 and 27, they have a meeting to discuss unrelated subjects,[2] but the Varennes incident changes their plans. Louis XVI's brother, the Count of Artois, and Calonne, a former minister to the French king, are present at the meeting, so the two rulers agree to sign a text known as the Declaration of Pillnitz.

In their joint statement, they assert that the French king's current situation is of interest to all European sovereigns and that they are ready to guarantee "the foundations of a monarchical government that is equally suitable to the sovereign's rights and the welfare of the French people."[3]

Even though some historians have claimed that the declaration was somewhat rhetorical, and not a concrete threat, aiming to evoke fear in the French revolutionaries and lead them to backtrack, it seems reasonable to suppose that the text was construed in France, if not in its literal sense, at least as a real threat of armed retaliation by the European monarchs.

The Constitution of 1791 did not solve the institutional deadlocks in France, nor the tension between Louis XVI and the Legislative. At the same time, the European powers were starting to make their move against

[1] Cf. the letter written by the then king, but censored by the French Legislature, which prevented it from being publicized after his recapture. In this letter, Louis XVI decries the popular societies' actions as being responsible for *l'anarchie et le despotisme* in France and asked the French people to place the king back in his place of prestige: *revenez à votre Roi, il sera toujours votre père, votre meilleur ami* (Capet in Roche-Tilhac, 1795, 145).

[2] The meeting, arranged before Louis XVI's escape, was intended to be a discussion on Poland's situation. The country had just ratified a new constitution establishing a constitutional monarchy after years of political instability (see Albert Sorel, "La Fuite de Louis XVI et les Essais d'Intervention en 1791—Varennes et Pillnitz," *Revue des Deux Mondes*, Third Period, t. 75 (1886)).

[3] Leopold II; Frederick William II in *Lettre*, 1791.

the French nation. The French crown sees this threat as a chance to restore the king's powers.

On December 14, the king threatens the Electorate of Trier: if the principality did not disband the groups of émigrés that threatened France by January 15, 1792, the Electorate would be considered an enemy of France. At the same time, Louis XVI sends a letter directly to the principality, explaining his proposal: "instead of a civil war, there would be a political war in Europe and this change would greatly improve the situation."[4]

Other groups were favorable to the war for distinct reasons. La Fayette saw it as an opportunity to oust the Jacobins. Part of the National Assembly's left also wanted the war. One of its representatives, Brissot, claimed that the foreign peoples were favorable to the French ideas and would thus embrace the Revolution once the conflict started. However, the imminence of war was avoided when Leopold invited the Electorate of Trier to dissolve the groups of émigrés.

One of the few voices that were openly against any kind of external war was Robespierre. The revolutionary figure asserted that war is the means through which the government concentrates even more power, especially in the hands of the Executive, that is, the king. Therefore, war should not be conceived as a way to liberate the European peoples, as Robespierre explained in one of his most famous quotes. In his speech on January 2, 1792, he declares:

> The most extravagant idea that can emerge in the head of a politician is the belief that to make a foreign people adopt one's laws and constitution, it takes only an armed invasion. No one likes armed missionaries; and the first advice given to them by nature and prudence is to repel them as enemies.[5]

After the Electorate of Trier's capitulation, the Assembly asks Emperor Leopold II to renounce any treaties that may threaten the French nation—in other words, to disavow the Declaration of Pillnitz. The Holy Roman Empire did not answer this French ultimatum. On the contrary, Austria and Prussia formed an official alliance by early February and on April 20, Louis XVI addresses the Assembly, proposing to declare war against the king of Hungary and Bohemia, Francis II, who succeeded Leopold II after

[4] Louis XVI quoted in Soboul, 1975, 236.

[5] Maximillien de Robespierre, *Œuvres Complètes de Robespierre.* v. 8 (Paris: Presses Universitaires de France, 1954), 82–83.

his death in March. By doing so, Louis XVI avoided declaring war against the whole empire. The proposition is approved with just a small dissent. This is the context necessary to analyze the speeches on (external) war and how they influenced the constitutional debates on the relations among the peoples.

Belissa presents the speeches about the war through the lenses of the right of the peoples.[6] While traditional historiography takes the disagreements over the war inside the Jacobin club as a mere difference in tactics instead of principles, the French historian endeavors to map the underlying political philosophies behind the existing positions.

In the war promoter camp, we have some distinct political groups: Brissotins, Girondins, and even future Montagnards, like Cambon. Their general tone is treating the war as a means to handle the political crisis, by uniting all these three groups. There are also some war enthusiasts, like Cloots, who defend the war as an emancipation of the peoples, but the bellicose speech is not very transparent.

In Belissa's reading, for Narbonne, Brissot, Vergniaud, and others, the war's purpose would be "that of order, tranquility, and the end of the Revolution. (...) [through] the union of both branches of government [the Legislative and Executive] in order to accomplish the 'national interests'."[7] Other kinds of justification are also present, such as the need for discipline within the army and the importance of regaining the wounded national glory. Some discourses also mention the emancipation of the peoples—a theme absent among moderate war promoters, but which is central to enthusiastic discourses, such as Cloots'.

Among the war enthusiasts, we have Roederer's speech on December 18 at the Jacobin Club—the same day as Robespierre's previously mentioned speech denouncing the war as a subterfuge sought by the Executive to concentrate more power. Roederer claims "we are not at peace. We are being attacked, won't we defend ourselves? (...) it is a war of the nobility against the people."[8]

The war would be against the princes, not against the peoples, and so it wouldn't be a war of conquest. But how can we reconcile this with the

[6] Marc Belissa, *Fraternité Universelle et Intérêt National (1713–1795): Les Cosmopolitiques du Droit des Gens* (Paris: Kimé, 1998).

[7] Belissa, *Fraternité Universelle et Intérêt National*, 269.

[8] Société des Amis de la Constitution, *Journal des Débats de la Société des Amis de la Constitution, Séance Aux Jacobins a Paris*, n. 113 (Paris: [s.n..], 1791), 3.

May 22 decree? A preventive war is announced as a kind of defensive war, as the hostilities by the European powers would confirm. The same discourse defends that the freed peoples be led to understand and utilize their newfound freedom: by the municipalization of their territories, by choosing the representatives of the people, and so on. According to Belissa, however, it was

> without a doubt, not only an attempt to 'popularize the war' among the Jacobins but also an ideological preparation for a war of conquest, embellished by the pretext of liberating the peoples.[9]

This position presupposes the idea of the people as a universal legislator, which is able and legitimized to control other peoples; in other words, it denies the sovereignty of the peoples and its reciprocity.[10]

The emphasis in the discourse against the war is exemplified by both Robespierre's speeches mentioned above, that is, the war would act as a distraction orchestrated by the Executive to strengthen itself: "it is during the war that the people forget the deliberations that essentially concern their civil and political rights and occupy themselves only with external events."[11] The war would be thus an artifice used by external enemies to bolster the Executive's despotism and conceal the internal enemies.

The patriotic criticism of war is based on the rejection of the idea of conquest and in the reciprocity of the right of the nations. Belissa presents an interesting contrast between the war promoters' discourses and, in his words, the patriotic discourse:

[9] Belissa, *Fraternité Universelle et Intérêt National*, 282.

[10] Belissa broadens his reading by analyzing the classical interpretations of this event. According to the French historian, Michelet and Jaurès had reduced the Girondin warmongering discourse to the emancipation of the peoples, but Belissa highlights at least three different versions: in the Assembly, the unification of the powers and the trust in the Executive; in the Jacobin Club, the need to defend oneself against aggression from the European monarchs; before the moderates, the need to restore the finances. This does not mean that the Brissotin position was incoherent or fallacious. In all three cases, we have the war as a way to redefine the power relations within the larger European terrain (Belissa, *Fraternité Universelle et Intérêt National*, 300–301). For a reading of the primary historiographical positions mentioned by Belissa, see Michelet, *Histoire de la Révolution Française*, t. 3 (Paris: Ernest Flammarion, 1893), 370 and 421, and Jaurès (dir.), *Histoire Socialiste*, 882–883.

[11] Robespierre, *Œuvres Complètes de Robespierre*, v. 8, 48.

> *confidence* is opposed by the *distrust in principle* against the Executive; *discipline* and respect to the generals are countered by *democracy in the army* and the arming of volunteers; *national honor* is matched by the *rejection of the politics of power*; lastly, *municipalization* is opposed by the *reciprocity of sovereignty among the peoples.*[12]

The events of July and August 1792 take place while these discussions are still ongoing, leading to the National Convention being summoned the following month. In early July 1792, the Prussian army, led by the Count of Brunswick and supported by an army of French emigrates under the leadership of the Prince of Condé, threatens to attack Paris unless the city submits to Louis XVI. Vergniaud and other deputies accuse the king and his ministers of treason, denouncing them as the masterminds behind this apparent imminent attack.

Brissot, in his July 26, 1792, speech before the National Legislative Assembly defends the position that the primary assemblies should not be convoked, and neither should any other sudden measure of institutional change be taken, such as adopting universal suffrage. It would be necessary, on the contrary, to defend the Constitution of 1791 and to find a solution to the issue of the king's treason within the institutional order already in place.[13]

Amidst maneuvers between the Girondins and the king, Robespierre and other Jacobins continue to attack the legitimacy of the monarch and the system implemented in 1791. Robespierre, in his July 29, 1792, speech before the Society of the Friends of the Constitution, defends the king's deposition and the renewal of the Legislative by the convocation of the primary assemblies:

> the main cause of our evils is in both the Executive and the Legislature; the Executive, which may lose the State, and the Legislature, which cannot or does not want to save it.[14]

Robespierre reiterates his criticism of the war as an artifice to instigate internal strife[15] and declares that, against despotism—seen by him as the usurpation of sovereign power—the only recourse would be to let the

[12] Belissa, *Fraternité Universelle et Intérêt National*, 290, emphasis in original.

[13] AP, t. XLVII: 160–163.

[14] Robespierre, *Œuvres Complètes de Robespierre*, v. 8, 409.

[15] Robespierre, *Œuvres Complètes de Robespierre*, v. 8, 418.

French people renew the delegated powers through the primary assemblies under universal suffrage.

With the publicization, on August 3, of the letters between the king and the Duke of Brunswick from July 25, the deadlock becomes short-lived. In the letter, signed by the Duke of Brunswick but written by Geoffroy de Limon,[16] the leader of the Prussian army threatens Paris with a "military execution" if any damage is done to the king, to the queen, or the royal family. Those who stood by the king and helped with the restoration of the order would be protected.

In response, almost all Paris sections demand the king's downfall. The Paris Commune organizes and mobilizes itself against the risk of a counter-revolution. The danger seems real, considering the Austrian advance and the king's escape plan. On August 9, 30 sections delegate powers to commissioners before the Commune to form an insurrectionary committee endowed with full powers. At the same time, the Assembly tries to reconvene without much success.

With the fall of the House of Bourbon, instead of stripping the king of his powers and terminating the French monarchy altogether, the National Assembly suspends the king from his functions, but decrees, on August 10, 1792, that a National Convention was to be elected by universal male[17] suffrage—this last point being approved the following day.

The topic of the relations among peoples is closely tied to two other debates: the war and the sovereignty of the people. After having presented the historical background for the debates between the end of 1791 and 1793, we should keep in mind that the constitutional debates over external relations, which include the subject of the war, took place during this heated period.

Between the Convention's first session in September 1792 and the final text approved on July 24, 1793, France invades the Belgian territory, dictates a relative adoption of the French regime in the occupied countries, declares war on Great Britain and the Dutch Republic, and possible treason by Dumouriez occurs.[18]

[16] On this episode, cf. H. A. Barton, "The Origins of The Brunswick Manifesto," *French Historical Studies* 5, n. 2 (Autumn, 1967): 158–160.

[17] However, we should note, as does Gauthier, that women did participate in the primary assemblies. Suffrage was denied to them, but not, in theory, participating in the Assembly (Gauther, *Triomphe et Mort*, 184–186).

[18] After supporting the kind and opposing the process held by the Convention, Dumouriez, by then the most important French general, and close to the Girondins starts to negotiate

We were able to see how the revolutionaries had widely different stances on the subject of war. These ideas reflected on how they think about the relationship between peoples during the war efforts.

The annexation of Savoy is a good example. Belissa highlights how the discussion over Savoy underlined the dispute over the concept of "national borders" and concluded:

> By pushing the argument to its final consequences, we arrive at a radical conclusion about popular sovereignty. If reunions are always preferable to an alliance between independent republics, France must impose a reunion with others in the name of the peoples' supposed interest.[19]

But this was not the only available option. Grégoire, who was responsible for writing the draft for the Savoy annexation decree, begins his speech by highlighting the impossibility of directly applying the same laws and Declaration to all peoples. It would always be necessary to subordinate their application to local circumstances.[20]

Grégoire's position should be read while taking into account the fact that the Convention was, at the time, welcoming representatives from Savoy's primary assemblies which declared the sovereignty of their people and their intention to unite themselves with France by way of "a diplomatic agreement drawn between two full and legitimate sovereigns."[21] We are thus far away from any French exceptionalism or nationalism which would justify an unrestricted conquest of the European territory. This, however, does not invalidate the fact that the final text of the decree is at least ambiguous, or even contrary to Grégoire's and the Savoy representatives' words.

This same ambiguity appears when we examine the decree and the discussion of December 15, about how the French army should act when occupying territories. The final text reveals the imposition of a series of rules by France to the occupied territories, without however a complete

with the enemy forces in an attempt to save himself from what he sees as his imminent demise. Dumouriez even arrests the French minister of war, Beurnonville, and four commissionnaires that were sent to check on this conduct, and delivers them to the enemy forces.

[19] Belissa, *Fraternité Universelle et Intérêt National*, 326–327.

[20] In Grégoire's words: "*comme de tous les temps, leur application est subordonnée à une foule de circonstances locales qui nécessitent des modifications.*" For the full quote, see AP, t. LIII, 610.

[21] AP, t. LIII, 617.

submission to the French nation.[22] Primary or communal assemblies were to be held to organize the provisional justice and administration. In other words, the people from the territory occupied by the French Republic would be responsible for inventing a new way of governing their territory. But there would be limitations. For example, article 3 of the decree excludes civil and military servants from the old regime from participating in these primary assemblies. Even when considering that such a limitation is circumscribed to one voting instance, it is still an evident case of French interference. Running against this kind of restriction, Basire takes the following stand at the Convention: "in this circumstance, you have no reason to violate the sovereignty of a people and the liberty of their choices; you run the risk, on the contrary, of alienating well-intentioned men from your cause."[23]

These diverse opinions on how to deal with pragmatic issues posed before the revolutionaries are also reflected in the constitutional proposals themselves. We can split the approach to the subject of external relations within the constitutional drafts into two main approaches. One is concerned with how to organize the government in regard to its relations toward other nations and peoples. The focus here is to determine which part of the government will fulfill each function, the relation between the Legislative and Executive in the external relations, and the role (or absence) of the people in the decision-making process involving other nations—the most important point being war and, subsidiarily, international treaties. The other is related to how the French revolutionaries understood the connections between external relations and the sovereignty of the peoples, including the colonial issue.

4.2 The War in the Constitutional Drafts

One of the most discussed topics was the declaration of war. Who was responsible for this declaration? Was there some kind of control over it? What motives were considered genuine for such a declaration to be made? During the debates over Chapter X of the Constitution, on June 15, 1793,

[22] François-Jean Baudouin (ed.), *Collection Générale des Décrets Rendus par l'Assemblée Nationale* (Paris: Baudoin, 1789–1795), v. 34, 73–76.

[23] AP, t. LV, 75.

the discussion about the declaration of war took most of the time of the debates.[24]

We saw how the debate about the declaration of war was also a debate about the Executive's place and limits. When Robespierre presents his opposition to the external war in 1791, he highlights how the conflict would serve to concentrate and increase the power exerted by the Executive through Louis XVI.

In the Constitution of 1791, the declaration of war was regulated under Chapter III, Section I, Article 2, which describes the exercise of power by the Legislative branch. According to this article, war could be declared only by a decree of the Legislative, following a proposal by the king. The decree was then sanctioned by the king. However, even if the Legislative rejected the king's proposal, the monarch was authorized to take the necessary measures to counter any existing hostilities.

The final text of 1793 completely subverts this logic. The debate over this topic of the Constitution is held in June 1793, that is, after the king's trial and the treason of Dumouriez. Robespierre's concerns, voiced in 1791, had been confirmed, at least apparently, and Dumouriez's case is mentioned by Thuriot.

The debates start with Azéma defending that the declaration of war was to be done only by way of a law. He argues that, if taxes can only be raised by law, such an important subject could not dispense with this requisite. Moreover, he states that "in all ancient Republics, the people deliberated over war and peace. During the first centuries of the French monarchy, the people were consulted in the assemblies."[25]

The argument is not properly disputed, and the debate revolves around what kind of war was at stake and how the slow Legislative process would affect something as urgent as a declaration of war. Ducos, Danton, Thuriot, and Génissieu make a distinction between a declaration of war and preparing for war against an external threat. It is however important to note that even these emergency preparations would be under the responsibility of the Legislative, a position that Thuriot and Danton declare without being challenged.

Another point of debate was the nature of war. Réal, Philippeaux, and Thuriot mention the possibility of an offensive war but they are amended by Jeanbon Saint-André, Billaud-Varenne, and Danton in two senses.

[24] AP, t. LXVI, 544–547 and t. LXVII, 141–142.

[25] AP, t. LXVI, 544.

Firstly, the French nation should waive all kinds of conquest (Billaud-Varenne). An offensive war, or a war of conquest, according to Jeanbon Saint-André, deserves to be faced with national horror: "a horror strengthened by a moral and healthy education (…), a war of this kind should be impossible in France."[26] Secondly, there should be no confusion between an offensive war—whose declaration by the Legislative should be barred—and a preventive war (Danton).

In a way, the same ambiguity mentioned above reappears in the debate. Even though denial of the war of conquest is present, the *conventionnels* still left a gray area. Between Billaud-Varenne's straightforward prohibition of any conquest and Danton's distinction between offensive war and preventive war, there lies a discursive gap that would be appropriated in many different ways throughout the Revolution.

In any case, we should not forget that the French representatives are leaving to the people, through the primary assemblies, the possibility of controlling the declaration of war. The same logic is repeated when discussing treaties. If war can only happen by law, and the Constitution specifies how the people can undo an act by the Legislative, a treaty—which is approved via a decree and without any legally pre-determined popular repeal procedure—isn't exempt of the possibility of popular control.

Responding to Génissieu's outcry, maintaining that any treaty should also be approved by law since the Executive and Legislative could concert to give part of the French territory to a foreign nation, Delacroix states: "but the people are here and through a general insurrection they will rigorously return them to order."[27] We should keep in mind that this debate happens just two weeks after the May–June 1793 uprising that led to the banishment of 28 Girondin deputies. The belief that a popular intervention could correct government actions thus seems well-founded.

Article 54 of the Constitution of 1793 defines what law is and, among the long list of its possible topics, we find the declaration of war.[28] That means that, based on articles 56–60, while a declaration of war can be

[26] AP, t. LXVI, 545.

[27] AP, t. LXVI, 547.

[28] We will come back to the legislative procedure in a later chapter. For now, we should keep in mind that there are two types of legislative texts issued by the Assembly: laws and decrees. Briefly, we can say that the law is the legislative work itself—allowing of the sanction by the people or opening up space for its repeal by the people—while the decree has a more reglementary or urgent aspect to it—depending on the topic. For example, while the declaration of war and civil legislation are examples of laws under the Constitution of 1793, the

revoked by the primary assemblies since it is a kind of law, a ratified treaty cannot be directly repealed by the will of the people. The Executive council (the national Executive body of the Constitution of 1793) has the exclusive attribution of naming the Republic's exterior agents and negotiating treaties, by articles 69 and 70. This second point was used, during the June 15 debates, as another opportunity to invoke the subject of the mistrust toward the Executive.

We saw above how Robespierre had expressed his opinion regarding the Executive in the debate on the subject of war. It was already evident at that time that his distrust did not limit itself to the person of the king, but that it extended to the place reserved for the Executive within the organization of government. But his skepticism was not shared, at least in the same degree, by his fellow *conventionnels*.

On June 16, 1793, debates over Chapter XIII of the Constitution, which regulated the Executive council, are held.[29] Ducos, for example, expressed his trust in the council for negotiating treaties. Any previous mistrust was justified only because the council was chosen by the king. There would be no reason to prevent the council from negotiating treaties once the body was to be selected by the people. Billaud-Varenne—who previously stated that treaties should be negotiated by the Legislative and ratified by the people—points to the fact that the council can become corrupted. The adopted solution is the one proposed by Robespierre. Giving the distrust toward the Executive, this body should restrict itself to negotiating the treaties, leaving the final ratification to the Legislative.

This debate and the final approved text, however, give us only a glimpse of all the possible solutions raised by the revolutionaries. For a group of constitutional proposals, the declaration of war and the ratification of treaties were to be treated uniformly. This uniformity, however, can have two different meanings. For Bacon-Tacon, both the attribution of declaring war and that of ratifying treaties should be with the Legislative, without the direct expression of the will of the people, even though the relations between the French and other nations are to be conducted by a group of ministers called the Executive Assembly.[30]

order to issue coins, unforeseen expenses, and the ratification of treaties are considered decrees.

[29] AP, t. LXVI, 573–576.

[30] Pierre Jean Jacques Bacon-Tacon (Comte de), *Plan Patriotique, ou Idée d'une Bonne Constitution Républicaine, en France* (Archives Nationales, Series AD/XVIIIC/262, n. 4), Articles 2 and 3.

But excluding the people from participating in the declaration of war or the ratification of treaties does not necessarily imply that there would be no popular sanction of laws in general, as Bacon proposes. The project by the Constitution Committee—presented on February 15 by Condorcet and Gensonné—and the project by the Committee of Public Safety—presented on June 10 by Hérault de Séchelles—both make the distinction between a law and a decree and consider the declaration of war and the ratification of treaties as kinds of decrees, not laws. However, the drafts never completely exclude the requisite of popular approval as a general rule.[31]

Not all drafts are explicit about the possibility of a constitutionally guaranteed form of popular intervention regarding the declaration of war. In his project, Saint-Just states that accidental acts of legislation and acts that are made necessary due to the circumstances would not be subjected to popular approval. He proposes that ratifying a declaration of war, treaties, and choosing ambassadors would be a direct attribution of the Legislative.[32] The general impression is that the declaration of war and the ratification of treaties are equated to the naming of ambassadors, and thus would exclude the need for approval by the people.

Conversely, some deputies bestow the right to sanction or reject the declaration of war upon the people and, in some cases, even extend this control to the ratification of treaties. Barailon's proposal, for example, confers some of the most comprehensive powers for the primary assemblies,[33] including the approval or rejection of a declaration of war or

[31] Comité de Constitution, *Projet de Constitution*, VII.II, Article 5, e Comité de Salut Public, *Projet de Constitution*, X, Article 3. Lambert takes the same position (Charles Lambert, *Plan de Constitution Républicaine, Précédé de Quelques Observations sur Celui que le Comité de Constitution a Présenté a la Convetion les 15 et 16 Février* (AP, t. LXII (April 17, 1793)), VII.II, Article 2 and Articles 9 e 10) and Daunou presents a similar position—the declaration of war and ratification of treaties are not listed as types of law (Pierre-Claude-François Daunou, *Essai sur la Constitution* (AP, t. LXII (April 17, 1793)), I.III, Article 1)—but he demands that the Legislative and Executive agree on declaring a war (Daunou, *Essai sur la Constitution*, II, Article 5).

[32] Antoine Louis Léon de Saint-Just, *Projet de Constitution* (AP, t. LXIII (April 24, 1793)), 1.XIV, Article 1, and 1.VII, Article 1.

[33] In his project, the name used is city assemblies. However, considering that they fulfill the same general function, I chose to use the term "primary assemblies." Generally, I follow this same rule when different authors use different names for the Executive or Legislative. These variations can have an important function when analyzing said political bodies. When we get there, I will use the names chosen by the authors, but when discussing other topics in which

treaty presented by the Executive. The Legislative would have no direct role in regard to external relations, even in the case of war.

Despite the diversity of proposals, a general undertone seems to be the reduction of the Executive role in the external relations, especially regarding the declaration of war. This mistrust is not limited solely to the issue of warfare, as we have seen how the Legislative or the people in general (through the assemblies) can be assigned a central role in ratifying international treaties.

Before analyzing the content and rationale of each proposal, it is important to stress how disrupting these proposals are. The revolutionaries seem to try to keep in the hands of the sovereign as many rights, faculties, and powers as possible—their limit can vary greatly between their positions. The reiterated proposals that leave it to the people the task of ultimately approving or rejecting, either preventively or repressively, the declaration of war or treaties demonstrate the intention to integrate the people in the establishing and the conduction of the external relations.

This intention is strictly tied to the cosmopolitical ambitions that circulated during the French Revolution, in all its variations. If, at first sight, it may seem unusual to a contemporary reader to leave this kind of decision to the people, we should keep in mind that the issue of international relations was very present during the revolutionary years that came before the constitutional debate—and the same can be said for the issue of the sovereignty of the people.

The question of warfare illustrates such a claim. The fear of international conspiracies, the mobilization of European courts, and the risk posed by the *émigrés* (as in the question of the Brunswick Manifesto) are all examples of international issues closely connected with the future course of the Revolution. It was thus not a matter of concern exclusive to general and deputies. The first section of the newspaper, the *Gazette nationale ou Le Moniteur universel*, titled *Politique*, dealt precisely with international politics and France's current political relations with other countries, especially the European ones.

The people and each citizen are necessarily linked to the course of the French Republic's external politics, and the necessity or possibility that they have the means to directly influence it stems from this fact. Delacroix was not wrong when he said that the people may, in the last resort, rise

those bodies appear, I will privilege the most widely used name to facilitate the reader's comprehension.

against a bad external policy adopted by the government, but the proposals to bring the people closer to the formulation of such policies reflect particular concerns and intentions of the revolutionaries.

The destiny of the French people was tied to the destiny of other nations, especially those around them. Not only because of the ongoing war and the existence of hostile monarchs surrounding France plotting to put an end to the French experiment on liberty and freedom but also because of an actual reciprocal relationship of fraternity and brotherhood between the French and other peoples. It was a relationship that could not be reduced to the relationship between peoples or nations, but that would reach even to the individual level. That is why it is so important for the individual citizen to participate in the formulation of the external policies. But what kinds of relations were established between peoples, nations, and individuals across borders?

4.3 External Relations and the Sovereignty of the Peoples

On March 23, 1793, the National Convention issues a decree declaring that the country of Porrentruy (roughly corresponding to the current region of Jura) would be united with the French Republic, stating "that it accepts the freely expressed will of the sovereign people of the country of Porrentruy in the general assembly of their representatives, held on the 8th of this month, to unite itself with France."[34] The text was the consequence of a prior decree issued on February 27, 1793, in which the Convention determined that the provisional Executive council should send one of its members to each country occupied by the Republic's troops to deal with each different people's claim to be united with France.[35]

In addition to Porrentruy, we have similar decrees relating to, among others, Tournaisis, Gand e Salm.[36] A couple of months before that, on November 19, 1792, the Convention had declared that the French nation "'will extend its fraternity and aid to all peoples that want to recover their

[34] Baudouin, *Collection Générale des Décrets*, v. 35, 475.

[35] Baudouin, *Collection Générale des Décrets*, v. 35, 299.

[36] Respectively: Baudouin, *Collection Générale des Décrets*, v. 35, 475–476; *Id.*, 315; and *Id.*, v. 35, 321. The first two regions are now part of Belgium and the last one is the current French department of Vosges.

freedom."[37] This ambiguity between this declaration and France's territorial expansionism (even if it appears to be legitimized by the annexed communities, as we have seen in the case of Savoy) is the ground upon which constitutional proposals regarding the construction of the young French Republic's external relations find their footing.

In the Portiez de l'Oise Collection, we find a letter from the "representatives of the Free State of the former Bishopric of Basel, gathered in a constitutional assembly in the castle of Porrentruy" to the French Republic's minister of external relations, together with a proclamation from that community.[38] In the letter, the representatives request the aid promised by the French in their November 19 decree and declare having broken the chains that linked them to the Bishop of Basel and to the Germanic Empire.

In their proclamation, the representatives reproduce the assembly formula used during the French Revolution. They begin by declaring themselves to be deputies of a specific community, to have verified the powers of the then present commissioners, and they continue by listing the violations perpetrated against the community. The laws subjecting them would not be the product "of the general will of the peoples that compose the community, but that of the princes, bodies, and the state that, by usurpation, have controlled different authorities over the peoples."[39]

To justify their break from the status quo, they point to previous treaties and court precedents that guaranteed reciprocal duties and rights between the prince and the people; these were breached, they claimed, only when they were beneficial to the people, for example, concerning the regulation of hunting and the use of common forests. In response, they were breaking their ties with the German emperor and the bishops of Basel, going back "to our primitive, imprescriptible and inalienable rights of freedom and independence" and constituting themselves as a free and independent republic.[40]

[37] Baudouin, *Collection Générale des Décrets*, v. 33, 205.

[38] Balê (Evêché de), *Copie de la Proclamation des Députés des États-Libres du Ci-Devant Evêché de Bâle, Reúnis en Assemblée Constituante au Château de Porentruy, le 27 Novembre 1792, l'An Premier de la République de la Rauracie ; Précédée de la Lettre du Ministre des Affaires Etrangères, a la Convention Nationale* (Portiez de l'Oise Collection, t. 262, n. 24). Basel was a Prince-Bishopric, that is, an ecclesiastic state under the Holy Roman Empire.

[39] Balê, *Copie de la Proclamation*, 3.

[40] Balê, *Copie de la Proclamation*, 4.

If there is any ambiguity in the revolutionary discourse regarding the right of the peoples, it didn't prevent revolutionary practices (like the people organizing in communal assemblies) and discourses (as in the relation between traditional rights, primitive rights, and the act of a people constituting itself as a republic) from being appropriated by neighboring countries, like Basel, and reworked through their own historical lens. The posterior annexation declared by the National Convention should not make us forget this in-between moment and its role in the understanding of the possibilities opened by that same ambiguity.

The Constitution of 1791 had not properly developed the topic of external relations. Under its Title IV, "Of the Relation of the French Nation with Foreign Nations," only two issues are mentioned: a waiver of any war of conquest and the use of the nation's powers against the liberty of other people. The remaining articles under this merely regulate the status of foreigners in Revolutionary France—their freedom of contract, succession rights, and subjection to French laws.

In the constitutional drafts sent to the Convention, the topic is discussed with varying degrees of depth. The chapter proposed by the Committee of Public Safety is adopted in its entirety. In the four articles under the same title as that of the Constitution of 1791, we find the two central principles that guided the constitutional debate on the rights of the peoples.[41]

Articles 118 and 120 put forth a double dimension of the principle of universal fraternity, regarding respectively the individual and the collective: "The French people is a natural friend and ally of the free peoples" and "'it offers asylum to foreigners who were banned from their home country for the cause of freedom, and refuses it to tyrants."

Article 119 outlines the principle of reciprocity within the international sphere: "It shall not intervene with the government of other nations; it shall not tolerate that other nations intervene in its own."

[41] Article 121 is of minor importance to this debate. It prohibits the possibility of making peace while the enemy occupies part of the French territory. Even if not applicable to the debate at hand, Robespierre's response to Mercier's critique is interesting: Mercier claims that "hardly do you have any just ideas about liberty and you already dare to place yourself at the same level as the Romans." Robespierre answers: "Where have you seen that these people that shed their blood for universal liberty is below the Romans, that were not heroes of liberty, but oppressors of all peoples?" (AP, t. LXVI, 676). This small quarrel illustrates how the place assigned to classical thinking and the Greek and Roman imaginary was not as one-dimensional as some commentators lead us to believe.

The adoption of this clause without any modifications is preceded by a presentation by Grégoire of his draft for a declaration of the right of the peoples followed by Barère's remark: "we should not extrapolate into philanthropic opinions."[42]

Grégoire presents only a draft of a declaration for the rights of the peoples. He does not present any draft of a declaration of the rights of men or a Constitution. Besides Grégoire, Blaviel is the only other deputy to do so. Among the constitutional drafts, Bonnemain's draft has a section detailing the relations among peoples and Wandelaincourt dedicates part of his text to the matter. Most of the drafts are limited to a short passage about the topic, as in the final text of the Constitution of 1793. A notable exception is Robespierre, who, on April 24, 1793, presents four constitutional articles on the topic of fraternity and mutual aid between peoples.[43]

Grégoire's speech, when re-presenting his draft in 1795, even if beyond our time frame, aptly summarizes the general tone of the 1793 project: "The law of sociability among peoples is none other than the natural law applied to humankind's grand corporations. It determines their rights, their duties; it traces its scope and limits."[44]

Natural law and humankind. These two ideas appear in Grégoire as categories through which one thinks and justifies a universal fraternity. In Belissa's interpretation, for Grégoire, Robespierre, and Saint-Just, "the nations are objectively tied up by a 'universal morality', against the position held by the majority of the members of the Gironde and the Mountain that a declaration of the natural rights of the peoples was a 'metaphysical abstraction'."[45] According to these two groups, it would not be possible to subordinate national sovereignty to natural law, as Grégoire proposes.

Grégoire's declaration bespeaks an apparent tension between universality and the sovereignty of the peoples. On the one hand, article 2 declares that each people is autonomous and sovereign in relation to the others, regardless of its size or territorial extension. On the other hand, the particular interest of each people is secondary to humankind's general interest, according to article 5.

[42] AP, t. LXVI, 679.

[43] Maximilien Marie Isidore de Robespierre, *Opinion* (AP, t. LXIII (April 24, 1793)).

[44] Henri Jean-Baptiste Grégoire (Abbé), *Discours, Déclaration du Droit de Gens* (AM, t. XXIV (April 23, 1793)), 294.

[45] Belissa, *Fraternité Universelle et Intérêt National*, 370.

We find a similar duality in Robespierre's April 1793 text. On the one hand, a people is sovereign and the government is its work and its property, as by article 14. On the other hand, those who oppress a nation are considered an enemy of all nations, and kings and aristocrats are considered "slaves revolted against the sovereign of the earth, that is humankind, and against the legislator of the universe, that is nature."[46] We should keep in mind, as we read these positions, that Robespierre was against an external war in the name of freedom for other peoples.

This tension, however, is only apparent. Robespierre and Grégoire affirm the prevalence of humankind and natural law, but that does not imply disregarding the particularities of each people or its sovereignty. This apparent problem will reappear when analyzing the relationship between natural law, a declaration of rights, and government acts—a topic we will return to when discussing Jaume and Gauchet's legicentrism hypothesis. How can we establish a dialogue between these two instances of the revolutionary discourse, that is, between natural law's universality and each people's own idiosyncrasies?

We can compare this line of thought with Blaviel's proposal, presented on June 24, 1793, the week after Grégoire's text was put forth. As Belissa notes, we can see a striking difference in the role assigned to natural law. For Blaviel, "man, in the state of nature, or outside society, has only faculties; and within the state of society, he has a right only to what is determined by the act of association."[47] Blaviel, however, makes a distinction between a declaration of the rights of men and a declaration of the right of the peoples. Only the latter enunciates universal and invariable rights. Both texts, that of Grégoire and that of Blaviel may seem similar at first glance. They both talk about the inalienable sovereignty and autonomy of each people, how each people can organize its own form of government without interference from other peoples, and they both state the binding aspect of treaties and alliances. There are, however, some important distinctions.

Firstly, Blaviel starts his text by declaring that "in matters of government, everything is relative,"[48] as he defends the position that we can't attest if a certain government is legitimate or if it enslaves its people, and

[46] Robespierre, *Opinion*, 257.

[47] Antoine-Innocent Blaviel, *Projet de Déclaration des Droits des Peuples, pour Servir de Bases a la Constitution Française* (AP, t. LXVII (June 24, 1793)), 246.

[48] Antoine-Innocent Blaviel, *Projet de Déclaration*, 246.

another government doesn't. This is the sense of his articles 3, 4, and 5, that state, respectively, that the peoples can delegate the exercise of their sovereignty in any way they find most convenient, that they can restrict the exercise of their freedom as they see fit, and that they can choose any kind of government they might prefer.

Grégoire claims, in articles 4 and 8, that each people can organize itself without any other people having the right to intervene in its government and that no government exists "according to the right of the peoples if not one grounded in equality and freedom." This same position is defended by Wandelaincourt, to whom "it is the folly of conquerors to try to give to all the peoples their laws and their customs" and that a republican should not claim the majesty of the nation to "submit other peoples to the beneficial laws that had regenerated it."[49]

A similar contrast can be made regarding the revolutionaries' view on international treaties. Article 12 of Blaviel's declaration states that the sole limitation is the rights of the other non-signatory peoples. In Grégoire's text, we find what may seem like an identical limitation, but phrased differently: "The leagues that have offensive warfare as their object, and the treaties or alliances that can hurt the interest of a people are an attack against humankind" (article 16).

These limitations, however, are only apparently similar. The textual difference seems relevant—the category "interest" used by Grégoire is potentially broader than "rights," as used by Blaviel, especially considering the latter's legalist position—but this is not the main distinction in our view. Instead, the main distinction lies in the fact that Grégoire connects those illegitimate treaties to a violation of the rights of humankind, that is, of natural rights.

Grégoire's text mentions repeatedly the idea of universal fraternity (universal morality as the link between the peoples and the common property of inexhaustible or innocent use goods between the peoples, respectively, articles 1 and 9) and of reciprocity (the ideas that a people should act as it would like the other peoples to act toward it and that attacking the liberty of one people is attacking the liberty of all peoples, respectively, articles 2 and 15). Nowhere does Blaviel's project point to such a

[49] Antoine-Hubert Wandelaincourt, *Observations sur le Plan de Constitution* (AP, t. LXVII (June 24, 1793)), 409, and *Suite des Observations sur le Plan de Constitution* (AP, t. LXVII (June 24, 1793)), 416.

connection. In his declaration of the rights of the peoples, peoples are merely autonomous, while in Grégoire's text they are interdependent.

Nevertheless, the notion of reciprocity and interdependency is not exclusive to Grégoire's and Robespierre's proposals. We can also find the use of these concepts in Chapter IX of Saint-Just's constitutional draft. Its first article declares that the French people are of all peoples and that their ships would protect foreign vessels from tempests. Also, article 8, which is comparable to Grégoire's article 16, declares that the French people "will not sign treaties that do not have as a purpose the peace and happiness of all the nations."

The notion of reciprocity, in fact, is not a particular Jacobin idea. In a draft by Bonnemain, a representative of the political center (also knows as The Plain)[50] we can find the statement that just like a sick individual has the right to receive aid from his peers, also the nation that suffers from natural disasters has the right to request the help of neighboring or allied nations. There is a "guarantee of reciprocity among nations"[51] that includes helping a nation that has been unjustly attacked—the only instance where the use of force is allowed against another people. While this kind of aid is a duty when the loss of property or goods is already consolidated, the victimized people has the right to recover what was lost, but other peoples have only the right but not the duty to directly aid them in this pursuit.

We can interpret this distinction as being closer to Grégoire and Robespierre's stance, for whom the universal fraternity entails the duty of mutual aid, but it does not imply the imposition of the natural law onto

[50] I adopt the classification made by Ollivier when presenting the deputies of the Conventions (Ollivier, "Les Projets Constitutionnels de 1793," 531). However, I do not use such qualification as a way to locate the individual text within the revolutionary political spectrum. Following Galy's reading, I do not believe that the separation between Girondins and Montagnards is particularly useful when interpreting the constitutional texts. On the contrary, attaching oneself to such a reading can hinder the hermeneutical work. In a similar sense, Galy warns us not to do a biographical interpretation of the texts: "Studying the life and mentality of their authors can explain little. Evidently, there are exceptions; we cannot understand Cloots' and Chabot's writings if we do not know that one was a madman and the other a fanatical figure, but in general, their work is independent" (Galy, *La Notion de Constitution dans les Projets de 1793*, 39). When reading Galy's final remark, we should keep in mind a warning made above regarding his somewhat prejudicial interpretation of some revolutionaries.

[51] Antoine-Jean-Thomas Bonnemain, *Instituts Républicains, ou Développement Analytique des Facultés Naturelles, Civiles et Politiques de L'homme* (Archives Nationales, Series Lb41, n. 2385), 38.

other peoples—even though Bonnemain's text seems to espouse a slightly more restrictive view on universal fraternity since he precludes supporting rebels opposing national sovereignty in other nations.

This notion of a natural brotherhood and universal fraternity can nevertheless take many forms. It can even serve as a justification for disregarding the sovereignty of other peoples. An example is in Anacharsis Cloots' position. According to Belissa,

> Cloots' cosmopolitics is conceived not as the accomplishment of federative relations of natural law, but as 'a political-institutional unification of States as they merge into a great Nation or Empire'. The issue of the reciprocity of sovereignty is alien to Cloots, as he considers every particular sovereignty to be a threat to humankind's universality.[52]

The fundamental difference between the ideas of Cloots and Robespierre lies in how they conceive sovereignty. For Cloots, sovereignty lies only in humankind as a whole. There is no sovereignty of the peoples. As the rights of men extend over to the totality of men, so does sovereignty. In this context, the notion reciprocity leads to very different results: "Two men, or two peoples, isolated on the earth can believe themselves to be sovereign; but as soon as they make contact, at the first sight of the *Rights of Men*, there is but one absolute will in the world."[53]

In other words, according to Cloots, the universal fraternity within the sphere of external relations does not operate between peoples, as it does for Grégoire or Robespierre, but among the individual members of humankind. That is the reason why Cloots asserts that "a people is an aristocrat in relation to other people; peoples are necessarily wicked; humankind is essentially good."[54] This idea is consistent with Cloots' philosophy, and not the work of a madman, as Galy claims.

The idea of fraternity also appears infrequently in other projects, albeit with more modest purposes, in comparison to the understanding of Grégoire, Robespierre, or Cloots. Boissel mentions this idea with the purpose of abolishing the right to war while preserving a natural right to answer and retaliation. Bourgois establishes a parallel between the

[52] Belissa, *Fraternité Universelle et Intérêt National*, 225.

[53] Anacharsis Cloots, *Bases Constitutionnelles de la République du Genre Humain* (AP, t. LXIII (April 26, 1793)), 391, emphasis in original.

[54] Cloots, *Bases Constitutionnelles*, 393.

fraternity among men and that among nations to justify his rejection of the right of conquest and limit warfare to an act of resistance.[55]

This does not mean that some version of fraternity is always present in the drafts. Beaulieu and Daunou, for example, waive the idea of a war of conquest without mentioning fraternity or any other similar principle.[56] Other drafts treat external relations as a mere extension of internal politics or may not even bear a specific chapter or section on the topic.[57]

The issue of universal fraternity leads us to the last topic in the constitutional debate about external relations of Year 3: the colonies.[58] Barlow aptly summarizes what appears to be an obvious consequence of French revolutionary thinking:

> As your nation has been the first in the world to solemnly forsake the horrible love for conquests, you should go one step further and declare that you no longer want colonies. That is but the necessary consequence of your first waiver; since the colonies are the result of conquests, and to seek a right over the seas would be to seek a perpetual right over the others.[59]

For Barlow, France would have no right of sovereignty over its colonies, therefore they should have the right to form their own governments without the interference or the intervention of their former colonizers.

The colonial issue is nonetheless unevenly discussed in the constitutional debate of Year 3. The topic had already been discussed during the Constitutional Assembly of 1791, and slavery and the colonial regime were maintained, but equal political rights were recognized for black

[55] Respectively: François Boissel, *Les Entretiens du Père Gérard* (AP, t. LXVI (June 17, 1793)), IV, Article 1; e Bourgois, *Plan de Constitution*, III, Articles 1 and 3).

[56] Claude François Beaulieu, *Nouvelle Rédaction de la Déclaration ses Droits et des Deux Premier Titres de la Constitution* (Archives Nationales, Series Lb41, n. 80), I, Article 18; Daunou, *Essai sur la Constitution*, Article 37.

[57] Respectively, Montgilbert's chapter on external relations, where the revolutionary states solely that a good constitution should be made and that would suffice (François-Agnes Montgilbert, *Avis au Peuple sur la Liberté et L'exercice des Droits, Contenu dans un Projet de Constitution Républicaine* (AP, t. LXVII (June 24, 1793)), 349), and in Daunou's and Jean-Antoine Debry's drafts.

[58] I will not directly discuss the black question at this point since it will be further explored in Chap. 5.

[59] Joël Barlow, *Lettre a la Convention Nationale sur les Vices de la Constitution de 1791 et sur l'Étendue des Amendements a y Porter, pour Lesquelles cette Convention a Eté Convoquée*. (AP, t. LIII (November 7, 1792), 296.

persons born of free parents.[60] In August 1791, the slave revolt in Saint-Domingue had begun and after the revolution of August 10, 1792, a group of soldiers from the United States of America call for the end of slavery, thus breathing a new life into the black question within the French Republic—a discussion that is directly related to the colonial issue. On August 22, 1792, the Convention issues a decree setting the number of representatives for each colony.[61]

The majority of the presented drafts do not mention the colonial issue. Out of the 205 selected documents, only 15 do so. Among the latter, only drafts presented by non-deputies go into greater detail in regard to this issue. Some proposals limit themselves to indicating the existence of some governmental body responsible for this subject,[62] while others merely mention the existence of colonies.[63]

Excluding these minimal approaches, we can identify two other groups: one which appears to legitimize the colonial regime, in continuity with the Constitution of 1791, and one which recognizes the sovereignty of the (former) colonial peoples. The first group does not reject the aforementioned decree issued on August 22, 1792. Rubigny, for example, incorporates the decree into his text by asserting that the number of deputies established in his Constitution doesn't include those representing the

[60] Cf. the sessions held on May 11 and 15, 1792. (AP, XV:476–524) and Baudouin, *Collection Générale des Décrets*, v. 14, 179–180.

[61] Baudouin, *Collection Générale des Décrets*, v. 31, 374–376. Also on the subject of how the Convention's representatives dealt with the colonies, cf. Matthieu Carlot, "Des Chemins Périlleux. "Le Voyage des Conventionnels des Colonies Vers Paris (1793–1794)," *Annales Historiques de la Révolution Française* 380 (June 2015).

[62] That is what happens in the text by Anonymous D. He mentions the existence of a minister of the navy and the colonies (Anonymous D, *La France Heureuse ou Tout le Monde Content*, Archives Nationales, Series AD/XVIIIC/262, n. 15, 17). Bourgois' draft also limits himself to state that the number of members for the Legislative body does not include those from the colonies (Bourgois, *Plan de Constitution*, II.V.1.1, Article 1). Cf. also Poultier's text (François-Martin Poultier [Poultier d'Elmotte], *Constitution Populaire* (AP, t. LXII (April 17, 1793)), V, Article 2).

[63] Some merely mention that the colonies exist, like Lanthenas and Régir: François-Xavier Lanthenas, *Bases Fondamentales de L'instruction Publique et de Toute Constitution Libre Ou Moyens de Lier L'opinion Publique, la Morale, L'éducation, L'enseignement, L'instruction, les Fêtes, la Propagation des Lumières et le Progrès de Toutes les Connaissances Au Gouvernement National Républicain* (AP, t. LXIV (May 10, 1793)), *projet* VII, Article 14; and Rey Régir, *Le Citoyen Rey Régir. Ordre du Jour* (Archives Nationales, F/17/1003), 2.

colonies;[64] this also means that the colonial representation in the Legislature would have no constitutional basis. The same can be said of Ragonneau but with an important addition: he claims that the colonies are a part of society, even if they are ruled by a particular kind of law.[65]

On the opposite end, we have—besides the aforementioned text by Barlow—three other main texts of note on this issue: Anonymous C, George Edwards, and Ruault. The first text (by Anonymous C) asserts that the colonies should adopt the regime of government that best fits them according to their wisdom and considering both their interests and those of France.[66] This document is not very clear and it would not be possible to claim that the author excludes the possibility of colonial independence.

This kind of ambiguity is not present in Edwards' or Ruault's texts. Even though Edwards starts his text by claiming that the colonies "will be represented according to their population in their motherland," creating their own laws and acting in agreement with the metropole, as in the English model, he declares that this link would last "only until it is made necessary to create separate nations because of their growth."[67]

Ruault begins by following a similar logic: the colonies would not be under the constitutional purview. However, instead of claiming that particular laws would be enacted at the colonies, Ruault states that the constitutional agreement would be sent to the colonies, so that they may freely appreciate its articles and choose whether or not to tie themselves to "their brothers in Europe."[68]

[64] Germain Rubigny, *Nouveau Système de Représentation Nationale, d'Assemblées et d'Élections* (AP, t. LXII (April 17, 1793)), IV, Article 3.

[65] See Ragonneau, *Plan d'une Nouvelle Constitution*, III, Article 7, and Ragonneau, *Plan d'une Nouvelle Constitution*, 260. The same logic appears in Lambert's text. He excludes the colonies from the uniform code of civil and criminal laws to be established for France and attaches them to a specific code to be created by the colonies themselves, but to be sanctioned by the Legislative body of the French Republic (Lambert, *Plan de Constitution Républicaine*, IX.I, Article 1).

[66] Anonymous C, *Plan d'une Constitution*, IX, Article 5. The text conditions the adoption of such a regime to the king's sanction—which indicates that the text was probably written before August 10, 1792.

[67] George Edwards, *Idées pour Former une Nouvelle Constitution, et pour Assurer la Prospérité et le Bonheur de la France et d'autres Nations* (AP, t. LIX (February 28, 1793)), 493.

[68] Alexandre-Jean Ruault, *Projet de Constitution de la République Française* (Portiez de l'Oise Collection, t. 176, n. 15), *extra titles*, 169.

Besides these proposals, I also include the text *Observation sur les colonies françaises dans leurs rapports actuels avec la France* (Observation on the French colonies concerning their current relations with France). The text, sent to the Convention and signed by "Demun," is dated November 21, 1792.[69] In this document, the author poses the question: "What right does France actually have to control its colonies, and in particular that of Saint-Domingue?"

The answer is categorical: none. His reasoning is based precisely on the concept of the sovereignty of the peoples, as expressed by Grégoire and Robespierre. The text mentions how, in 1788, individual landowners came to the Estates-General in France but points out that "almost near totality of Saint-Domingue population never recognized such deputation" and that the only way these particular deputies could become general representatives was by the "almost unanimous will of the population." The place of the natural law is therefore categorically asserted: "[the] unalienated and inalienable natural right that the colonies have to govern themselves."[70]

The text appears to contradict itself when, in its last words, it claims that the colonies do not want independence, but only the authority they believe to be indispensable. Yet, all the remainder of the text undoubtedly supports the argument for the severance of colonial domination.

What Barlow, Anonymous C, George Edwards, Ruault, and Demun have in common is the application of the principle of the sovereignty of the peoples, as seen under articles 6 and 7 from Grégoire's declaration, to the colonial issue. The colonies emerged through France's intromission, but they could not be reduced to a mere overseas French department. A people already occupies said territory and has the right to decide its own future. The revolutionaries state so even as Saint-Domingue is in a full-fledged insurrection, and the Convention itself had just sent representatives to subdue this movement.

The contradiction is self-evident, which demonstrates the multiplicity of voices within the Convention. There is no unequivocal consensus even inside the particular political groups. Ruault and Lambert are both

[69] Even considering that the text does not directly mention the constitutional moment, its submission date and content make it reasonable to take it as part of the constitutional debate. The text is signed simply by "Demun." There is no first name or further clues as to who the author would be. It is perhaps an anonymous text sent under a pseudonym, but we have no way of knowing it for sure.

[70] J.-J. Demun, *Observation sur les Colonies Françaises Dans Leurs Rapports Avec la France* (Archives Nationales, Series AD/XVIIIC/336, n. 2), 19, 20, and 23.

members of the Gironde, but they profess almost antagonistic views on how to handle external relations.

However, some of the ambiguities are only apparent. As we've stated before, Grégoire and Robespierre's notions could be (mistakenly) read as contradictory. How can one assert the primacy of natural law and still disallow intervening in despotic regimes?

The recourse to natural law to justify the colonies' independence, as in the text by Demun, poses no problem. The same can be said of Cloots' position. If there is but one natural law determining the rights of men, the idea of a universal family encompassing the whole of humankind under the same political regime seems like a logical conclusion. However, this framework shows its complexity when we recognize that Grégoire, Robespierre, and Cloots share a common lexicon—for example, the idea of a universal family or humankind.

But the use of such terms should not mislead us. When the revolutionaries talk of humankind, universal family, universal morality, sovereignty, and the sovereignty of the peoples, they are not necessarily referring to the same things. Even the texts that recognized the legitimacy of colonial rule—as mentioned above—proclaimed the inalienable and imprescriptible sovereignty of the people.

The main apparent ambivalence lies in how to reconcile the articles 5 and 8 with articles 2 and 3 of Grégoire's text. In other words, the private interest of a people is subordinated to the general interest of the human family and there may be no government according to the rights of the peoples if not one grounded in equality and freedom. But, at the same time, the peoples are autonomous and sovereign and should treat one another as they would hope to be treated themselves.

This means that subjecting private interests to the general interest does not *a priori* entail a rationally deductible general interest functioning as a perfect moral duty enforceable upon all peoples. The subjection still exists but it can only work endogenously. When it operates from an external source—as in Robespierre's quote about armed missionaries—the general interest of the human family is itself put at risk.

Grégoire also aims, as stated by Cloots in a more radical wording, for some kind of international community or integration. In the speech presenting his draft declaration, on April 23, 1795, Grégoire talks about a monetary and measurement unification as a means of moralization. The word "moral" is crucial here since the integration—not the same as uniformization—would work by adhering to a universal morality, not by its imposition.

The converge of a people's private interest and the human family's general interest would come by the diffusion of the ideas of universal morality and fraternity, as in Edward's proposal of a "general assembly of the whole world" as a means for "men to learn to love all humankind."[71]

Another way of understanding their stance is by identifying freedom as the first and foremost value to be protected. The main principle in natural law would be that of respecting reciprocal freedom. It is a version of liberalism that is strikingly different from today's political philosophy take on the subject, as it situates equality and reciprocity as necessary links within the notion of freedom.

With that in mind, we may go back to question of the declaration of war and interpret some of the aforementioned positions—those that strongly rejected external warfare and condition even a defensive war to the people's approval—as a manifestation of this supremacy of freedom.

In regard to the debate on external relations, this principle of reciprocal freedom implies that the sovereignty of a given people can't be deducted from the outside. That is why the notion of natural borders, sustained by Thuriot and Jeanbon Saint-André is contrary to this liberal philosophy of natural law. Not only does this notion impose something like the supposed interest of the peoples, as noted by Belissa,[72] but it also deprives the peoples of their self-delimitation, that is, the faculty of constituting themselves as a separate entity from the French people.

This is the confusion that we find when discussing the cases of Basel and Savoy. While these communities seemed to express themselves as autonomous groups, constituting themselves as independent entities, the Convention recognized them as new departments within the French Republic. The same problem is found in Cloots' idea of a universal community, as in both cases only a part of the totality—albeit the majority—has the full authority to determine the limits of that totality. It matters little if this authority is moral (as in Cloots) or factual (as in the annexation decrees issued by the Convention), the logic in action is the same.

To return to Moyn's position on the French Revolution, if there is a nationalistic character within the juridico-philosophical debates during the French Revolution, the small time frame of Year 3 is already enough to show us that this is but one of many schools of thought circulating at the time. It is not possible to label the whole French Revolutionary experience as one opposed to cosmopolitanism.

[71] Edwards, *Idées pour Former une Nouvelle Constitution*, 493.
[72] Belissa, *Fraternité Universelle et Intérêt National*, 327.

Appendix

Historical References for the 1792–1793 Debates

Explanatory Notes

1. Whenever possible, the drafts are cited by article or chapter and article, not by page.
2. I reference the anonymous texts' authors as "Anonymous A" to "Anonymous U" to more easily reference them in the main text of this book.
3. Since this is an abridged version of the original thesis, not all of the texts listed below are mentioned throughout the main text. I chose to include them in the references for fellow researchers interested in the topic.
4. The final and approved text of the Declaration and Constitution of Year 1 of the Republic are cited as *Declaration* and *Constitution*. The other primary texts are listed below.

Parliamentary Notes, Newspapers, and Legal Texts

Archives parlementaires de 1787 à 1869 (First series). Paris: Paul Dupont, 1867–2021. [cited as "AP," followed by tome number, page, and the document's date, when available]

Baudouin, François-Jean (ed.). *Collection Générale des Décrets Rendus par l'Assemblée Nationale*. Paris: Baudouin, 1789–1795, 67 v. [A digital version is available through: https://collection-baudouin.univ-paris1.fr].

Drafts

Anonymous C. *Plan d'une Constitution Libre et Heureuse selon Justice, Raison et Sagesse, Trouvé Chez M. Laporte*. Archives Nationales, Series AD/XVIIIC/219, n. 14.

Anonymous D. *La France Heureuse ou Tout le Monde Content*. Archives Nationales, Series AD/XVIIIC/262, n. 15.

Bacon-Tacon, Pierre Jean Jacques (Comte de). *Plan Patriotique, ou Idée d'une Bonne Constitution Républicaine, en France*. Archives Nationales, Series AD/XVIIIC/262, n. 4.

Balê (*Evêché* de). *Copie de la Proclamation des Députés des États-Libres du Ci-Devant Evêché de Bâle, Reúnis en Assemblée Constituante au Château de Porentruy, le 27 Novembre 1792, l'An Premier de la République de la Rauracie ; Précédée de la Lettre du Ministre des Affaires Etrangères, a la Convention Nationale*. Portiez de l'Oise Collection, t. 262, n. 24.

Barlow, Joël. *Lettre a la Convention Nationale sur les Vices de la Constitution de 1791 et sur l'Étendue des Amendements a y Porter, pour Lesquelles cette Convention a Eté Convoquée*. AP, t. LIII (November 7, 1792), 286–297.

Beaulieu, Claude François. *Nouvelle Rédaction de la Déclaration ses Droits et des Deux Premier Titres de la Constitution*. Archives Nationales, Series Lb41, n. 80.

Boissel, François. *Les Entretiens du Père Gérard*. AP, t. LXVI (June 17, 1793), 613–642.

Bonnemain, Antoine-Jean-Thomas. *Instituts Républicains, ou Développement Analytique des Facultés Naturelles, Civiles et Politiques de L'homme*. Archives Nationales, Series Lb41, n. 2385.

Bourgois, Nicolas. *Plan de Constitution Proposée a la République Française*. AP, t. LXIII (April 24, 1793) 259–279.

Cloots, Anacharsis. *Bases Constitutionnelles de la République du Genre Humain*. AP, t. LXIII (April 26, 1793) 389–403.

Comité de Constitution. *Projet de Constitution*. AP, t. LVIII (February 15, 1793) 602–609.

Comité de Salut Public. *Projet de Constitution du Peuple Français*. AP, t. LXVI (June 10, 1793) 260–264.

Edwards, George. *Idées Pour Former une Nouvelle Constitution, et Pour Assurer la Prospérité et le Bonheur de la France et d'autres Nations* AP, t. LIX (February 28, 1793) 482–498.

Daunou, Pierre-Claude-François. *Essai sur la Constitution*. AP, t. LXII (April 17, 1793) 350–370.[73]

Demun, J.-J. *Observation sur les Colonies Françaises Dans Leurs Rapports Avec la France*. Archives Nationales, Series AD/XVIIIC/336, n. 2.

Grégoire, Henri Jean-Baptiste (Abbé). *Discours, Déclaration du Droit de Gens*. AM, t. XXIV (April 23, 1793) 294–296.

Lambert, Charles. *Plan de Constitution Républicaine, Précédé de Quelques Observations sur Celui que le Comité de Constitution a Présenté a la Convetion les 15 et 16 Février*. AP, t. LXII (April 17, 1793) 434–466.

[73] The document is subdivided as follows: *Projet de Déclaration*, *Bases de l'Établissement en France*, *Constitution ou Définition et Distribution des Pouvoirs dans la République Française*, and *Principes de la Législation en France*.

Lanthenas, François-Xavier. *Bases Fondamentales de L'instruction Publique et de Toute Constitution Libre Ou Moyens de Lier L'opinion Publique, la Morale, L'éducation, L'enseignement, L'instruction, les Fêtes, la Propagation des Lumières et le Progrès de Toutes les Connaissances Au Gouvernement National Républicain.* AP, t. LXIV (May 10, 1793) 456–505.

Montgilbert, François-Agnes. *Avis au Peuple sur la Liberté et L'exercice des Droits, Contenu dans un Projet de Constitution Républicaine.* AP, t. LXVII (June 24, 1793) 328–339.

Poultier, François-Martin [Poultier d'Elmotte]. *Constitution Populaire.* AP, t. LXII (April 17, 1793) 482–492.

Ragonneau. *Plan d'une Nouvelle Constitution.* AP, t. LXIV (May 6, 1793) 252–259.

Régir, Rey. *Le Citoyen Rey Régir. Ordre du Jour.* Archives Nationales, F/17/1003, n. 211.

Robespierre, Maximilien Marie Isidore de. *Opinion.* AP, t. LXIII (April 24, 1793) 197–198.

Ruault, Alexandre-Jean, *Projet de Constitution de la République Française.* Portiez de l'Oise Collection, t. 176, n. 15.

Rubigny, Germain. *Nouveau Système de Représentation Nationale, d'Assemblées et d'Élections.* AP, t. LXII (April 17, 1793) 561–570.

Saint-Just, Antoine-Louis-Léon de. *Projet de Constitution.* AP, t. LXIII (April 24, 1793) 200–215.

Wandelaincourt, Antoine-Hubert. *Observations sur le Plan de Constitution.* AP, t. LXVII (June 24, 1793) 409–415.

Wandelaincourt, Antoine-Hubert. *Suite des Observations sur le Plan de Constitution.* AP, t. LXVII (June 24, 1793) 415–420.

References

Barton, H. A. "The Origins of The Brunswick Manifesto." *French Historical Studies* 5, n. 2 (Autumn, 1967): 146–169.

Belissa, Marc. *Fraternité Universelle et Intérêt National (1713–1795): Les Cosmopolitiques du Droit des Gens.* Paris: Kimé, 1998.

Blaviel, Antoine-Innocent. *Projet de Déclaration des Droits des Peuples, pour Servir de Bases a la Constitution Française.* AP, t. LXVII (June 24, 1793), 246–248.

Capet, Louis. "Déclaration de Louis XVI a Tous les Français, a Sa Sortie de Paris." *Le Procès de Louis Xvi, Ou, Collection Complette, des Opinions, Discours et*

Mémoires des Membres de la Convention Nationale, sur les Crimes de Louis XVI, edited by Jean-Charles Poncelein de Roche-Tilhac, 136–146. Paris: Debarle, 1795.

Carlot, Matthieu. "Des Chemins Périlleux. Le Voyage des Conventionnels des Colonies Vers Paris (1793–1794)." *Annales Historiques de la Révolution Française* 380 (June 2015): 3–23.

Galy, François. *La Notion de Constitution dans les Projets de 1793*. Paris: Editions Albert Mechelinck, 1932.

Gauthier, Florence. *Triomphe et Mort de la Révolution des Droits de l'Homme et du Citoyen*. Paris: Éditions Syllepse, 2014.

Leopold II; Frederick William II. "Déclaration." In *Lettre de Monsieur, et de M. le Comte d'Artois, Au Roi Leur Frère, Avec la Déclaration Signée a Plinitz, le 27 Août 1791, par l'Empereur & le Roi de Prusse*, 7. [s.l.; s.n.], 1791.

Michelet, Jules. *Histoire de la Révolution Française*, t. 3. Paris: Ernest Flammarion, 1893.

Ollivier, Nathalie. "Les Projets Constitutionnels de 1793." PhD Diss. Université Panthéon-Assas, 2002.

Robespierre, Maximillien de. *Œuvres Complètes de Robespierre*, 10 v. Paris: Presses Universitaires de France, 1910–1967.

Soboul, Albert. *The French Revolution*. New York: Vintage Books, 1975.

Société des Amis de la Constitution. *Journal des Débats de la Société des Amis de la Constitution, Séance Aux Jacobins a Paris*. Paris: [*s.n.*.], 1791–1793. http://gallica.bnf.fr/ark:/12148/cb327995128/date.item.

Sorel, Albert. "La Fuite de Louis XVI et les Essais d'Intervention en 1791 – Varennes et Pillnitz." *Revue des Deux Mondes*, Third Period, t. 75 (1886) 314–346.

CHAPTER 5

Facets of the Executive Branch

Où se sont concentrés les ennemis secrets de la liberté?
—Barère

The first topic of the 1793 debates on the organization of the revolutionary government I will discuss is the Executive branch. First, I will focus on the distinct role played by the judicial apparatus, in comparison with its contemporary functions. For example, in most drafts, the Judiciary system is seen as part of the Executive branch and not as a separate branch or power. The role allotted to the Judiciary will serve as introduction to the many subtle differences among the proposals for the Executive branch itself.

In the next chapter, I will analyze the proposals for the Legislative branch and how they connect to this chapter's topic through a common theme to be found in the drafts and during the debates: how to ensure that the law and the government both are the work of the people and not of a cabinet aristocracy. The apparently inverted order—most drafts present the Judiciary after the Executive branch and the Executive branch after the Legislative branch—will lead to the final chapter, in which the relations between citizenship, sovereignty, and the Republic in the 1793 drafts will be analyzed.

E. Baker, *Human Rights and Humanity's Rights During Year Three of the French Revolution*,
https://doi.org/10.1007/978-3-030-99508-9_5

5.1 Judiciary

The need to reform the justice system was not an invention of the 1793 revolutionaries. Legibre demonstrates that the issue was widespread in the 1789 *cahiers*, even the ones written by the nobility.[1] Before that, Louis XVI had already started a timid reform through an edict from May 1788, inspired by Lamoignon's attempts to rationalize the confusing medieval judicial system.[2]

Between the start of the Revolution and the Year 3 drafts, the judicial system went through many changes. Even though the changes in substantive law are outside my object of analysis, some facts from that period are important for an understanding of the context in which the Convention's debate was taking place.

Leuwers stresses the importance of the laws from August 16 to 24, 1790, and highlights two main points: the suppression of *lettres de cachet* (orders by the king that could lead to imprisonment or exile without the right to a trial) and the introduction of the figure of the arbitrator who is freely nominated by the involved parties without recourse to the state judicial system and without a prior agreement between them.[3]

These changes were complemented by the decree of August 4, 1789, which abolished seigneurial justice and other nobiliary privileges associated with the judicial system.[4] The aim was already to diminish Executive influence over the Judiciary and bring the Judiciary closer to the people. The attempt to prevent undue influence went both ways, as Article 13, Title II, of the 1790 reform shows:

> The judicial functions will be distinct, and they will always remain separated from administrative functions. Judges will not be allowed, under penalty of characterizing abuse of authority, to disturb, in any manner whatsoever, the

[1] A. Legibre, "1789, la justice dans tous ses états," in *Une Autre Justice: Contributions a l'Histoire de la Justice sous la Révolution Française*, dir. Robert Badinter (Paris: Fayard, 1989) 39.

[2] A. Legibre, "1789, la justice dans tous ses étas," 41–43.

[3] "freely appointed; jurists or not, they examined the facts and gave an arbitral decision that was later imposed by an order from the president of the district's tribunal, it was not possible to appeal to the Judiciary, except if the possibility of said appeal was explicitly accorded between the parties" (Hervé Leuwers, "Rendre la justice á la Nation. Révolution constituante et réforme judicaire (1789–1791)," in *La Révolution Française: Une Histoire Toujours Vivante*, ed. Michel Vovelle (Paris: Tallandier, 2010), 126.

[4] BAUDOUIN, v. 1, 52–53.

operation of the administrative bodies or to cite the administrators for reasons related to their functions.

This continuity between the abolishment of feudalism and judicial reform is also present in the resistance by the already sitting judges and courts, including those who were recently elected.[5] This is why Jean Bart claims that the August 4 abolition was an illusion.[6]

The 1791 Constitution follows the same general outline. It reinforces the downfall of the judicial apparatus that was inherited from the *Ancién Regime*. Chapter V of Title III regulates the judicial branch [*Pouvoir Judiciaire*]—the term itself will disappear from the 1793 Constitution and will not appear in the majority of the drafts.

While the August 16 to 24, 1790, laws go into detail about the organization of the Judiciary and the legal procedures that should be followed, the 1791 constitutional text is limited to providing the Judiciary's general characteristics and reiterating some of the previous changes, such as the role of the arbitrator (Article 5) and the election of judges by citizens (Article 2). Some topics are included which were absent in the 1790 judicial reform, but appeared in 1793, such as the Court of Cassation [*cour de cassation*] (Article 19).

This didn't eliminate the mistrust toward "men of the law" [*hommes de loi*], which remained a point of contention during Year 3, as we can tell from a December 1792 text by Henri Bacal, called *Du Nouvel Ordre Social*:

> The so-called men of justice were one of society's greatest plagues. They overturned the legislative power of nations and favored the despotism of a single person. They constituted themselves as authorities and created a Judiciary.[7]

However, there is an important distinction between the 1791 and 1793 constitutions. In the former, Article 23 in the chapter on the Judiciary establishes that there is a high national court which is responsible for judging crimes committed against the general security of the state and crimes committed by members of the Executive branch. This court is not

[5] Jean-Jacques Clere, "L'Abolition des Droits Féodaux en France," Cahiers D'histoire (Revue d'Histoire Critique) 94–95 (2005).

[6] Jean Bart, "L'Abolition de la Féodalité et des Priviléges, ou des Illusions de la Nuit du 4 Août 1789," in *La Révolution Française*, ed. Michel Vovelle.

[7] Bancal, *Du Nouvel Ordre Social*, 411.

mentioned in the final 1793 text, but it appeared in a good number of proposals: the initial draft by the Constitution Committee and the draft by the Committee of Public Safety respectively proposed a jury or a grand national jury with similar attributions.

These institutions are generally understood to be part of the Judiciary. This is how Galy and Ollivier interpret similar institutions that appear under different names, such as censorship tribunal, censors, court of cassation, national court, and others, as will be analyzed in further detail.[8]

However, Ollivier and Galy make the mistake of grouping those initiatives under the general theme of control of Legislative and/or Executive activities. Ollivier expressly states that

> It is impossible to talk about constitutionality review in relation to the constitutional drafts of 1794. [...] The legal imprecision of the notion of constitution prevents the development of an idea of normative hierarchy.[9]

Reading the Year 3 drafts through the contemporary lens of judicial or constitutionality review prevents a better comprehension of what was actually at stake. The issue wasn't the organization of the Judiciary. That kind of interpretation is already weakened by the above-mentioned notion that, in 1793, the Judiciary was not generally seen as a branch or separate power. In some cases, the proposals seem to approach the administration of justice, if this category is considered in the terms presented by the revolutionaries, but as the next chapter will show, those institutions are more closely related to the institutionalization and guarantee of popular sovereignty.

For example, the national jury proposed by the Constitution Committee can be understood in this way, while the censors (a different institution) are indeed part of the Judiciary. This hypothesis is reinforced by the fundamental qualitative distinction between accountability for abuse of authority committed by the people's representatives and rulings on judicial appeals against criminal or civil cases.

In their discussions of those institutions, the revolutionaries were concerned with developing institutions that could be held accountable by the public, from which unfaithful representatives could be purged, and that

[8] See Galy, *La Notion de Constitution dans les Projets de 1793*, 135ff, and Ollivier, *Les Projets Constitutionnels de 1793*, 397ff.

[9] Ollivier, *Les Projets Constitutionnels de 1793*, 447.

can undo acts and laws against the rights of men and citizens. They were not discussing a better design for the Judiciary system, as Galy and Ollivier claim. The Judiciary played a much more modest role in the 1793 drafts.

This does not mean the topic was of no interest to the revolutionaries. According to Royer, the *conventionnels*' interest in the issue was undeniable. Different was their focus. Instead of worrying about the separation or independence of powers, it was their aim to simplify forms and procedures and to popularize the justice system.[10]

This claim can be illustrated by taking a look at an anonymous draft with the title *Quelques idées sur une Constitution populaire pour un grand État* and Barailon's text.[11] In the latter, section VII, titled *Des censeurs* (On censors), must be considered. In the draft, there are two relevant chapters: *De la censure du people* (On the people's censorship) and *Des conservateurs de la Constitution* (On the keepers of the Constitution).

Both texts focus on regulating the operations of the Judiciary, but with important distinctions. Barailon divides the administration of justice in three main sections: justice of the peace and arbitrators for civil suits; police courts for most crimes; and national courts, including a jury, responsible for judging appeals against the police court's decisions and directly ruling on a limited number of crimes.[12] In all cases, their members were elected and held a four-year mandate.[13]

The Judiciary, in Barailon's text, only deals with disputes between private persons. The censors, however, have a starkly different role, although they are also elected. They are "the eyes, the watchmen of the city." They correspond with representative bodies and monitor everything that is related to the common good, especially "the political and moral life of public servants"[14] and anything that could suffocate the republican spirit.

[10] Jean-Pierre Royer, "Le 'Pouvoir Judiciaire' dans la Constitution de 1793," in *La Constitution du 24 Juin 1793: L'Utopie dans le Droit Public Français? (Actes du Colloque de Dijon, 16 et 17 Septembre 1993)*, coord. Françoise Naudin-Patriat (Dijon: Editions del'Universite de Dijon, 1997): 308.

[11] Respectively, Anonymous E, *Quelques Idées sur Une Constitution Populaire pour un Grand État* (AP, t. LXIII (April 24, 1793)), and Barailon, Jean-François, *Projet de Constitution Présenté a la Convetion Nationale* (AP, t. LXVII (June 24, 1793)).

[12] Respectively: Barailon, *Projet de Constitution Présenté a la Convetion Nationale*, IX, Articles 2–7; X, Articles 3–4; and X, Articles 2–3.

[13] Barailon, *Projet de Constitution*, VI, Article 16.

[14] Respectively: Barailon, *Projet de Constitution*, VII, Article 1; Barailon, *Projet de Constitution*, VII, Articles 7–9.

They are not concerned with private conflicts or mere transgressions of civil or criminal law.

Anonymous E's text contains a similar distinction. The draft does not present a separate section on the administration of justice, as in Barailon's text. It tackles the topic with its discussion of the magistrates for the communes and the magistrates for the departments. In addition to fulfilling other roles, one is responsible for analyzing disputes between citizens and the other for deciding and executing rulings.[15]

Both are not to be confused with the keepers of the Constitution. The keepers have the power to exclude up to ten members from a given session of the Legislative council, they serve as prosecutors in high treason cases, and they can be assigned to defend the integrity of the Republic through an act of law, in the case of a conspiracy or disorder.[16]

Their role, although not exactly the same as that of Barailon's censors, is not part of the administration of justice. The name "keepers of the Constitution" is not a reference to the legal text called "Constitution," but to the constitution of the organization of government and its location within the broader organization of society.

This hypothesis is reinforced by the debates on the Committee of Public Safety's proposal for a grand national jury and the way they developed. For example, Thirion responds to the proposal by stating: "there already exists such a court, it is the public opinion."[17] Hence we cannot agree with Ollivier's claim that the absence of some kind of judicial or constitutionality review was due to the lack of proper legal technique or knowledge. What is at stake are different views on the role that the law fulfills, by the government and by the institutions—be they social institutions or institutions created by law.

Before we proceed with an analysis of the constitutional proposals, we should consider how the drafts of the declaration of rights address the issue. When the Judiciary branch is explicitly mentioned, it tends to be in a generic form that merely describes its general role. One example of this can be found in Chevret's text. He states that one of the general aims of the constitution is to define the administration of justice "that has as its

[15] Respectively: Anonymous E, *Quelques Idées sur Une Constitution Populaire pour un Grand État*, Article 49 e Anonymous E, *Quelques Idées*, Article 54.

[16] See Anonymous E, *Quelques Idées*, Articles 81, 83, and 84.

[17] AP, t. LXVI, 576.

aim to give each one their due and is related, whether in a civil or criminal context, to people, things and actions."[18]

Few drafts address the topic in greater detail. One case is *Anonymous O*, whose proposal includes an article on the organization of the Judiciary, which determines that all judges, whether responsible for criminal or civil cases, are to be chosen in an assembly of their fellow citizens.[19]

Chevret's claim appears in most drafts. Few treat the administration of justice as a separate power or branch. Two notable exceptions are Boissy d'Anglas and Thorillon.[20] The former says that "Judiciary power is essentially distinct and separate from legislative power and from Executive power."[21]

[18] One example of this can be found in Chevret's text. It states that one of the general aims of the constitution is to define the administration of justice "that has as its aim to give each one their due and is related, whether in a civil or criminal context, to people, things and actions" (Jean Chevret, *Principes de Sociabilité, ou Nouvel Exposé des Droits et des Devoirs de l'Homme et du Citoyen, Suivies d'Observations Importantes, Relatives aux Propriétés, a la Liberté du Commerce & a la Proportion du Prix des Subsistances avec les Facultés des Citoyens* (Archives Nationales, Series Lb41, n. 2883), 14).

[19] The provision is mentioned in Anonymous O [Par Cosmopolite], *Discours Fraternel et Instructions a mês Citoyens pour Les Mettre a la Hateur des Républicains: Ouvragre Nouveau sur les Droits de l'Homme et du Citoyen, d'Après des Principes Physiques et Moraux* (Archives Nationales, Series Lb41, n. 2982), Article 19. The text also restricts judicial activity in a way similar to what will be encountered in the constitutional proposals we will discuss later on. The text warns citizens not to see judges and officials as "proxies for the sovereignty to enforce the law against those who broke it" (Anonymous O [Par Cosmopolite], *Discours Fraternel et Instructions*, 30).

[20] The expression *pouvoir judiciaire* (Judiciary power) also appears in other drafts, as in Bacon-Tacon's text (Bacon-Tacon, *Plan Patriotique*, IV), who does not explicitly state it to be a separate branch. Lambert's proposal, on the other hand, asserts: "Judiciary power is essentially distinct and separate from Legislative power and Executive power, both of which cannot, in any case or under any pretext, usurp its functions" (Lambert, *Plan de Constitution Républicaine*, IX.I, Article 4).

[21] François-Antoine Boissy d'Anglais (Comte de), *Constitution* (AP, t. LXII (April 17, 1793)), IX.I, Article 1. Thorillon declares, in his discussion of the law, that "it would be monstrous for the Executive power, which ensures that [the law] is respected, to have the power to serve justice... That which serves it is an independent power from that which ensures it" (Antoine-Joseph Thorillon, *Idées ou Bases d'une Nouvelle Déclaration des Droits de l'Homme, de Cette de ses Devoirs et d'une Nouvelle Constitution pour la République Française, où l'on Traite, entre Autres Choses, de la Liberté, de l'Égalité, des Insurrections, de l'éducation Nationale, du Code Civil, et Notamment des Enfants Naturels, de l'Adoption, d'une Seule Substitution Officieuse, de l'Organisation d'un Nouvel Ordre Judiciaire, etc.* (AP, t. LXII (April 17, 1793)), §14, 591).

However, if we read the three texts carefully (*Anonymous O*, Boissy d'Anglas, and Thorillon's), we realize the proposals are not so different. Boissy d'Anglas, in the same article, partially transcribed above, declares that the Executive branch must ensure that the Judiciary acts in accordance with the law. Thorillon states that the judge is no interpreter of the law, but merely the one who enforces it.

So even the drafts that recognize the existence of a Judiciary power as such—separate from the Legislative and the Executive power—circumscribe its role to the mere enforcement of the law. This does not mean it is irrelevant to think of the Judiciary as a separate branch, but it serves to show that the generic claim made by the drafts' authors is not all there is to consider. The ways in which they actually managed the administration of the justice system must be explored to comprehend where it fits into the broader picture of governmental organization.

Royer points out the two main strategies for bringing the justice system closer to the people, adopted during the constituent debate: the jury and arbitration.[22] Both topics dominate the debates and the ways in which the issue was treated in the Convention will shine a light on the different positions on the role of the Judiciary that abounded during Year 3.

The debates on June 17, 19, and 20, 1793, were dominated by this subject. The main protagonist was Cambacères, who went on to coordinate the writing of the Civil Code of 1804 by Tronchet, Bigot de Préameneu, Portalis, and Maleville.[23]

However, the first controversy was raised on June 16, 1793, during the discussion of Chapter XVIII of the Committee of Public Safety's draft. It was a small but apparently unresolved debate that revealed a third topic.

Guyomar stated that it was necessary to declare that the justice of the peace was to be elected by the primary assemblies. Mathieu agreed, since "the primary assemblies are not involved in national acts and the election of a justice of the peace is not a national act, its functions are limited to the township."[24] The debate is not postponed or resumed later on, but it

[22] Royer, "Le 'Pouvoir Judiciaire' dans la Constitution de 1793," 309.

[23] For a brief summary of the 1804s code history, see Saman Safatian, "La Rédaction du Code Civil," Napoleonica 1, n. 16 (2013). For a more philosophically focused discussion on the concept of right by its writers, in contrast with the alleged legiscentrism of the revolutionary period, see Pierre Serrand, "La Loi Dans la Pensée des Rédacteurs du Code Civil," *Droits* 2, n. 42 (2005).

[24] AP, t. LXVI, 579.

relates to the discussion on the place of the Judiciary in society and the existence of a Judiciary power—two topics which this chapter will return to later.

5.1.1 *The Jury*

During the conventional debates, Cambacères is the main proponent of the idea of extending the jury to civil lawsuits. He starts his defense with the following words: "Citizens, justice is the social body's first debt."[25] The representative says the jury is as useful in the civil sphere as it is in the criminal sphere because it prevents the judges from acting unjustly.[26] Cambacères tries to anticipate the critique. For example, in anticipation of the possible claim that it is harder to differentiate facts from the law in civil suits, Cambacères proposes that the facts can be established previously, by an investigation or a report written by specialists.

The debates about the civil jury are mixed together with the debate on arbitration, but we can identify the objections against the civil jury in the June 17 debates. Bentabole, Thuriot, and Couthon essentially have the same proposal. As Couthon states, "the institution of the civil jury is a sublime institution, but you are not yet ready to receive it."[27] Hérault de Séchelles, responsible for the Committee of Public Safety's proposal, had been assigned to present a new formulation for the articles on civil justice and starts his June 19 speech by repeating the same position. The civil jury is a wonderful institution, but inapplicable to the present practice of French legislation and customs.[28]

One of the few voices in favor of the civil jury is Barère. He is the only representative that was also present during the 1790 debates and had already defended the institution on that occasion.[29] Barère based his position on a distrust of the "men of law" that justified the judicial reforms of previous years: "Where are the secret enemies of liberty concentrated? Inside the courts. Who opposes the Republic if not the men of law? These kinds of men are sterile when it comes to society and they do not produce anything useful."[30] Civil jury would be "the only way to guarantee the

[25] AP, t. LXVI, 597.
[26] AP, t. LXVI, 591.
[27] AP, t. LXVI, 598.
[28] AP, t. LXVI, 706.
[29] Royer, "Le 'Pouvoir Judiciaire' dans la Constitution de 1793," 310.
[30] AP, t. LXVI, 709.

rights of the people and the surest way to protect ourselves against the aristocratic race of the men of law."[31]

Civil jury appears in a good number of proposals. At least nine drafts include some kind of jury or jurors within the administration of civil justice. However, when the term "jury" is used, it does not necessarily mean the same thing.

In some texts, a division of labor among jurors is proposed. Chabot creates two different bodies. A jury composed of teenagers responsible for ruling on the facts and a jury of older citizens to rule on rights.[32] Daunou limits the jury's tasks to assessing the facts and leaves the legal analysis to arbitrators.[33] Poultier makes a similar suggestion but adds a caveat that appears in many other drafts (even in those which do not discuss the jury): no authority can prevent the parties from appealing to arbitration.[34]

Civil jury is also defended by Bacon, Bourgois, Debry, Dupont, George Edwards, and the draft submitted by the Committee of Public Safety. There are some minor differences,[35] but I will concentrate on how the jurors are selected.

The Constitution Committee, Dupont, George Edwards, Daunou, and Debry each proposes a different procedure for choosing the jurors: by election; by random drawing; by decision of the assembly of the neighboring district; or chosen by the parties themselves.[36]

In the June 19 debates, Robespierre claims the proposal of the Committee of Public Safety and the idea to create a civil jury are

[31] AP, t. LXVI, 710.

[32] François Chabot, *Projet d'Acte Constitutif des Français* (AP, t. LXVII (June 24, 1793)), V, Articles 2–3.

[33] Daunou, *Essai sur la Constitution*, V.II, Articles 3–4.

[34] Poultier distinguishes between jurors who deal only with facts (Poultier, *Constitution Populaire*, VIII, Article 3), leaving the proper legal aspect to the judges. But he still extends the involvement of the jury to parts of the justice system, such as the appeal court (Poultier, *Constitution Populaire*, VIII, Article 11) and the justice of the peace (Poultier, *Constitution Populaire*, VIII, Article 12). See also Poultier, *Constitution Populaire*, VIII, Article 17.

[35] Bacon limits the jury to accepting the complaint (Bacon-Tacon, *Plan Patriotique*, IV, Article 4). Bourgois believes the jury should just deliberate before the judges (Bourgois, *Plan de Constitution*, III.IV, Article 5).

[36] Respectively: Comité de Constitution, *Projet de Constitution*, X.II, Article 8 (I should point out that the Committee of Public Safety's proposal was that the civil jury only decides against previous decisions by arbitrators, and doesn't act as a lower court); Duplantier, *Réflexions sur le Scrutin*, X, Article 6; Edwards, *Idées pour Former une Nouvelle Constitution*, 491; and Daunou, *Essai sur la Constitution*, V.II, Article 3; and Jean-Antoine Debry (Baron), *Projet de Constitution* (AP, t. LXIII (April 24, 1793)), Article 14.

fundamentally the same. The former is for judges who are elected by the people to rule on fact and law. The latter is to divide the body into two different groups of citizens: one that decides on the facts; the other on legal interpretation. Both are to be chosen by a public official—which according to Robespierre is worse than leaving it directly to the people: "If your jurors are not chosen by the people, they are worth less than the present judges; if they are, the institution has no other advantage than to multiply the number of judges, to decide on the facts and on the law.[37]

It is important to clarify this. Royer says Robespierre's position contradicts the stance he took during the 1790 debates, when he was in favor of the civil jury.[38] However, this (apparent) change in position can be seen in a different light.

On both occasions, what was at stake was the relation between the organization of the justice system and the popular government. In his April 7, 1790, speech, Robespierre spoke in favor of extending the jury's operations to include civil cases. In some versions of the speech, Robespierre repeats the above-mentioned distinction between fact and law,[39] but we can find his main argument in favor of the extension in the *Anciên moniteur*: "The judges of permanent courts, with their terrible power to judge, will necessarily adopt a bodily stance all the more dreadful as, joined by pride, it will turn into despotism."[40]

So, in 1790 Robespierre discusses civil jury within the broader context of fighting against the judicial caste. Defending civil jury meant making a break with the aristocracy of the judicial order. This problem isn't part of the 1793 debates, at least not in the same manner. The judges put forward by the Committee of Public Safety's proposal were citizens who had already been elected by other citizens. Just like the civil jurors from 1790, the 1793 judges did not need any special qualification. They only needed the vote of confidence from their fellow citizens. It is for this reason that Robespierre can claim in 1793 that the civil jury simply results in a multiplication of the number of judges—a critique which is also expressed in Couthon's speech on June 19, 1793.[41]

[37] AP, t. LXVI, 710.

[38] Royer, "*Le 'Pouvoir Judiciaire' dans la Constitution de 1793*," 310.

[39] Robespierre, *Œuvres Complètes de Robespierre*, v. VI, 307–308.

[40] AM, t. IV, 67.

[41] AP, t. LXVI, 710–711.

5.1.2 *Arbitration and Choosing Those Who Judge*

The relation between the people and civil justice is also central to the debates on arbitration, as we can tell from Robespierre's speech from June 17, just before the issue was sent back to the committee for analysis:

> Nobody discussed the true heart of the issue: it is not about which tribunals we will have, but what kind of judges. We demand they are appointed by the people and are called judges; others want them to be chosen by the parties, and those we call arbitrators.[42]

Robespierre connects his critique of compulsory arbitration to the renewal of French customs. While France is not free of its *royalisme*, it is not possible to implement compulsory arbitration.[43] He anticipates the critique that the judge could be as corrupt as the arbitrator. The judge who neglects his duties is set off by the publicity of trials and the constant vigil of the republican people, while "arbitration is, by its nature, a work hidden within cabinets."[44]

The discussion and its outcome are nevertheless confusing. The Convention ends up adopting a mixed system that involves a justice of the peace and public arbitrators. An anonymous representative from the Convention observes that "public arbitrators are judges under a different name."[45]

The statement rings true, as it is extremely hard to identify the difference between the two. It should be kept in mind that prohibiting arbitration is never even discussed as an option. The quarrel is, at least in some cases, between having arbitration as the only "judicial" recourse available (compulsory arbitration), or having an institutionalized and free justice system for those who do not want to make use of arbitrators. The first option has few supporters.[46] So the debate centers on how to organize the second option.

[42] AP, t. LXVI, 600.

[43] In his words: "it can only serve a people whose customs and institutions are simple, and we are making the law for a people whose customs for a long time will remain unpurged of the leaven with which royalism has infected them" (AP, t. LXVI, 598).

[44] AP, t. LXVI, 599. The original French expression was *ouvrage de cabinets*, but the literal translation "work of cabinets" does not convey what I interpreted to be Robespierre's claim.

[45] AP, t. LXVII, 24.

[46] One example is Boissy d'Anglas. His draft presents a parallel system which involves a justice of the peace and arbitrators. The latter would only rule on cases which are outside the

The debates, Robespierre's critique and the available drafts make it clear that the terminology used for the institution is not important. The issue is how to appoint those who are going to judge. Robespierre's worry is that the administration of justice could be captured by the interests of the rich and that a Judiciary caste might arise. To prevent such an outcome, the selection procedure is of central importance.

Most proposals involve some kind of periodic appointment by the people. The Constitution Committee's draft, for example, introduces a yearly replacement of the justice of the peace who is responsible for civil cases and a biannual change for the judges and the prosecutor in criminal courts.[47] A good number of other texts follow the same direction as the Committee of Public Safety's and Boissel's proposal.[48]

former's competence (Boissy d'Anglas, *Constitution*, IX,II, Article 2). The task of determining it is a matter of future legislation (Boissy d'Anglas, *Constitution*, IX,II, Article 2), but Boissy d'Anglas' general idea is using the justice of the peace as a first filter before sending the case to compulsory arbitration. Other examples can be found in: Gleizal (who considers arbitration compulsory for lawsuits up to a certain value—Claude Gleizal, *Projet de Décret sur les Elections, les Assemblées Primaires, le Corps Législatif, le Conseil Exécutif, l'Administration de Département, les Municipalités, les Tribunaux, l'Arbitrage et les Bureaux de Pacification* (AP, t. LXII (April 17, 1793)), VII.7, Article 2); Pénières (who proposes compulsory arbitration for all cases, regardless of value—Jean-Agustin Pénières, *Plan et Projet de Constitution pour la République Française* (AP, t. LXII (April 17, 1793)), *administration de la justice*, Article 2); and Pressavin (who also defends compulsory arbitration, even for rulings on appeals—Jean-Baptiste Pressavin, *Projet de Constitution* (AP, t. LXVII (June 24, 1793)), 386).

[47] See Comité de Constitution, *Projet de Constitution*, X.I, Article 3; Comité de Constitution, *Projet de Constitution*, X.II, Article 3; and Comité de Constitution, *Projet de Constitution*, X.III, Article 9.

[48] Rosanvallon makes a minor mistake when he claims that Hérault de Séchelles' draft (the Committee of Public Safety's proposal) does not determine direct election for the judges (Rosanvallon, *La Démocratie Inachevée*, 76). Both de Séchelles' proposal and the Constitution's final text provide for the direct election of the justice of the peace (Comité de Salut Public, *Projet de Constitution*, XVII, Article 2, and *Constitution*, Article 88). The only difference is that the final version also includes public arbitrators who are appointed by the electoral assembly, instead of directly chosen by the people (*Constitution*, Article 91). Barailon suggests biannual elections for the judges (Barailon, *Projet de Constitution*, VI, Articles 2 and 16). The variation is the duration of their term. There are proposals for four years (Gleizal, *Projet de Décret*, VII.1, Article 4) and five years (Daunou, *Essai sur la Constitution*, V.II, Article 2, and V.III, A 2). But most drafts only provide for the existence of an election procedure, leaving its extension for future regulation or following the same rules applied to the representatives. The other drafts which propose the election of the officials responsible for judging are Anonymous P, *Essai sur la Constitution Française par un Citoyen du District de Montivilliers, Départment de la Seine Inférieure* (Archives Nationales, Series Lb41, n. 2993), 6); Beaulieu, *Nouvelle Rédaction*, II, Article 5; Beffroy de Reigny, *La*

There are some interesting variations which trigger reflections on the issue presented by Robespierre and Bancal's warning from December 1792. One is the suggestion of installing certain prerequisites for who may exercise the role of judge or arbitrator. In Beffroy de Reigny's text, all court judges are to be elected, but they must haves a minimum age of 55 years and a minimum of 10 years of previous experience in other public service jobs.[49] George Edwards declares, moreover, that judges must be specialists, which seems to imply they should be jurists.[50]

Yet those ideas are an exception. The almost unanimous proposal is that judges, arbitrators, or jurors are chosen by the people and in most drafts this happens by direct election. The meaning and place assigned to the law by the revolutionaries will be discussed in further detail in Chaps. 5 and 6, but it can already be stated here that the idea that judges should be freely chosen by the people derives, in part, from the notion that the law is a product, property, and knowledge belonging to all. The republican spirit is more important than the technicalities in any reading of the legal text.[51]

Constitution de la Lune, LXVIII, 244–245); Bourgois, *Plan de Constitution*, III.I, Article 6; Cappin, *Projet de Constitution*, X, Article 10; Lambert, *Plan de Constitution Républicaine*, IX.I, Article 3; Theodore Le Sueur, *Idées sur l'Espèce de Gouvernement Populaire qui Pourrait Convenir à un Pays de l'Étendue et de la Population Présumée de la France. Essai Présenté a la Convention Nationale par un Citoyen* (AP, t. LXII (April 17, 1793)), I.XI, Article 1; Poultier, *Constitution Populaire*, VIII, Article 14; Ruault, *Projet de Constitution*, IX, Article 2; and Wlriot (de Tours), *Hommage a la Convention d'un Projet de Gouvernement Républicain a Donner a la France* (AP, t. LXII, April 17, 1793) 576.

49 Beffroy de Reigny, *La Constitution de la Lune*, LXVIII, 244–245.

50 Edwards, *Idées Pour Former une Nouvelle Constitution*, 490. I do not believe we should consider Chabot's proposal as part of the same group. As mentioned before, Chabot proposed a two-jury system. One is composed of adolescents who decide on the facts, and another is composed of senior citizens who apply the law itself. There is no professional requirement necessary (as in Edwards and Reigny). Even the age requirement is somewhat relative, as it depends on the age distribution within each circumscription.

51 The criminal justice system receives practically the same treatment and variations, so it isn't necessary to simply repeat the same proposals. For example, in the final text, the Constitution provides for the electoral assemblies to appoint the judges (*Constitution*, Article 97). In the Constitution Committee's proposal, they are elected by the people (Comité de Constitution, *Projet de Constitution*, X.III, Article 9), as in—for example, Danou (Daunou, *Essai sur la Constitution*, V.III, Article 2) and Lambert (Lambert, *Plan de Constitution Républicaine*, IX.I, Article 3). The only topic with some greater degree of variation compared to the civil justice system is what we would today call "due process clauses." The topic falls outside the scope of my research, but I can point to the Constitution Committee's draft as an example that pays particular attention to the topic. It abolishes the death penalty for private crimes (Comité de Constitution, *Projet de Constitution*, X.III, Article 1), prohibits a

5.1.3 *Justice and the Executive Branch*

The issue of the appointment of judges serves as an introduction to our analysis of the Executive branch. As I have pointed out, aside from a few exceptions, the justice system as a whole is seen as an extension of the Executive body and not as a separate power or institution. However, the possibility of the Executive branch directly interfering in the administration of justice is almost non-existent in the proposals.

There are only three exceptions. The option of having the Executive branch directly appointing judges only appears in Anonymous P's draft, in which the justice of the peace is chosen by municipal officials and by so-called notables.[52] The other two exceptions are cases in which the act of judging itself is left to members of the Executive body. That is the case of Ducastellier's proposal, in which civil and criminal lower courts' rulings are carried out by municipal officials, who themselves are directly elected by the people in their primary assemblies.[53]

The last exception is less clear-cut. Anonymous E's text presents the magistrates of the commune and the magistrates of the department. They both play a role in administrative, police, and judicial matters. But regarding the election of those officials, the text suggests that, although they are called similarly, the task of judging and the task of administering are entrusted to different people.[54]

These are isolated cases. Therefore, even if there is a discourse which apparently denies that judicial rulings are independent from the Executive body, in practice, there seems to be little to no link. On the contrary, the predominant notion is that the different functions performed by the government are autonomous actions. A good number of drafts provide for some kind of autonomy—for example, the Constitution Committee's text, as well as Calès' and Daunou's commentaries.[55]

person to be tried more than once for the same act (Comité de Constitution, Projet de Constitution, X.III, Article 8), guarantees legal aid (Comité de Constitution, *Projet de Constitution*, X.III, Article 7), aside from other substantive and procedural provisions. For more information of the criminal justice system during the French Revolution, see P. Lascousme and P. Poncela, "Classer et Punir Autrement, les Incriminations sous l'Ancien Regime et sous la Constituante," in *Une Autre Justice*, dir. Robert Badinter, 73–104.

[52] Anonymous P, *Essai sur la Constitution Française*, 6.

[53] Ducastellier, *Le Drapeau de l'Indépendance*, Article 17.

[54] Anonymous E, *Quelques Idées*, Article 49, 51, and 55.

[55] See: Comité de Constitution, *Projet de Constitution*, X.I, Articles 5–6; Jean-Marie Calés, *Notes* (AP, t. LXII (April 17, 1793)), X.I, Articles 5–6; and Daunou, *Essai sur la Constitution*, V.I, Articles 3–4.

In the few instances in which some kind of interference appears, it isn't related to the content of the ruling, but in response to the abuse of authority perpetrated by judges. Bourgois and Constantini both assign the task of supervising the administrative and judicial bodies to the council of the government, denouncing any misfeasance and abuse of power to the Legislative body.[56] This kind of control is related to the point raised earlier, that neither judges nor members of the administrative bodies are allowed to interpret the law.

This autonomy isn't always expressly stated, but it can also be discerned from the way the texts structure the appeal system. This mainly happens through the revision of the merits of a given lawsuit. The operation is generally resolved within the organization of the justice system itself and does not redirect the decision to an external body. Depending on the draft, the justice of the peace and the arbitrators form different appeal structures, as can be seen in the Constitution's final version, but also in the proposal by the Constitution Committee, Bacon-Tacon, and Beffroy de Reigny.[57] In some texts, as we can see in the proposal by the Committee of Public Safety, the matter is left to the forthcoming Legislature.[58]

Therefore, the idea that the organization of the justice systems belongs to the Executive branch should not be understood as the complete opposite to what we today call the separation of power. For a better understanding of what it means to claim that the Judiciary and the Executive power are one and the same, I will finally turn my attention to the revolutionaries' view on the matter.

[56] Bourgois, *Plan de Constitution*, II.V.I.2, Article 4 and Antoine Constantini, *Correspondance du Citoyen Constantini avec le Citoyen Monge, Ministre de la Marine, Concernant les Approvisionnemens des de la République Française, Suivi d'un Projet de Décret sur l'Organisation du Pouvoir Exécutif* (Archives Nationales, Series Lb41, n. 566), 2, Article 27.

[57] See: *Constitution*, Articles 87 and 93; Comité de Constitution, *Projet de Constitution*, X.II, Article 8; Bacon-Tacon, *Plan Patriotique*, IV, Article 6; and Beffroy de Reigny, *La Constitution de la Lune*, LXVIII, 243. Bourgois also declares the appeal is a matter internal to the juridical bodies themselves, with the caveat that there must be some kind of supervision by the council of government (Bourgois, *Plan de Constitution*, III.III, Articles 1, 2, 5 and 8). Faure's and Lagrange and Dupin's proposals also provide for an appeal that is decided by the neighboring department's court (Pierre-Joseph-Denis-Gauillaume Faure, *Observations sur le Gouvernement de France, Relativement Au Plan du Comité de Constitution* (AP, t. LXIII (April 24, 1793)), 287; Lagrange et Dupin, *Projet de Constitution* (AP, t, LXIV (May 6, 1793)), Article 58) or, as in the latter's proposal for civil cases, by ambulatory judges (Lagrange et Dupin, *Projet de Constitution*, Article 81).

[58] Comité de Salut Public, *Projet de Constitution*, XVII, Article 6.

5.2 The Executive Council and the Administrative Bodies

Ollivier summarized, "the executive role, associated with the power of the king, is understood as a potential enemy of the people. That is why the authors try to define its duties as much as possible."[59] It should be noted that Louis XVI's trial and execution took place during the first month of the Convention's operation.

The first mechanism that was proposed to diminish the risk posed by a too dominant Executive power was to transform it into a collegial body. Almost all proposals follow this rule. There are three exceptions. Anonymous D proposes a *primat*. Hazard's text provides for the lifetime mandate of a *regens executor*. Ducastellier's draft includes a procedure for choosing the king, in case the people opt for a monarchy.[60]

But even in those cases there are limits to the power exercised by the monopersonal executive: Hazard establishes a procedure for dismissing the *regens executor*; Anonymous D restricts the *primat* to a two-year mandate and stipulates that the department responsible for choosing the authority must change each time. These two forms of control—short mandates and the possibility of recall—also appear in the proposals for a collegial Executive body. Duscastellier establishes a selection procedure in which one person is chosen by each department, thus forming an electoral body which then appoints ten people from among its members. The older person among those ten becomes king.

[59] Ollivier, "Les Projets Constititionnels de 1793," 372.

[60] See Anonymous D, *La France Heureuse*, 13; Hazard, *Vues d'un Patriote Présentées à la Convention Nationale* (Archives Nationales, Series Lb41, n. 2391), 10–11; and Ducastellier, *Le Drapeau de l'Indépendance*, 244. In the first draft, the term *primat* seems to have been imported from the political organization of the Catholic Church, in which the word *primat* is used in reference to the prelate just below the archbishop (Jean-François Féraud, *Dictionnaire Critique de la Langue Française*, t. 3 (Marseille: Jean Mossy, 1787), 241). In a way, we could also include Anonymous T's text in this list, as it is the only one which proposes the continuation of the monarchy. But the author restricts the monarch's power by removing all the prerogatives from the 1791 Constitution, such as the veto power and the civil list. A similar example can be found in Anonymous S' proposal to bring back the royal family and Anonymous U's claim that creating a republic is impossible in France, because of its size and its corrupted customs.

As Jean-Pierre Duprat summed up, "the absence of a head is perceived, within the democratic context, as a necessary condition that determines the organization of the Executive branch."[61]

5.2.1 *Choosing the Executive Council*

Ollivier puts forward that the principal point of discussion about the Executive council[62] was its selection procedure. According to the author, the issue is usually interpreted as an opposition between the draft submitted by the Constitution Committee and the final approved text—with the former proposing direct elections and the latter arguing the decision be made by the Legislative body, either by way of electoral assemblies or not.[63]

Rosanvallon, in his comparison of Hérault de Séchelles' draft (which was subsequently used as a starting point for the final text) and Condorcet—in other words, a comparison between the Committee of Public Safety's proposal and the Constitution Committee's—states that the former is "less democratic than the latter, which creates space for a system of direct elections."[64]

However, Ollivier highlights that the Constitution Committee's draft did not propose an independent Executive branch. In addition to the collegiality of the Executive body and its selection procedure, there were other ways of subordinating to the Legislative body. The distinction between administration and enforcement of the law (not law enforcement) must be kept in mind. A greater connection between the Executive council and the Legislative body doesn't necessarily imply some severe subordination of the secondary administrative bodies.

[61] Jean-Pierre Duprat, "Le 'Monstre Acephale' dans la Constitution de 1793," in *La Constitution du 24 Juin 1793*, coord. Naudin-Patriat, 244. Duprat's text presents an interesting discussion of the role to be played by the ministers, especially in the proposals submitted by the committees. The central point of contention is their separation, or not, from the Executive council. For those interested in the topic, his chapter in the compendium organized by Naudin-Patriat is recommended.

[62] To standardize the text, I chose the term "executive council" to refer to the collegial body responsible for exercising the Executive power. The texts themselves use a variety of terms, such as "executive commission" (Louis-François Mont-Réal, *Projet de Constitution* (AP, t. LX (March 2, 1793)), V), "executive agency" (Louis Léfebure, *Constitution du Gouvernement pour la Nation Française* (Archives Nationales, Series Lb41, n. 2391), 2), and "supreme Executive power" (Duplantier, *Réflexions sur le Scrutin*, V).

[63] Ollivier, "Les Projets Constititionnels de 1793," 379.

[64] Rosanvallon, *La Démocratie Inachevée*, 76.

There are two main issues to discuss in relation to the Executive branch: its selection procedure, considering its relationship with democratic practices, following Rosanvallon's cue; and the possible subordination of the Executive branch to the Legislative body. The second topic will be addressed later in this chapter, when I will discuss the relationships between the powers, which lead to a third topic: control mechanisms with regard to the Executive branch proposed in the different drafts.

On the selection procedure, it should be noted that there was practically no actual debate about Article 63 of the 1793 Constitution. The short debate on Chapter XII (On the Executive council) happened on June 16, 1793, and the exchange was limited to Thuriot, Poullain-Granprey, Levasseur, and Hérault de Séchelles.

The text initially put forward corresponds with the final version. They both stipulate that the electoral assemblies each choose one candidate, and then the Legislative body selects 24 people among those. Thuriot proposed that the Legislative body have more freedom—it should be able to appoint up to 12 members not previously chosen by the electoral assemblies. His argument is that the assemblies can perfectly select virtuous men, but they may be inapt for the task at hand. The discussion that follows is brief. Poullain de Grandprey is against the proposal and Levasseur comes up with a middle ground: 12 are to be selected by drawing lots, but Hérault de Séchelles opposed such a proposal "because that procedure was fatal to Athens."[65]

The use of drawing lots may have been a minor topic during the conventional debates, but the proposal appears in a good number of drafts. One example is Constantini's text. He suggests an Executive power composed of 85 members, distributed in groups of ten, for each of the eight departments. The remaining five are limited to take part in the deliberations.[66] Each assembly presents a given number of names that amount to

[65] AP, t. LXVI, 573. On the same passage, we have the revolutionary's justification for the drawing by lots: "in my opinion, the best way that can be adopted by a democratic government." The selection of magistrates by drawing lots will reappear in the discussion on the selection procedure for the Legislative branch.

[66] Respectively: Constantini, *Correspondance du Citoyen Constantini avec le Citoyen Monge*, Article 1, Article 3, and Article 8. In relation to Article 3, the eight listed departments were: Interior Affairs, War, Finances, Navy, Public Contributions, Diplomacy, Commerce, and Agriculture.

680 electables, who gather and draw the names of the 85 effective members of the Executive branch.[67]

Lantenhas gives a generic response to the proposal of selecting public officials by drawing lots. In his words, "wanting luck to choose is the same as choosing your own food by lot; it is the belief that we will precisely find in that way what is convenient to our health."[68]

Despite Lanthenas' critique, we can find two drafts presented by other representatives in which the drawing of lots is proposed. Ruault's text describes a drawing procedure in which the list of drawables is not constructed by the primary assemblies, as was the case in the three drafts by non-representatives mentioned before. Instead, the drawing happens among the members of the Legislative body itself.[69] Cappin, in an isolated case, universalizes the drawing of lots to encompass all electoral procedures. In his draft, the communes always choose twice the number of people for the available vacancies, followed by a drawing which decides who takes the post.[70]

In a way, Lantenhas' critique is not applicable to these proposals. All of them include a previous selection procedure. The drawing itself is limited to a small number of candidates. It must be remembered that, as a general rule, elections were open to all citizens, so anyone could be chosen to take a seat in the Executive branch.[71] But the drawing itself only happened after a severe, in most cases popular, screening process.

The discussion on drawing lots shows us the concern the authors of the drafts have for giving actual shape to democracy through the selection

[67] Constantini, *Correspondance du Citoyen Constantini avec le Citoyen Monge*, Article 7. There is a similar proposal in Dunouy's text (Jean-Honoré Dunouy, *Organisation d'un Nouveau Pouvoir Exécutif* (Archives Nationales, Series AD/XVIIIC/262, n. 14.), 9–10) and in Lafont's draft (Lafont, *Nouveau Mode de Nomination aux Emplois de la République* (AP, t. LXIV (May 6, 1793)), 246. In both cases the primary assembly chose twice the number of available vacancies and appointments were made through a process of drawing lots.

[68] François-Xavier Lanthenas, *Des Elections et du Mode a Elire par Listes Epuratoires* (AP, t. LXIV (May 10, 1793)), 513.

[69] Ruault, *Projet de Constitution*, VII.I, Article 1.

[70] Cappin, *Projet de Constitution*, XV, Article 4.

[71] There are some exceptions, as a small number of proposals include some kind of precondition to the job—in addition to the usual requirements, such as citizenship, a minimum age, residing within the French territory, and, almost unanimously, being male. For example, Anonymous D states that the *primat* should be chosen among former ministers and ambassadors (Anonymous D, *La France Heureuse*, 15) and governors among former general directors (Anonymous D, *La France Heureuse*, 22).

procedure for the members of the Executive council. One way of doing this is through drawings. The other is through direct elections by the primary assemblies, as proposed by the Constitution Committee. According to Ollivier's count, the second proposal had the greatest number of adherents among the draft authors, compared to those who believed the Legislative branch should be nominating the members.[72] Even though I disagree with some of Ollivier's ways of categorizing proposals,[73] I agree with her identification of these two main options presented by the revolutionaries. There are two residual groups. Seven drafts call for electoral assemblies and five for the absorption of the Executive powers into the Legislative body.[74]

The Legislative body's role, or lack of it, in choosing the members of the Executive council relates not only to the selection procedure itself, but also to the issue of the control mechanisms for the Executive power. As described above, there is a profound mistrust of what the revolutionaries see as the Executive branch's tendency to amass power. The participation of the Legislative branch is a way to try to prevent this abuse of power. This participation, however, does not necessarily imply some kind of submission of the Executive branch to the Legislative branch. To discuss this point further, I will return to Rosanvallon's claim that the Committee of Public Safety's proposal is less democratic than the proposal of the Constitution Committee.

As a preliminary remark, I should point out that the term "democracy" does not necessarily mean the same thing when Rosanvallon employs it and when the French revolutionaries utter it. In his trilogy on France's

[72] Twenty-five people would propose direct elections, while 19 would leave the decision to the Legislative body (Ollivier, "Les Projets Constititionnels de 1793," 380).

[73] For example, the author does not include Bacon on her list, although he provides for the Legislative body to select the Executive Assembly (Bacon-Tacon, *Plan Patriotique*, III, Article 2). According to my count of who says the Legislative body should have the final say, there are 16 proposals (Bacon, Beffroy de Reigny, Boissel, Brunel, Cloots, Coupé, Daunou, Dupont, Edwards, Kersaint, Lambert, Montgilbert, Pénières, Pressavin, and Wandelaincourt). There are 24 proposals for direct election by the primary assemblies, including those which propose to draw lots after an initial selection by the assemblies (Anonymous D, Anonymous E, Anonymous H, Barailon, Beaulieu, Blaviel, Bonnemain, Bourgois, Cappin, Constantini, Cusset, Debry, Desacy, Duplantier, Dupont, Faure, Gleizal, Lagrange et Dupin, Lesuer, Lefebure, Poultier, Rouzet, Thorillon, and Wlroit).

[74] Respectively: Calès, Boissy d'Anglas, Defrance, Mont-Réal, Oudot, Rubigny, and Saint-Just; and, calling for the concentration of power, Albouys, Chabot, Merry, Ragonneau, and Seconds.

political history, the *politologue*, Rosanvallon starts by discussing suffrage in France and then focuses on its relation to the idea of a people and their sovereignty.[75] In the following years, Rosanvallon expands his reflections beyond French history,[76] but in all these instances there is no doubt that "democracy" is a positive notion in Rosanvalon's point of view. Therefore his evaluation of the Committee of Public Safety's draft is undoubtedly negative.

For the revolutionaries, however, "democracy" is not necessarily associated with positive values. In part, democracy and representation were seen as opposites. In Robespierre's speech from May 10, 1793, this is expressed in his claim that the section should be organized "in a way equidistant from the storms of absolute democracy and the perfidious tranquility of representative despotism."[77]

Today this perhaps translates to the contradiction between representative and direct democracies, as evidenced by the clashes between *sans-culottes* and the Mountain group about which political model to adopt,[78] but this does not mean that the revolutionaries thought this debate was internal to the notion of democracy itself.

The opposition between representation and democracy appears in some representatives' speeches during the 1793 constituent debate. For instance, Pétion, debating the forms of government, states that the government should be representative but with democratic elements, such as the right to censor and the impermanence of magistrate positions.[79] Chabot asserts the democratic principle lies in not delegating what the people can do by themselves.[80] This also seems to be Hérault de Séchelles' position, who, when talking about the need for the popular sanction of all legal bills, says

[75] See: Pierre Rosanvallon, *Le Sacre du Citoyen: Histoire du Suffrage Universel En France* (Paris: Gallimard, 1992), *Le Peuple Introuvable* (Paris: Gallimard, 1998), and *La Démocratie Inachevée*.

[76] Rosanvallon's research trajectory can be followed in his series of courses given at the *College de France* starting in 2000. For example, his courses "What is a democratic society" (2009–2011) and "Democracy: outline for a general theory" (2011–2014).

[77] AP, LXIV:430.

[78] Josemar Machado de Oliveira, "Governo Revolucionário e Movimento Popular: A Contradição Entre a Democracia Representativa e a Democracia Direta Durante o Ano II (1793–1794)," In *Anais Eletrônicos do III Congresso Internacional Ufes/Université Paris-Est/Universidade do Minho: Territórios, Poderes, Identidades*, ed. A. P. Campos et al. (Vitória: GM Editora, 2011), 1–11.

[79] AP, LXIV:627.

[80] AP, t. LXVI, 540.

"the French Constitution cannot be exclusively *representative*, because it is no less *democratic* than it is representative."[81]

In this sense, the Committee of Public Safety's proposal is less democratic, as it does not provide for the direct election of the Executive council by a direct vote of the primary assemblies. However, less democratic here only means that the choice of magistrates does not come about by way of direct vote by citizens. In the revolutionaries' world view, suffrage was not a value in and of itself, but that doesn't mean they rejected the idea that the people should choose their administrators. In the Committee of Public Safety's draft, municipal officials are to be chosen directly by the assemblies of the communes, while departmental and district administrators are to be appointed by the electoral assemblies.[82]

Even considering those who, like Pénières, propose that the Executive council should be chosen directly by the Legislative body, without any mediation by the electoral assemblies, the selection of the non-national administration is as a rule entrusted to the primary assemblies.[83]

5.2.2 *Local and Regional Administrations*

No proposal suggests that the administrative bodies and the Executive council belong to different powers, branches, or functions within the government. In all texts, they both focus on the same issue of administering and enforcing the law. Why then distinguish between the two spheres?

The texts themselves do not elaborate on the subject. One of the few exceptions is the explanatory memorandum for the Committee of Public

[81] AP, t. LXVI, 259. The italics are part of the original archival texts.

[82] Saint-Just's draft follows a similar logic by providing for the direct election of the communities' councils (small-scale administrative bodies) and the indirect election, through electoral assemblies, of the directories of each *arrondissement* (Saint-Just, *Projet de Constitution*, XVI, Article 2; and, Saint-Just, *Projet de Constitution*, XV, Article 1). Boissy d'Anglas' text stipulates that the electoral assemblies elect the Executive council, while the primary assemblies are responsible for choosing municipal and departmental administrators (Boissy d'Anglais, *Constitution*, VII.I, Article 2; and, Boissy d'Anglais, *Constitution*, VII.II, Article 22).

[83] Pénières, *Plan et Projet de Constitution*, *Administration de section* e *administration de canton*. See also: François-Agnes Montgilbert, *Projet des Lois Constitutionnel* (AP, t. LXVII (June 24, 1793)), III and IV) and Lambert's draft (Lambert, *Plan de Constitution Républicaine*, IV, II). In a similar spirit, see George Edwards (Edwards, *Idées pour Former une Nouvelle Constitution*, 488).

Safety's draft. This statement was read by Hérault de Sécheles on June 10, 1793 and included this long, but interesting section:

> That we are not to be reprimanded for, on the one hand, having maintained the electoral assemblies after having paid homage to the sovereignty of the people and their right to vote. We believed it to be essential to establish a strong distinction between the representation on which the laws and decrees depend upon, in other words, the destiny of the Republic; and the appointment of a large number of public officials for whom, on the one hand, it is indispensable to be aware of their dependance on their origin and their roles, and on the other hand, that the people themselves must recognize that, most of the time, they are not in a position to choose, either because they don't know a great number of capable individuals in the cantons, or because their roles are of a simple and unique nature; or, finally, because the counting of their votes would take up too much time and effort. That was our intention, to leave it up to the electoral assemblies to choose all the posts other than those of representatives or the grand national jury.[84]

Hérault de Séchelles is therefore aware of the apparent contradiction between proclaiming the sovereignty of the people and right to vote. To justify his proposal, he creates a distinction between representation (from which the law originates) and the appointment of public officials. Then de Séchelles continues his argument by justifying the recourse to electoral assemblies with the claim that the people would face difficulties appointing capable citizens to the different administrative roles and that constant elections are bad, since they take too much time and impose delays. Oudot proposes a possible solution to the first problem: the electoral assemblies could choose from a list of people, made up of an initial roster elaborated by the primary assemblies, to run in a final election.[85]

However, the two arguments presented by Hérault de Séchelles seem to deviate from the main reason for making use of electoral assemblies. The people should occupy themselves only with the selection procedure for members of the Legislative body and leave the rest to another institution to elect. Why then does the draft he presented in the name of the Committee of Public Safety provide for the direct election of municipal officials—a choice that is maintained in Article 79 of the final text?

[84] AP, t. LXVI, 258.

[85] Charles-François Oudot, *Règles Générales Pour les Elections dans les Assemblées Primaires* (AP, t. LXVII (June 24, 1793)), 364–365.

As discussed previously, selecting those administrative agents who act in closer proximity to individuals and their communities, such as the municipal official in the Committee of Public Safety's text and the community council in Saint-Just's proposal, is a choice which is always delegated to the popular assemblies, even in those proposals in which the author provides for electoral assemblies and even when it is the Legislative branch which directly appoints the Executive council.

This does not mean, however, that the revolutionaries thought those public functions had some kind of representative character. Article 3 of Chapter XV of the Committee of Public Safety's proposal and Article 82 both expressly state that municipal administrators and officials are not representatives of the people.

During the June 16, 1793 debate, when the Convention discusses said article, Robespierre proposes that the article be scrapped completely. He claims "that Article appears to be absolutely useless, because the true character of representatives of the people is determined by the nature of their functions.[86] Although he maintains a somewhat isolated stance during the conventional sessions, Robespierre systematically positions himself against the idea that the people are represented by their congressmen. According to him, legislators and administrators are, all of them, the people's mandataries. Not their representatives. The nature of their institutional role determines the character of their activities—a point I will further explore in the next chapters.

Neither Robespierre's view nor the moderate position taken by the majority in the Convention appear to make any essential difference between municipal administration and other administrative spheres. There may be differences in their respective powers, but all instances have to do with law enforcement.[87]

One possible solution for this apparent dilemma is to simply claim that Hérault de Séchelles' defense is insincere or false. This would exclude the incompatibility of direct election of municipal officials from his

[86] AP, t. LXVI, 578.

[87] The Committee of Public Safety's draft and the final text of the Constitution both leave this issue up to future legislation (Comité de Salut Public, *Projet de Constitution*, XVI, Article 6, and TA, Article 83), but many proposals do determine the division of powers among the different administrative bodies. For instance, the Constitution Committee's and Saint-Just's proposal both regulate the matter in detail (Comité de Constitution, Projet de Constitution, IV.I, Article 10; Saint-Just, *Projet de Constitution*, XVI, Article 6).

explanation to avoid showing the flaw in his reasoning. But even if such an interpretation is accepted, it still doesn't explain why they opted for direct election.

There are two possible explanations. The first is to take Hérault de Séchelles at his word. The contradiction is apparent: the elective principle would exist, but it simply could not be universalized to encompass each and every post. Hérault de Séchelles' claim that constant elections or meetings of the people in primary assemblies tire them and have negative effects on the overall functioning of the government is a common theme during the debates and in the constitutional drafts. Both Robespierre and Guyomar declare as much.[88] Thibadeau adds that because of the size of the communes, only rich citizens would take part in the elections frequently, due to the cost of travel and the time away from work. In his words, it leads to an "aristocracy of rich or scheming men."[89]

Those statements express two practical concerns that imply the need to limit suffrage: possible damages to the economy and the possibility of creating a political aristocracy. This is far removed from the abstractionism thesis raised by Moyn and Douzinas that I presented in the first chapter. Or I could say that abstractionism is exercised by those who proposed universal suffrage, as the Constitution Committee did, because they could simply consider the vote as a value in and of itself, without weighing its pros and cons. Following such reasoning, the most democratic proposal in Rosanvallon's view, is precisely the view that doesn't pay as much attention to the socio-historical circumstances of the time.

Another reason could be considered. The Committee of Public Safety's concern that the constitutional text expressly stated that the municipal administrators and officials were not representatives means there was at least some fear that those public agents might see themselves as representatives of the people or could usurp powers that belong to the Legislative branch. This is the same reason which justified the ban on the Executive council or administrative bodies to interpret or modify the law.[90] Although

[88] AP, t. LXVI, 550 and 552. Furthermore, Robert claims such constant gatherings ruin the state, as they would keep the people away from commerce and agriculture (Pierre-François-Joseph Robert, *Discours* (AM, t.16 (April 27, 1793)), 231).

[89] Thibadeau, Antoine-Claire (Comte), *De La Division Du Territoire* (AP, t. LXVII (June 24, 1793)), 402.

[90] For example, see Articles 65 and 82 of the final text of the Constitution Committee's draft (Comité de Constitution, Projet de Constitution, IV.I, Article 19).

Robespierre alone claimed those rules were dispensable, because the limits of government functions derive from the nature of the function and not from an article in the Constitution.

5.2.3 Controlling the Executive Council and the Administrative Bodies

Ollivier lists three different ways that ensure the Executive council is held accountable: short mandates; controlling the missions; and recall and dismissal procedures.[91] The last two are forms of control exerted by the Legislative power and/or by the people. Municipal officials, or corresponding roles mentioned in the different proposals, are the administrative bodies which are closest to direct supervision by the people. On the other hand, administrators of the districts, communes, departments, and other administrative spheres that have a wider range are necessarily removed from the majority of the people who are under their administration, making popular oversight harder to enforce.

Although there are various kinds of control mechanisms proposed, the main one is that of popular oversight, but this is harder to implement in the larger administrative spheres. The risk of municipal officials who circumvent popular supervision is smaller, considering their proximity to the people. This hypothesis is corroborated by the way some of the proposals organize the administrative functions between the different spheres. While the Constitution Committee, which had proposed direct elections for all administrations, leaves the distribution of direct contributions to the departmental administrations[92]—just as the 1791 Constitution did, Saint-Just, who is the only member of the Committee of Public Safety to present a separate text, leaves those tasks to the council of the community[93]—a body which corresponds with the municipal officials of the final approved text.

The closer relation between municipal agents and the people is also mentioned in Barailon's proposal. In addition to distributing the citizens' contributions, municipal officials in Barailon's proposal are also

[91] Ollivier, "Les Projets Constititionnels de 1793," 383.

[92] Comité de Constitution, *Projet de Constitution*, IV.I, Article 10.

[93] Saint-Just, *Projet de Constitution*, XVI, Article 6. Daunou's proposal also lists the allocation of contributions at a local level as part of the municipal bodies' role (Daunou, *Essai sur la Constitution*, IV.III, Article 3).

responsible for making laws publicly known, for spreading the republican spirit, and for instilling love for the country.[94] Other drafts propose different institutional arrangements in a similar vein, such as Boissy d'Anglas' draft which provides for municipal administrators to directly receive petitions from the citizens.[95]

The difference in proximity parallels the difference in the distribution of the people. According to Verpeaux, this derives from the need to keep the roles distinctly separate.[96] The author criticizes the way the final text of the 1793 Constitution subordinated local administrations. The local administrations were to be a mere extension of the central body, which erases the duality that connected municipal bodies to local interests. In Verpeaux words, "the 24 June 1793 Constitution apparently ignores the duality of roles, at least in the name of the exasperation of the idea of unity."[97]

Nonetheless, Verpeaux does not consider the direct election of municipal officials as possible proof, or at least indicative of the fact that those officials were indeed recognized as agents linked to local interests. The separation into levels that, according to the author's argument, seems to imply that municipal officials should be elected through a two-tier procedure, is precisely what compels their election to be direct. As for the administration, the separation into levels can be brought into relation with the proximity of the official to the citizens and the direct local interests.

This greater proximity of municipal officials and the people may justify the Convention's choice for direct appointment through primary elections, but it does not imply that oversight and supervision are restricted to those citizens' direct actions.[98]

[94] Barailon, *Projet de Constitution*, II.XIII, Article 6.

[95] Boissy d'Anglais, *Constitution*, VII.II, Article 5.

[96] Michel Verpeaux, "Des Corps Administratifs et Municipaux," in *La Constitution du 24 Juin 1793*, coord. Naudin-Patriat, 274. The author refers to the distinction between the administration (two-level elections through electoral assemblies) and the justice system (direct election through primary assemblies). However, the argument seems incomplete, as the municipal officials are directly elected.

[97] Verpeaux, "Des Corps Administratifs et Municipaux," 277.

[98] Before exploring the control mechanisms proposed for the Executive council and administrative bodies, a side note on the previous argument. I do not intend to claim that the choice to exclude direct election of the members of the Executive council and other administrative bodies is better or immune to criticism. I am not defending Hérault de Séchelles' position. But unlike what some of the commentators are doing, I am attempting to identify the internal logic behind those proposals. This internal logic cannot be comprehended with-

The general notion of oversight was already expressed in Article 82 of the final document, in which administrators did not carry any representational weight and were barred from modifying or suspending the acts of the Legislative body.[99] Verpeaux reminds us that this disposition is not exclusive to the Committee of Public Safety's proposal. Even if not in the same exact formulation, it is also part of the Constitution Committee's and Boissy d'Anglas' proposals.[100] The author claims the article aims to combat federalism by preventing local administration from becoming independent from the central authorities.[101]

There are, however, two exceptions to this general rule: Wandelaincourt and Coupé. Wandelaincourt provides for a kind of reglementary power which the Executive branch may exert: "to give particular orders and establish provisional regulations."[102] Coupé states that, once the basis is firmly set, the necessary rules could be constructed by the assemblies and administrations.[103] But they were not proposing independent administrative bodies. In Wandelaincourt's proposal, the Executive body was nominated by the Legislative body. Coupé does not distinguish between Legislative and Executive bodies at the national level, assigning to both of them what he calls the role of mandatory assemblies.[104]

out reference to the concrete situation in which the revolutionaries were inserted. They had practical problems that needed, or so they thought, an immediate response. Implementing the proposed institutions was part of the answer, for example, to issues such as the concentration of power in the hands of the Executive branch (as Louis XVI attempted after 1789) and the possible difficulties that a daily elective calendar might create.

[99] The same logic already appeared in the 1791 Constitution. Section II, Chapter IV of the document determined: "Article 2. Administrators have no representational character. They are agents, temporarily elected by the people to perform administrative duties under the supervision and authority of the King"; "Article 3. They may not interfere in the exercise of the Legislative power, suspend the execution of laws, or encroach in any manner upon the judicial order or upon military arrangements or operations."

[100] Respectively: Comité de Constitution, *Projet de Constitution*, III.IV.III, Article 3; Boissy d'Anglais, *Constitution*, VII.I, Articles 2 and 3.

[101] Verpeaux, "Des Corps Administratifs et Municipaux," 275–276.

[102] Wandelaincourt, *Observations sur le Plan de Constitution*, 411.

[103] Jacques-Marie Coupé (Abbé), *Idée Simples de Constitution*, (AP, t. LXVII (June 24, 1793)), 269.

[104] Respectively: Wandelaicourt, *Observations sur le Plan de Constitution*, 411; Coupé, *Idée Simples de Constitution*, 267.

The oversight mechanism for the Executive branch, however, is not limited to this constitutional article.[105] In addition to the general prohibition on intervening in acts by other powers or bodies, there is a pyramidal control in which the Legislative body sits at the top. The general outlines can be found in the final text.

In this structure, the Executive council monitors the general administration, including all subordinate administrative bodies, while the Legislative body personally oversees the members of the Executive council.[106] In both situations, the final constitutional text does not extend this to include the right to decide on the matter. The Legislative body simply has to submit the issue to the appropriate courts. The Executive council is limited to filing a complaint with the Judiciary authorities against those administrative officials.[107]

Although the Committee of Public Safety's proposal and the final text both leave the matter of regulating the subordination structure and the division of roles between members of the administrative bodies to future legislation,[108] most proposals provide for a pyramidal structure of subordination.

The Constitution Committee's proposal divides the regional administration into three levels: department, commune, and section of the commune. The commune is subordinated to the departmental administration and the section's administration is assigned to an official subordinated to the commune.[109] In the same text, the most common mechanism proposed to ensure the regional administration's subordination to the

[105] There are also oversight mechanisms for other public functions, not only for the Executive power, such as revocation. These procedures will be analyzed in the next chapter.

[106] Respectively, *Constitution*, Article 65 and Article 71. On the final point, the Legislative power could formalize a complaint against members of the Executive council, in cases of malfeasance.

[107] In this last case, it should be pointed out that the right to denounce the Executive council does not seem to include the right to denounce members of other administrative bodies. However, it is possible that this option was considered to be part of the general power of oversight over the general administration (*Constitution*, Article 65). On the other hand, if that was so, it would not be necessary to provide for that control in relation to the agents assigned to the Executive council and such a point is not raised during the debates.

[108] Comité de Salut Public, *Projet de Constitution*, XVI, Article 6; and *Constitution*, Article 83.

[109] Respectively Comité de Constitution, *Projet de Constitution*, IV.I.I, Article 7; Comité de Constitution, *Projet de Constitution*, IV.I.I, Article 1.

Executive council appears: the council's nomination of a national commissioner to act jointly with the departmental administration.[110]

In the Constitution Committee's draft, the agent's roles are confined to communicating with the Executive council; supervising the enforcement of the law; and requiring the enforcement of the law. In other texts this power is extended or even reduced. For instance, in Barailon's proposal, the national commissioner can temporarily suspend the enforcement of administrative decisions deemed detrimental to the city, until there is a final ruling by the Executive council. Conversely, in Daunou's constitutional proposal, while the national commissioners are also chosen by the Executive council, they are limited to corresponding with the Executive council and monitoring the enforcement of the law. This political choice seems to be the general rule and is also present, in an analogous fashion, in the relation between Judiciary bodies and the treasury.[111]

This pyramidal subordination also forms part of the frequent creation of an intermediary body between the departmental and municipal administrations, responsible for supervising the latter while being monitored by the former. If no intermediary is created, the role is fulfilled by the department itself. That's the architecture which, for example, Boissy d'Anglas proposes when he subordinates the department to the Executive council and the municipal administration to the departmental body. The departmental administration could annul administrative acts of lower administrations, if they are against the letter of the law, and can provisionally suspend

[110] Comité de Constitution, *Projet de Constitution*, IV.I.I, Article 15. I will use the generic term "national commissioner" for this role, but the name itself can vary. Barailon talks about "national inspectors" (Barailon, *Projet de Constitution*, II.V, Article 28ff), for example. The important point is that the person is chosen by the Executive council, even if there are limitations to the appointment, and is to act jointly with some of the subordinated administrative bodies as an extension of the Executive council.

[111] See: Barailon, *Projet de Constitution*, II.V, Article 29; Daunou, *Essai sur la Constitution*, III, Article 2; Daunou, *Essai sur la Constitution*, V.II, Article 5; Bourgois, *Plan de Constitution*, V.I.4; Cappin, *Projet de Constitution*, V, Article 4. On the related disposition with regard to the Judiciary, see, among others: Mont-Réal, *Projet de Constitution*, VIII, Article 1; Lambert, *Plan de Constitution Républicaine*, V.III, Article 3; Boissy d'Anglais, *Constitution*, VIII, Article 1. On the treasury, see this reduced list of examples: Ruault, *Projet de Constitution*, IX, Article 23; RAG, XII, Article 6; Lambert, *Plan de Constitution Républicaine*, IX.II, Articles 19 and 20; Gleizal, *Projet de Décret*, V.II. Article 2; Daunou, *Essai sur la Constitution*, V.II, Article 2.

sub-administrators, about which the Executive council makes final decisions. Similarly, the Executive council can annul decisions made by lower administrations, if they go against public order, and can suspend administrators for acts or conduct that goes against national interest.[112]

The same logic is followed in almost all proposals in which intra-administration subordination is regulated.[113] Some texts are limited to simply stating that oversight is organized by degree.[114] There are, however, some different ways of handling intra-administrative control. Barailon, for example, uncommonly gives the Executive council the right to definitively dismiss or dissolve lower administrations.[115]

On the other side, there are those who prohibit the Executive council or lower administrative bodies from directly intervening in their subordinates' activities. Bourgois states that departments are not allowed to intervene in matters entrusted to the local administration. They can only present the matter to the Legislative or Executive council, and the latter

[112] Boissy d'Anglais, *Constitution*, VII.I, Articles 5 and 6; Boissy d'Anglais, *Constitution*, VII.I, Articles 6 and 7. Boissy d'Anglas is one of the few who uses the term "national interest," which is practically absent from the constitutional proposals. The dismissal of administrators, however, was decided by the Legislative power, except when the official was directly nominated by the Executive council (Boissy d'Anglais, *Constitution*, VI.I, Article 10). Some proposals, and that is not the general rule, do not provide for that limitation and allow the Executive council to directly dismiss officials who are nominated by their respective subordinate administrations—the Constitution Committee's text follows this line (Comité de Constitution, *Projet de Constitution*, V.I, Article 11).

[113] For instance, see Cappin, *Projet de Constitution*, V, Articles 9, 10, and 11); Comité de Constitution, *Projet de Constitution*, IV.I, Articles 17 and 18, and V.I, Articles 8, 9, and 10; Dunouy, *Organisation d'un Nouveau Pouvoir Exécutif*, 13; Jacques-Antoine-Paul Duplantier, *Réflexions sur le Scrutin a Etablir pour l'Élection des Représentants et des Magistrats du Peuple Français* (AP, t. LXVII (June 24, 1793), VIII, Articles 5 and 6; Lambert, *Plan de Constitution Républicaine*, Articles 8, 13, and 14; Ragonneau, *Plan d'une Nouvelle Constitution*, XI, Article 10; and Durand-Maillane, *Examen Critique du Projet de Constitution*, IV.I, Articles 10 and 11. Durand-Maillane is the only one that expressly permits the sub-administrator to appeal to the Executive council against the annulment of his activities by the departmental administration. Lambert has a similar provision for resolving intra-administration conflicts, but prohibits any appeal that bypasses the superior administration (Lambert, *Plan de Constitution Républicaine*, IV.I, Articles 23 and 24).

[114] A good example is Bonnemain, *Instituts Républicains*, V, 26, but see also: Debry, *Projet de Constitution*, Article 19; Joseph-Marie Cusset, *Projet de Décret sur la Constitution* (AP, t. LXIII (April 29, 1793)), IV, Article 12); Gleizal, *Projet de Décret*, VI, Article 8; and Poultier, *Constitution Populaire*, VI, Article 5.

[115] Barailon, *Projet de Constitution*, II.V, Article 22.

may present a formal complaint against illegal acts to the Legislative power, as well as temporarily suspend those involved.[116]

Daunou uses similar language, but goes one step further. According to him, even the Legislative power cannot intervene in matters attributed to the Executive council. It can only determine how the Executive council's members can be held accountable.[117] This is an isolated case, since the idea of an Executive body independent from the Legislative body was not common among the revolutionaries.

The revolutionaries' political views on the Judiciary must be kept in mind. Even though some of them directly place the Judiciary within the Executive branch, there are very few examples of any kind of effective control of judicial decisions by the superior administrative bodies. Daunou's text provides for the Executive council to suspend members of Judiciary bodies who are under suspicion of malfeasance and Constantini permits the council to suspend rulings, but his proposal is an isolated case. Even in these two cases the Executive council does not have the final say. Daunou proposes to send the matter to the Legislative body and Constantini proposes that the council sends the matter back to the courts.[118] In the Constitution Committee's draft, the Executive council is limited to a monitoring function. At most, it can send those rulings it considers tainted by excesses to the Judiciary censors.[119]

This overview already reveals the relative independence of the Judiciary function from the Executive bodies and administrations, as I suggested at the beginning of this chapter.

The pyramidal subordination is fundamentally a subordination to the Legislative power, since the Executive council, as a general rule, answers to it.[120] However, this doesn't mean the revolutionaries permit the

[116] Bourgois, *Plan de Constitution*, II.V.IV.4, Article 6; and II.V.IV.2, Article 2. Similarly, Gleizal determines that once the Executive council makes a suspension on the basis of a serious administrative act, the matter must be passed on to the Legislative power for a final say (Gleizal, *Projet de Décret*, VI, Article 12). Pressavin makes a similar proposal (Pressavin, *Projet de Constitution*, 386).

[117] Daunou, *Essai sur la Constitution*, 358.

[118] Respectively: Daunou, *Essai sur la Constitution*, III, Article 2; Constantini, *Correspondance du Citoyen Constantini avec le Citoyen Monge*, 2, Article 27.

[119] Comité de Constitution, *Projet de Constitution*, V.I, Article 7; Comité de Constitution, *Projet de Constitution*, V.I, Article 12. Lambert also repeats the same idea (Lambert, *Plan de Constitution Républicaine*, V.I, Article 15).

[120] In addition to those drafts, we can also point to Boissy d'Anglais, *Constitution*, VI.I, Article 8, VI.II, Article 1, and V.II, Article 2; Bonnemain, *Instituts Républicains*, IV, 25;

Legislative power's *motu proprio* to dissolve the Executive council or lower administrative bodies or even dismiss their members.

There are a few texts in which such harsh measures do appear—only in Montgilbert's and Bacon-Tacon's proposals.[121] According to the other texts, the Legislative body can allow for a member of the Executive council to be tried, but it is not responsible for the judgment. The final text adopts this solution, as well as the Constitution Committee's and Constantini's texts.[122]

Even when they consider the subordinate role of the Executive council in relation to the Legislative power and the mistrust of the Executive branch, the revolutionaries appear to practice restraint in their creation of legislative oversight mechanisms for the Executive branch. There are even three drafts which propose that the Executive council can interpellate the Legislative branch.

Poultier gives the Executive council the right to consult the Legislative power in case of doubts, unforeseen issues, or mistakes.[123] This appears to reinforce the supremacy of the Legislative body, but the proposal also suggests that the Executive council may identify and point out mistakes allegedly committed by the Legislative body.

The other two examples are more straightforward. Pressavin permits the Executive council to present a complaint against decrees it deems to be contradictory to the Constitution or contrary or dangerous to public affairs. The Legislative branch itself can rule on the matter and can't refuse

Bourgois, *Plan de Constitution*, II.IV.IV.1, Articles 9, 10, and 17; Duplantier, *Réflexions sur le Scrutin*, V, Article 14, and VI, Article 5.

[121] For Montgilbert's proposal, see Montgilbert, *Projet des Lois Constitutionnel*, Article 35. Bacon seems to allow for the dissolution of an administration which has committed acts contrary to the letter of the law (Bacon-Tacon, *Plan Patriotique*, V, Article 4). This possibility for the dissolution of the entire administrative body by the Legislative power is found only in these two drafts, but there are some intermediary proposals. Ruault, in a similar fashion, provides for the suspension of officials by the Executive council, in case of repeated disobedience or an act which compromises public safety and order, but the final decision on the suspension is made by the Legislative power (Ruault, *Projet de Constitution*, VII.VIII, Articles 6 and 10).

[122] Comité de Constitution, *Projet de Constitution*, V.I, Articles 21, 27, and 28; Constantini, *Correspondance du Citoyen Constantini avec le Citoyen Monge*, 2, Article 20; *Constitution*, Article 74. See also Lambert (Lambert, *Plan de Constitution Républicaine*, V.III, Article 18). Cloots has a similar take on the matter. He states that ordinary courts should be responsible for ruling on abuse of authority, "*lèse*-society" and "*lèse*-nation" cases (Cloots, *Bases Constitutionnelles*, 395).

[123] Poultier, *Constitution Populaire*, V, Article 28.

to deliberate on it.[124] Saint-Just proposes the Executive council can submit to the people any decree it believes to be contrary to the Declaration, if it has been issued with less than 251 votes.[125]

I will expand on these proto-judicial reviews in the next chapter. The important point to highlight here is that the Executive branch's subordination to the Legislative branch, even when it is unambiguously defended by the revolutionaries in their proposals and speeches, did not lead to an institutional arrangement that gave the Legislative body effective control of the Executive council or lower administrations.

In the next chapter I will discuss the different proposals for popular control over the government. They will mirror some of the mechanisms proposed in relation to the Executive branch or involve some broader proposition for internal control. For example, Debry states that any public official can be suspended by the Legislative body, but if the official was elected by the people, a jury will be needed to rule on the dismissal or incapacity of this person. Poultier states that the departmental administration, as it was nominated by the people, can only be dissolved by them.[126] Gleizal is the only one who places the decision in the hands of the primary assemblies—apart from the general right of revocability that will be studied in the next chapter—as they have the final word in the case that the Executive council disagrees with the Legislative body's decision to suspend one of its members.

Appendix

Historical References for the 1792–1793 Debates

Explanatory Notes

1. Whenever possible, the drafts are cited by article or chapter and article, not by page.
2. I reference the anonymous texts' authors as "Anonymous A" to "Anonymous U" to more easily reference them in the main text of this book.

[124] Pressavin, *Projet de Constitution*, 386.

[125] Saint-Just, *Projet de Constitution*, XIII, Article 8.

[126] Debry, *Projet de Constitution*, Article 22 and Poultier, *Constitution Populaire*, VI, Article 2.

3. Since this is an abridged version of the original thesis, not all of the texts listed below are mentioned throughout the main text. I chose to include them in the references for fellow researchers interested in the topic;
4. The final and approved text of the Declaration and Constitution of the Year 1 of the Republic are cited as *Declaration* and *Constitution*. The other primary texts are listed below.

Parliamentary Notes, Newspapers, and Legal Texts

Archives parlementaires de 1787 à 1869 (First series). Paris: Paul Dupont, 1867–2021. [cited as "AP," followed by tome number, page, and the document's date, when available]

Anciến moniteur (Réimpression de l'), *Seule Histoire Authentique et Inaltérée de la Révolution Française depuis la Réunion des États-Généraux jusqu'au Consulat (Mai 1789–Novembre 1799)*, 31 t. Paris: Henri Plon Imprimeur-Éditeur, 1862–1863. [cited as "AM," followed by tome number, page, and the document's date, when available]

Baudouin, François-Jean (ed.). *Collection Générale des Décrets Rendus par l'Assemblée Nationale*. Paris: Baudouin, 1789–1795, 67 v. [A digital version is available through: https://collection-baudouin.univ-paris1.fr].

Drafts

Anonymous D. la *France Heureuse ou Tout le Monde Content*. Archives Nationales, Series AD/XVIIIC/262, n. 15.

Anonymous E. *Quelques Idées sur une Constitution Populaire pour un Grand État*. AP, t. LXIII (April 24, 1793), 296–302.

Anonymous O [Par Cosmopolite]. *Discours Fraternel et Instructions a mês Citoyens pour les Mettre a la Hateur des Républicains: Ouvragre Nouveau sur les Droits de l'Homme et du Citoyen, d'Après des Principes Physiques et Moraux*. Archives Nationales, Series Lb41, n. 2982.

Anonymous P. *Essai sur la Constitution Française par un Citoyen du District de Montivilliers, Départment de la Seine Inférieure*. Archives Nationales, Series Lb41, n. 2993.

Bacon-Tacon, Pierre Jean Jacques (Comte de). *Plan Patriotique, ou Idée d'une Bonne Constitution Républicaine, en France*. Archives Nationales, Series AD/XVIIIC/262, n. 4.

Bancal, Jean Henri (Bancal des Issarts). *Du Nouvel Ordre Social.* AP, t. LV (December 24, 1792), 409–423.
Barailon, Jean-François. *Projet de Constitution Présenté a la Convetion Nationale.* AP, t. LXVII (June 24, 1793):187–220.
Beaulieu, Claude François. *Nouvelle Rédaction de la Déclaration ses Droits et des Deux Premier Titres de la Constitution.* Archives Nationales, Series Lb41, n. 80.
Beffroy de Reigny, Louis-Abel. *La Constitution de la Lune, Rêve Politique et Moral, par le Cousin-Jacques.* Archives Nationales, Series Lb41, n. 706.
Boissy d'Anglas, François-Antoine (Comte de). *Constitution.* AP, t. LXII (April 17, 1793), 291–315.
Bonnemain, Antoine-Jean-Thomas. *Instituts Républicains, ou Développement Analytique des Facultés Naturelles, Civiles et Politiques de L'homme.* Archives Nationales, Series Lb41, n. 2385.
Bourgois, Nicolas. *Plan de Constitution Proposée a la République Française.* AP, t. LXIII (April 24, 1793) 259–279.
Calés, Jean-Marie. *Notes.* AP, t. LXII (April 17, 1793) 319–325.
Cappin [or Capin], Joseph. *Projet de Constitution.* AP, t. LXIV (May 6, 1793) 235–243.
Chabot, François. *Projet d'Acte Constitutif des Français.* AP, t. LXVII (June 24, 1793) 261–266.
Chevret, Jean. *Principes de Sociabilité, ou Nouvel Exposé des Droits et des Devoirs de l'Homme et du Citoyen, Suivies d'Observations Importantes, Relatives aux Propriétés, a la Liberté du Commerce & a la Proportion du Prix des Subsistances avec les Facultés des Citoyens.* Archives Nationales, Series Lb41, n. 2883.
Cloots, Anacharsis. *Bases Constitutionnelles de la République du Genre Humain.* AP, t. LXIII (April 26, 1793) 389–403.
Comité de Constitution. *Projet de Constitution.* AP, t. LVIII (February 15, 1793) 602–609.
Comité de Salut Public. *Projet de Constitution du Peuple Français.* AP, t. LXVI (June 10, 1793) 260–264
Constantini, Antoine. *Correspondance du Citoyen Constantini avec le Citoyen Monge, Ministre de la Marine, Concernant les Approvisionnemens des de la République Française, Suivi d'un Projet de Décret sur l'Organisation du Pouvoir Exécutif.* Archives Nationales, Series Lb41, n. 566.
Coupé, Jacques-Marie (Abbé). *Idée Simples de Constitution.* AP, t. LXVII (June 24, 1793) 266–279.

Cusset, Joseph-Marie. *Projet de Décret sur la Constitution*. AP, t. LXIII (April 29, 1793) 599–601.
Daunou, Pierre-Claude-François. *Essai sur la Constitution*. AP, t. LXII (April 17, 1793) 350–370.[127]
Debry, Jean-Antoine (Baron). *Projet de Constitution*. AP, t. LXIII (April 24, 1793) 238–241.
Ducastellier, M. *Le Drapeau de l'Indépendance sous lequel les Français Doivent se Réunir à l'Assemblée Conventionnelle*. AP, t. LXIII (April 24, 1793) 241–259.
Dunouy, Jean-Honoré. *Organisation d'un Nouveau Pouvoir Exécutif*. Archives Nationales, Series AD/XVIIIC/262, n. 14.
Duplantier, Jacques-Antoine-Paul. *Réflexions sur le Scrutin a Etablir pour l'Élection des Représentants et des Magistrats du Peuple Français*. AP, t. LXVII (June 24, 1793) 309–310.
Durand-Maillane, Pierre-Toussaint. *Examen Critique du Projet de Constitution, Présenté a la Convention par son Comité, avec un Ordre Nouveau dans le Plan*. AP, t. LXII (April 17, 1793) 374–388.[128]
Edwards, George. *Idées Pour Former une Nouvelle Constitution, et Pour Assurer la Prospérité et le Bonheur de la France et d'autres Nations* AP, t. LIX (February 28, 1793) 482–498.
Faure, Pierre-Joseph-Denis-Gauillaume. *Observations sur le Gouvernement de France, Relativement Au Plan du Comité de Constitution*. AP, t. LXIII (April 24, 1793) 279–292.
Gleizal, Claude. *Projet de Décret sur les Elections, les Assemblées Primaires, le Corps Législatif, le Conseil Exécutif, l'Administration de Département, les Municipalités, les Tribunaux, l'Arbitrage et les Bureaux de Pacification*. AP, t. LXII (April 17, 1793) 411–420.
Lafont. *Nouveau Mode de Nomination aux Emplois de la République*. AP, t. LXIV (May 6, 1793) 245–246.
Lagrange et Dupin. *Projet de Constitution*. AP, t, LXIV (May 6, 1793) 248–252.
Lambert, Charles. *Plan de Constitution Républicaine, Précédé de Quelques Observations sur Celui que le Comité de Constitution a Présenté a la Convetion les 15 et 16 Février*. AP, t. LXII (April 17, 1793) 434–466.

[127] The document is subdivided as follows: *Projet de Déclaration*, *Bases de l'Établissement en France*, *Constitution ou Définition et Distribution des Pouvoirs dans la République Française* and *Principes de la Législation en France*.

[128] Includes: *Projet de Déclaration*, 379–384; and *Projet de Constitution*, 384–388.

Lanthenas, François-Xavier. *Des Elections et du Mode a Elire par Listes Epuratoires.* AP, t. LXIV (May 10, 1793) 510–513.

Léfebure, Louis. *Constitution du Gouvernement pour la Nation Française.* Archives Nationales, Series Lb41, n. 2391.[129]

Le Sueur, Theodore. *Idées sur l'Espèce de Gouvernement Populaire qui Pourrait Convenir à un Pays de l'Étendue et de la Population Présumée de la France. Essai Présenté a la Convention Nationale par un Citoyen.* AP, t. LXII (April 17, 1793) 548–570.

Mont-Réal, Louis-François. *Projet de Constitution.* AP, t. LX (March 2, 1793) 615–620.

Montgilbert, François-Agnes. *Projet des Lois Constitutionnel.* AP, t. LXVII (June 24, 1793) 352–362.

Oudot, Charles-François *Règles Générales Pour les Elections dans les Assemblées Primaires.* AP, t. LXVII (June 24, 1793) 364–368.

Pénières, Jean-Agustin. *Plan et Projet de Constitution Pour la République Française.* AP, t. LXII (April 17, 1793) 477–482.

Pressavin, Jean-Baptiste. *Projet de Constitution.* AP, t. LXVII (June 24, 1793) 380–390.

Poultier, François-Martin [Poultier d'Elmotte]. *Constitution Populaire.* AP, t. LXII (April 17, 1793) 482–492.

Ragonneau. *Plan d'une Nouvelle Constitution.* AP, t. LXIV (May 6, 1793) 252–259.

Robert, Pierre-François-Joseph. *Discours.* AM, t. 16 (April 27, 1793) 230–231.

Ruault, Alexandre-Jean, *Projet de Constitution de la République Française.* Portiez de l'Oise Collection, t. 176, n. 15.

Saint-Just, Antoine-Louis-Léon de. *Projet de Constitution.* AP, t. LXIII (April 24, 1793) 200–215.

Thibadeau, Antoine-Claire (Comte). *De la Division du Territoire.* AP, t. LXVII (June 24, 1793) 400–403.

Thorillon, Antoine-Joseph. *Idées ou Bases d'une Nouvelle Déclaration des Droits de l'Homme, de cette de ses Devoirs et d'une Nouvelle Constitution pour la République Française, où l'on Traite, entre Autres Choses, de la Liberté, de l'Égalité, des Insurrections, de l'éducation Nationale, du Code Civil, et Notamment des Enfants Naturels, de l'Adoption, d'une Seule Substitution Officieuse, de l'Organisation d'un Nouvel Ordre Judiciaire, etc.* AP, t. LXII (April 17, 1793) 582–598.

[129] A shorter version was published in the *Ancien Moniteur* on April 24, 1793 (AM, t. XVI, 202).

Wandelaincourt, Antoine-Hubert. *Observations sur le Plan de Constitution.* AP, t. LXVII (June 24, 1793) 409–415.
Wlriot (de Tours). *Hommage a la Convention d'un Projet de Gouvernement Républicain a Donner a la France.* AP, t. LXII (April 17, 1793) 574–582.

References

Badinter, Robert (dir.). *Une Autre Justice: Contributions a l'Histoire de la Justice sous la Révolution Française.* Paris: Fayard, 1989.
Clere, Jean-Jacques. "L'Abolition des Droits Féodaux en France." *Cahiers D'histoire (Revue d'Histoire Critique)* 94–95 (2005): 135–157.
Féraud, Jean-François. *Dictionnaire Critique de la Langue Française, 3 t.* Marseille: Jean Mossy, 1787–1788. http://catalogue.bnf.fr/ark:/12148/cb16986415s
Galy, François. *La Notion de Constitution dans les Projets de 1793.* Paris: Editions Albert Mechelinck, 1932.
Naudin-Patriat, Françoise (coord.). *La Constitution du 24 Juin 1793: L'Utopie dans le Droit Public Français? (Actes du Colloque de Dijon, 16 et 17 Septembre 1993).* Dijon: Editions del'Universite de Dijon, 1997.
Oliveira, Josemar Machado de. "Governo Revolucionário e Movimento Popular: A Contradição Entre a Democracia Representativa e a Democracia Direta Durante o Ano II (1793–1794)" In *Anais Eletrônicos do III Congresso Internacional Ufes/Université Paris-Est/Universidade do Minho: Territórios, Poderes, Identidades (Territoires, Pouvoirs, Identités)*, ed. A. P. Campos *et al.* Vitória: GM Editora, 2011.
Ollivier, Nathalie. "Les Projets Constitutionnels de 1793." PhD Diss. Université Panthéon-Assas, 2002.
Robespierre, Maximillien de. *Œuvres Complètes de Robespierre*, 10 v. Paris: Presses Universitaires de France, 1910–1967.
Rosanvallon, Pierre. *La Démocratie Inachevée: Histoire de la Souveraineté du Peuple en France.* Paris: Gallimard, 2000.
Rosanvallon, Pierre. *Le Peuple Introuvable.* Paris: Gallimard, 1998.
Rosanvallon, Pierre. *Le Sacre du Citoyen: Histoire du Suffrage Universel En France.* Paris: Gallimard, 1992.
Safatian, Saman. "La Rédaction du Code Civil." *Napoleonica* 1, n. 16 (2013): 49–63.
Serrand, Pierre. "La Loi Dans la Pensée des Rédacteurs du Code Civil." *Droits* 2, n. 42 (2005): 31–48.
Vovelle, Michel (ed.). *La Révolution Française: une Histoire Toujours Vivante.* Paris: Tallandier, 2010.

CHAPTER 6

The Legislative Body

L'approbation du souverain est le murmure de la foule.
—François Galy

In my analysis of the revolutionaries' views on the Judiciary and the Executive, I have hinted at the Legislature's superior and supervisory position. I have also shown how this position had a double function and meaning: as institutional design and as a symbolic enunciation. Especially in regard to the Justice system, the powers assigned to the Legislative body[1] to effectively interfere in judicial rulings were non-existent or, at most, restricted to a small number of projects, depending on the interpretation. In comparison with the Executive council, the scope of actions of the Legislature differs considerably and a sizable portion of the previously mentioned drafts directly include the Legislature in the selection of council members. This logic, however, is not repeated in local and regional spheres, where the administrative bodies are less subject to some kind of direct control by the Legislature, even if some indirect mechanisms are in place. Even the Executive council has a good deal of independence.

[1] Considering the different names chosen for this body among the Year 3 projects, I will mostly use the nomenclature adopted in June 24, 1793, final text.

E. Baker, *Human Rights and Humanity's Rights During Year Three of the French Revolution*,
https://doi.org/10.1007/978-3-030-99508-9_6

Even if we recognize that the different parts that compose the forms of government proposed in 1793 held a greater deal of independence than the historiography usually recognizes, the Legislative body's centrality in the Year 3 institutional design is undeniable. At this point, we should go back to one of the typical readings of this phenomenon: the idea of legiscentrism, especially as proposed by Gauchet and Jaume. But we should not confuse legiscentrism with the centrality of the Legislative body.[2] I will present some initial remarks on this relationship and this distinction, but I will only develop it in further detail in the last chapter.

Also, as a background to the Year 3 debates on the Legislative body, we have the question of representation.[3] Whereas political philosophy issues are more implicit than openly discussed in the projects and debates on external relations, the Justice system, the Executive branch, and administrative bodies, controversies around the Legislature bring philosophical debates more directly to the forefront, one of them being the issue of representation.

This, however, does not mean that we have a large corpus of theoretical debates on representation. As Galy points out, when analyzing the 1793 constituent debate on representation:

> The authors of these projects were neither original thinkers, nor theoreticians. There was no time or inclination, during a revolution, to think about political problems in a disinterested manner. First and foremost, the aim was to write a votable project.[4]

Both legiscentrism and representation will be better discussed in the following chapter, but we can see echoes of this debate here.[5]

[2] As shown in my first chapter when discussing Jaume and Gauchet's ideas.

[3] In this chapter, we will see why some revolutionaries, notably Robespierre, did not agree with using the term "representation" to describe the work of the Legislative body. However, I will use the term in its broader sense until I get to the point of the discussion where the relevant distinctions can be explained.

[4] Galy, *La Notion de Constitution dans les Projets de 1793*, 94.

[5] It is by articulating the legiscentrism hypotheses as exposed by Gauchet and Jaume with the problems regarding representation that we can better comprehend categories such as citizenship and sovereignty, both topics to be discussed in the next chapter. I will not, however, engage with the debates on representation taking place in the eighteenth-century France, as that is beyond the purpose of this book. For a good presentation of these discussions, as well as a detailed study on some revolutionaries' take on the subject, see Michel Ganzin, ed., *Le*

The participants in the Year 3 constituent debates had in mind at least two models of representation. The first one was the representation-mandate model of the General Estates, as in 1789, when local primary assemblies wrote their *cahiers* instructing the deputies who were then sent to Paris. These assemblies handed to their deputies a set of relatively specific demands and problems, which seemed to restrict these representatives' freedom of action.[6] After that, we have the representative model adopted by the 1791 Constitution.

In the 1791 Constitution, the National Legislative Assembly was the main body responsible for exercising the Legislative power. The Assembly was unicameral and elected for a two-year term by the electoral assemblies, and it was composed of 745 representatives chosen from the 83 departments, as well as the deputies assigned to the colonies.[7] These 745 representatives were divided in three groups: 247 were chosen in a territorially based system (three for each department and one for Paris); 243 deputies were chosen in proportion to each department's population; and the remaining 243 according to the direct taxes collected by each department.

In 1791, there was no direct election of representatives by the primary assemblies, nor a direct mandate by primary or electoral assemblies, nor any possibility for these local bodies to interfere in the legislative procedure. The National Assembly passed the laws, and the king sanctioned them. If he vetoed them, two consecutive Legislatures had the possibility of overruling such a decision.[8] The king could also suggest issues for the Assembly to discuss.[9] We have a model of representation that is clearly distinct from the one adopted by the General Estates and closer to what we think today as parliamentary representation.

In between these two models, we have the August 10, 1792, insurrection. On July 25, the Assembly had established that the primary assemblies

concept de représentation dans la pensée politique (Aix-en-Provence: Presses Universitaires d'Aix-Marseille, 2003).

[6] I use the word "seemed," because the *Tiers'* deputies were responsible for the path chosen by the General Estates in 1789 and it is not possible to say that their actions were directly guided by the assembly that had chosen them.

[7] See Title III (On the Public Powers), Chapter 1, of the 1791 Constitution.

[8] Title III, Chapter III, Section III, explains the royal sanction and veto procedure.

[9] Title III, Chapter III, Section I, presents the National Assembly's attributions and Section IV the relationship between the king and the Assembly.

were permanent, after the July 11 *la patrie en danger*[10] proclamation. Ollivier claims that this shows how the subsequent National Convention was legitimized by the insurrection itself. The Convention had established a relationship, albeit an ambiguous one, with the exercise of sovereignty by the primary assemblies, between the need for a representative regime and the implementation of a direct democracy.[11]

Even if I disagree with Ollivier's use of the term "direct democracy," since it is not a part of the revolutionaries' lexicon,[12] it is not possible to disregard the relationship between the people and the primary assemblies that we see by late 1792 when discussing the Year 3 constituent debates on the organization of the Legislative.

As Galy points out, in 1793 not a single project proposed a purely representative system, nor a direct government model.[13] It is by understanding how these different elements interact with each other that we can better comprehend the Year 3 proposals for the Legislative body.

A good starting point is the discussion on the formation of the Legislature. As I've mentioned before, the 1791 Constitution had little more than 700 deputies indirectly elected by the primary assemblies through the electoral assemblies, according to three criteria: territory, population, and taxation. If we look only to the 1793 final text, we would see the adoption of solely the populational criterion and the rejection of the indirect election model with the electoral assemblies.

6.1 The Formation of the Legislative Body

The June 12, 14, and 15 debates were centered around the constitutional chapters on the Legislative body, and they brought forth some of the issues presented in the drafts. After an initial argument over the correct individual-to-deputy ratio in each territorial district,[14] the Convention debated if one department could choose a deputy from another department. For Charles Delacroix, this would lead to an "aristocracy of reputation"—a motion seconded by Génissieu.[15]

[10] Roughly translatable as "the country is in danger." See AP: 46, 342 (*Décret du 11 juillet 1792*).

[11] Ollivier, *Les Projets Constitutionnels de 1793*, 267.

[12] Ollivier highlights this herself (Ollivier, *Les Projets Constitutionnels de 1793*, 268).

[13] Galy, *La Notion de Constitution dans les Projets de 1793*, 83.

[14] AP, t. LXVI, 454–455.

[15] AP, t. LXVI, 518.

This idea of some kind of aristocracy being formed inside and by the Legislative was also raised by Poullian de Grandprey in regard to another topic. For him, the Convention should ban reelection, because "of all aristocracies, the most dangerous one is the aristocracy of popularity."[16] Against both positions, Garrau, Boyer-Fronfrède, and Thuriot present the same objection: the best defense against aristocracy is respecting the sovereignty of the people.[17]

Among the projects, the scope of concerns and possibilities is broad. The total number of deputies, how to choose them, the existence (or not) of a mandate, and how to control the representatives; all these issues are approached in varied ways. However, a small number of elements seem to be constant. Only one project—Anonymous A—proposed a bicameral system.[18] All other proposals are for a unicameral Legislature, but this does not mean that similar preoccupations are not present.

The rejection of bicameralism is a consequence of the revolutionaries' wish for a Legislative body that acted as one. Internal rivalries inside the Legislature could stain the idea of government they seemed to hold. Two distinct chambers would mean the most radical kind of internal schism, but not the only one. There were at least two other internal divisions that the revolutionaries had already experimented: the coexistence of distinct political groups, including a special division inside the National Assembly chamber, and the tension between the committees within the Legislature.

Both questions show up in the drafts. Even though only a small minority expressly rejects some of these inner tensions, it is interesting to see what they have to say. Beffroy de Reigny and Saint-Just are two of those who are against the division of the Legislative body into committees, and Desacy is the only who risks proposing a solution to the internal division in political groups: randomly assigning seats.[19]

This serves to show us how far the revolutionaries' concern over internal strifes within the Legislature could go. However, such a position did

[16] AP, t. LXVI, 519.

[17] AP, t. LXVI, 518, 519. Garrau also claims that Delacroix' position would promote federalism.

[18] With a four-year term and reciprocal veto powers balancing each other (Anonymous A, *Cit. ***. Réflexions Sur Les Bases D'une Constitution…Présentées Par Bresson*, Archives Nationales, Series AD/XVIIIC/257, n. 20, 61).

[19] Respectively: Beffroy de Reigny, *La Constitution de la Lune*, 96; Saint-Just, *Projet de Constitution*, I.VI, Article 12; Claude Louis Michel Desacy, *Additions Au Plan de Constitution, Présentées a la Convention Nationale* (AP, t. LXII (April 17, 1793)), 370.

not mean a lack of oversight in relation to the Legislature. Different control mechanisms were discussed, and we will see them later in this chapter. Furthermore, the fact that these solutions to internal tensions appear in a small number of proposals seems to indicate that the revolutionaries, though they openly adopted a unitary logic for the Legislature, were not willing to impose extreme institutional arrangements just to take this unity to its final consequences, even if only for practical purposes.[20]

In opposition to the 1791 model, the rule in the 1793 texts was proposing the direct election of the deputies by the primary assemblies, as Dufriche-Valazé highlights in this May 6 report summarizing all the drafts sent to the Analysis Committee.[21] Only two texts keep the old system of nominations by the electoral assemblies: Ruault and Rubigny. The former's proposal is very close to the 1791 model; it keeps not only the indirect suffrage, but also the election criteria by territory, population, and contribution.[22]

Ragonneau also keeps that tripartite logic of representation and adds a restriction that is also proposed by Charles Delacroix during the debates: a deputy could be chosen among the citizens registered in a voting department.[23] Thorillon is the only other person who defends such a limitation, but he is careful to expressly reject the creation of a federative republic.[24]

The aspect that varies the most among the drafts, in regard to the election of the deputies, is how they are selected and how long their term should last.[25] On the latter issue, the longest term proposed is of six years with an election for half the Legislature each three years (proposed by Léfebure). The most common proposal is for a two-year term, followed by

[20] The division of the Legislative body into committees is an example of a practical mechanism to improve legislative work and it is expressly introduced by some of the proposals, such as Poultier (*Poultier, Constitution Populaire*, IV, Article 7).

[21] AP, LXIV:207–209. Dufriche-Valazé mentions the existence of several drafts that appear to have been lost, such as texts by Degravers, Dalzan, Tripier, and Goulu-Privé.

[22] Ruault, *Projet de Constitution*, 88. We cannot confound indirect elections with the creation of specific requirements in order to participate in the voting procedures. For example, Anonymous D restricts the right to vote for deputies only to citizens labeled as "notables" (Anonymous D, *La France Heureuse*, 102). This is a matter that is closely related to citizenship and will be discussed in the next chapter.

[23] Ragonneau, *Plan d'une Nouvelle Constitution*, 550.

[24] Thorillon, *Idées ou Bases d'un Nouvelle Déclaration*, 605 and 602.

[25] Another factor that varies a lot is the number of deputies. However, I chose not to enter into details on this point, as I have understood it not to be relevant to my general discussion. For a detailed view on the topic, see Ollivier, *Les Projets Constitutionnels de 1793*, 541ff.

a one-year term—the option adopted in the final text. The technique of only changing half the members every half-term is also common.[26]

The discussion about the term's duration was a debate on legislative accountability. Ollivier explains how shorter terms were conceived as accountability mechanisms for the members of the Executive council.[27] We can apply the same reasoning to the Legislature, as seen in Robespierre's text on the representative government, in which the revolutionary extends the use of short terms for all public officials.[28]

The idea that this control mechanism should also be applied to the Legislature points, or at least seems to point, to a certain mistrust in relation to its members. It was not a mistrust directed only against the Executive, even if, as we saw in the last chapter, it was surely stronger in the latter case. The general option for a closer control over the Legislature's work by the people should not be mixed with the attempt to allegedly improve the quality of the representatives.

[26] For two-year terms, we have: Anonymous D, *La France Heureuse*, 9–10; Bacon-Tacon, *Examen Impartial des Bases de la Nouvelle Constitution* (AP, t. LXIII (April 29, 1793), 601–604), II, Article 10; Barailon, *Projet de Constitution*, II. IV, Article 2; Beffroy de Reigny, *La Constitution de la Lune*, 112; Boissel, *Les Entretiens du Père Gérard*, II, Article 21; Boissy d'Anglas, *Constitution*, V.I, Article 5; Bourgois, *Plan de Constitution*, II.V.I.1, Article 5; Chabot, *Projet d'Acte Constitutif*, III, Article 3; Coupé, *Idée Simples de Constitution*, 268), Gleizal (Gleizal, *Projet de Décret*, III, Article 7), Lafont (Lafont, *Nouveau Mode de Nomination*, 246), Lagrange et Dupin (Lagrange et Dupin, *Projet de Constitution*, Article 6); Ruault, *Projet de Constitution*, 35; Saint-Just, *Projet de Constitution*, I.V, Article 3; and Thirion, *La Pierre Angulaire* Article 6. For one-year terms, we have: Anonymous P (Anonymous P, *Essai sur la Constitution Française*, 39), Cappin (Cappin, *Projet de Constitution*, VII, Article 5), Constitution Committee (Comité de Constitution, *Projet de Constitution*, VII, Article 1), Daunou (Daunou, *Essai sur la Constitution*, II, Article 1); Jean-Antoine Debry, (Baron), *Projet de Constitution* (AP, t. LXIII (April 24, 1793)), Article 30, Montgilbert, *Projet des Lois Constitutionnel*, VI.I, Article 2), Pénières, *Plan et Projet de Constitution*, *Des élections*, Article 4) and Jean-Louis Seconds, *Art Rationnel Politique. De l'Art Social ou des Vrais Principes de la Société Politique (Quatrième Cahier)* (AP, t. LXII (April 17, 1793)) 543). For the renovation of half the Legislative body every half-term, we have: Anonymous D, *La France Heureuse*, 9–10; Chabot, *Projet d'Acte Constitutif*, III, Article 3; Gleizal (Gleizal, *Projet de Décret*, III, Article 7), Lafont (Lafont, *Nouveau Mode de Nomination*, 246). Direct criticism of this proposal comes from Garnier, but only indirectly, as he claims that a one-third renovation would simply lead to the incoming minority following the remaining majority (Jacques Garnier [de Saintes], *Aperçu de Réflexions sur la Constitution* (Archives Nationales, Series Le38, n. 2302), 4).

[27] Ollivier, *Les Projets Constitutionnels de 1793*, 383.

[28] Maximilien Marie Isidore de Robespierre, *Discours sur le Gouvernement Représentatif par Maximilien* Robespierre *Prononcé à la Tribune de l'Assemblée Nationale* (Archives Nationales, Series Le38, n. 245), 14.

Keeping in mind that being able to vote and being able to be voted coincide in the final text,[29] a small number of drafts, however, establish additional requirements for a citizen to be elected as a member of the Legislature. Anonymous D, for example, restricts the representative role solely to patricians and voting rights only to the notables (as a general rule, citizens over 50). Boissy d'Anglas sets a minimum age of 25 years old.[30]

These are, however, isolated cases. The general rule is to respect the sovereignty of the people, to paraphrase Garrau and Thuriot's previous quotation. There is one particular case of restricting the citizen's freedom to choose that escapes the logic present in the previous restrictions. Le Suer proposes that each administrative unit (he calls them circles) choose 12 deputies and at least eight of them should belong to the first class of proprietors, known as *minus possidentes*.[31] As the name already makes clear, this was not the class of the well-off citizens, but of those with meager funds. Instead of privileging the rich, Le Suer inverts the censitary logic of the 1791 Constitution and privileges the poor.[32]

This concern with improving the quality of the representatives was not that widespread in the proposals. We see a different case if we look at the concern with improving the quality of the representation itself. If we look at the bigger picture instead of the individual level, a good number of drafts propose different mechanisms to improve the Legislative body. The two most common mechanisms discussed are the electoral procedure and an oversight mechanism for the Legislature.

[29] *Constitution*, Article 28.

[30] Respectively Boissy d'Anglas, V.I, Article 18 e Anonymous D, *La France Heureuse*, 9–10). I will discuss citizenship in the next chapter, in which we will see the complex citizenship system proposed by Anonymous D. We have other similar proposals, for example, Anonymous E, for whom deputies should have previously been at least departmental magistrates (Anonymous E, *Quelques Idées*, Article 64). Beffroy de Reigny comes up with an extensive list of requirements: being or having been married; never having been formally accused of defamation; never having been a general, etc. (Beffroy de Reigny, *La Constitution de la Lune*, 104–105). This concern with separating military power from the government appears only sparsely in the proposals.

[31] Le Sueur, *Idées*, I.IV, Article 2.

[32] The 1791 Constitution required the payment of a certain amount of taxes in order to be considered an active citizen, which was the only class of citizens allowed to take part in the electoral assemblies and to be elected to the national representative body.

6.2 The Electoral Procedure

As for the electoral procedure, the revolutionaries came up with many different proposals for how the suffrage should be organized. For example, Daunou proposes two voting lists: one for nominations, and other for excluding names from the election.[33] A good number of drafts propose successive votes, including the Constitution Committee text: a first one in order to form a preparatory list; and a second vote for the election itself.[34] We also get three successive votes in Chabot, and even four different ballots in Lanthenas.[35]

There are many other examples of multiple ballots,[36] but the most interesting topic is the appearance, once again, of drawing lots as part of the selection procedure. It appears, for example, in Cappin's and Lafont's drafts. Both propose that assemblies elect double the number of vacancies, and the final selection would be made by drawing lots.[37] In comparison with drawing lots for official posts in the Judiciary, the Executive council, or administrative bodies, this proposal is not common in regard to the Legislative body, which points to an intention to keep representation closer to the sovereign's control.

This intention appears also to be present in the different ways the revolutionaries try to come up to guarantee the integrity of the vote. This issue can be divided into two topics: publicity, or not, of the vote, and how to guarantee that citizens effectively know for whom they are voting. The

[33] Respectively, by relative majority and by absolute majority (Daunou, *Essai sur la Constitution*, I.II, Articles 1ff).

[34] Comité de Constitution, *Projet de Constitution*, III.III, Article 1.

[35] Lanthenas, *Des Elections et du Mode a Elire par Listes Epuratoires*, 511 and Chabot, *Projet d'Acte Constitutif*, III, Article 3. In both cases, we have the same logic. Firstly, four times or three times, respectively, the number of seats would be chosen, and consecutive votes would reduce the number one by one until a deputy was chosen.

[36] Pressavin defends two votes: first choosing three times as many candidates as the number of seats, and a second and final vote (Pressavin, *Projet de Constitution*, 389). Pénières proposes that each primary assembly would choose three people in order to form a list that was to be sent to all the communes. The communes would then choose two names, and at least one of those should be from outside the canton (Pénières, *Plan et Projet de Constitution*, *Des élections*, Articles 8–11), inverting the logic of proposals that restrict the choice to the voting department.

[37] Cappin, *Projet de Constitution*, XV, Article 4; Lafont, *Nouveau Mode de Nomination*, 246.

first point comes up during the June 12 debates in response to the committees' drafts, both of which stated that voting should be nominal.[38]

In Dufriche-Valazé's report on the primary assemblies, presented on May 6, 1793, the revolutionary notes that, even though some proposals recommend votes should be vocalized by the citizens, the most adequate solution would be adopting a secret ballot since part of the citizens could feel somewhat constrained if they were forced to declare their votes out loud. The rapporteur, however, defends that such voting procedure would be the most compatible with republican customs and that subsequent Legislatures should be free to modify the procedure.[39]

With the presentation of the Committee of Public Safety draft, the debate gains new strength. Réal is the first one to speak. He affirms that demanding the vote to be signed or spoken out loud harms the freedom to vote. The revolutionary had previously sent a draft highlighting this same position: voting out loud favored the rich and public servants, both of which would come to have more influence over the voters.[40] Salle's draft expresses a similar opinion by claiming

> to which abuses would lead such institution if it was accepted by a people which has the need for commerce and the arts, where a multitude of workers who frequently depend on a singular individual would be forced to vote against their conscience and follow the interest of their bosses, under penalty of disgrace and of losing their livelihood?[41]

Dufriche-Valazé's idea—that the public vote proposal was more suitable to republican customs—is also present in Jeanbon Saint-André's speech and appears to gather support, as none explicitly rejects the open ballot system for violating any republican principles or natural rights.[42]

Danton agrees that greater publicity is more suitable to the people but points out that the freedom to vote should also include the freedom of the way to vote: "I note that only transparency and publicity are the natural

[38] Comité de Constitution, *Projet de Constitution*, III.III, Article 2; Comité de Salut Public, *Projet de Constitution*, V, Article 6.

[39] AP, LXIV:208.

[40] See his speech in AP, t. LXVI, 452, and for his draft's take on the subject, see Guillaume-André Réal, *Réflexions sur le Meilleur Mode d'Élection* (Archives Nationales, Series AD/XVIIIC/261, n. 14), 4. Bourgois, who does not intervene during the debates, also proposes a secret ballot in his draft (Bourgois, *Plan de Constitution*, V.I, Article 1).

[41] Jean-Baptiste Salle, *Examen Critique de la Constitution* (AP, t. LXVII (June 24, 1793)), 392.

[42] AP, t. LXVI, 452.

nutrients of freedom."[43] In light of what seems to be a conjunction of a theoretical argument (freedom to vote) and a practical argument (it would not be suitable in the current situation in France), the final option is to leave the decision of choosing how to vote to the citizens.[44]

On the last topic regarding the electoral procedure, we have Gleizal and Oudot's proposals. The former proposes that each municipality form a list of dignified citizens and then the candidates would take part in a debate one month before the election.[45] Oudot adopts a hybrid system in which the electoral assembly was to come up with a list of candidates solely to make it easier for the citizens to get to know them, while the final say would be handed back to the primary assemblies.[46] Analogous measures also appear in Lafont, Pénières, and Beffroy de Reigny. In general, the primary assemblies are allowed, even if implicitly, to discuss before the vote.[47]

Since no party system was in place, or even the formal registration of candidacies, these authors propose different ways through which the citizens would get to know the electables. The residual appearance of such concern seems to indicate that it was a secondary matter to most revolutionaries. The general tone is in favor of freedom in the voting procedures and the vote itself.[48]

This concern with balancing the regulation of public spaces and freedom shows us that the drafts' authors, be they deputies at the Convention or not, were especially preoccupied with coming up with an institutional design that favored the virtuous choice, whether this meant guaranteeing the virtue of the elected ones or, above all, guaranteeing the virtue of the choice itself. The constant reference to the idea of a republic and

[43] AP, t. LXVI, 453.

[44] *Constitution*, Article 16.

[45] Gleizal, *Projet de Décret*, II, Articles 5 and 7.

[46] Oudot, *Règles Générales*.

[47] Lafont states the candidates should register three months before the elections (Lafont, *Nouveau Mode de Nomination*, 246). Duplantier has a similar proposal, in which a list of candidates would be formed one month before the election (Duplantier, *Réflexions sur le Scrutin*, 310). Pénières provides for a three-month assembly (Pénières, *Plan et Projet de Constitution*, Article 6). Beffroy de Reigny requires candidacies to be previously registered, but prohibits any kind of electoral propaganda (Beffroy de Reigny, *La Constitution de la Lune*, 116).

[48] This tension between willing to closely regulate versus leaving room for freer governmental procedures also shows up in other topics. The main one, to be discussed in the next chapter, is how to organize the primary assemblies and how they would work.

republicanism in the drafts can be read as reinforcing this hypothesis.[49] The final text, however, opts for letting the people free in their choices of representatives, as do the majority of the drafts. In Thuriot's words, during the June 15, 1793, debates:

> We should not disregard the fact that every time we have an assembly of men, there will be passions, and the discussion of topics of great interest will provoke violent shocks. But such reasons should not make one ignore the sacred principle of sovereignty.[50]

Guaranteeing virtue and the quality of choice would be the result of preserving and guaranteeing the sovereignty and the freedom of its holder, the people.

6.3 Control of the Legislative Body, Censorship, and Censors

Understanding how the revolutionaries conceived of the oversight of the Legislative body is a central piece in comprehending the political philosophy underpinning the Year 3 constituent debates. The Legislature is the main governmental body. Although we have seen that the subordination of the Judiciary and the Executive to the Legislature was not that pronounced, unarguably the almost totality of the drafts presented put the Legislature as the central governmental piece in creating and maintaining the French Republic and the natural rights of men.

This realization points to an important discussion. Is the Legislature the main actor responsible for this performance or is it (only) the main governmental actor? The ideas regarding the Legislature bring us closer to understanding the role played by the people in the Republic under construction. On this issue, the oversight of the Legislative debates can help us better comprehend what was at stake—as well as two other related topics I will cover in the next subsection (sanction and the legislative procedure).

If the Legislature was responsible for monitoring and controlling the Executive council and the administrative bodies, as well as the Judiciary, albeit to a lesser degree, who or what monitored and controlled the

[49] I will cover this topic below, but it is important to notice that this term appears in the most different drafts. For example, in Beffroy de Reigny (Beffroy de Reigny, *La Constitution de la Lune*, 54), Thorillon (Thorillon, *Idées ou Bases d'un Nouvelle Déclaration*, 584), and Saint-Just (Saint-Just, *Projet de Constitution*, I.I, Article 1).

[50] AP, LXVI: 519.

Legislature?[51] The revolutionaries propose a plethora of answers to this question, some of which I have already briefly mentioned—the censors and national tribunals.

The issue was virtually absent from the 1791 Constitution. Only two articles dealt with the representatives' inviolability, guaranteeing immunity for their opinions and allowing for their detention in cases of *flagrante delicto*, with the procedure only continuing with an authorization by the Legislative body.[52]

The Constitution of 1793 has similar provisions, but with a slight difference. While the 1791 text plainly stated, when presenting substantive immunities, that "the nation's representatives are inviolable," the 1793 text presents no such phrase.[53] On the contrary, the Declaration of the Rights of Men and the Citizen that precedes it states that "crimes committed by the mandataries of the people and their agents shall never remain unpunished. No one has the right to claim to be more inviolable than other citizens."[54] The Declaration of 1789 had no similar provision.

This change seems to point to the revolutionaries' willingness to differentiate as little as possible representatives from citizens and to guarantee that abuses by the former would be prosecuted and punished. The limits to congressional immunity act as a first aspect of the oversight of the Legislative body.

The topic is treated identically in the Constitution Committee's and Committee of Public Safety's proposals, as well as in a number of other drafts.[55] The same goes for the need for previous authorization by the Legislative body in order to criminally prosecute its members.[56]

[51] For the issue of oversight on matters of war and external relations, see Chap. 2.

[52] Articles 7 and 8, Section V, Chapter 1, Title III (on public powers).

[53] In his constitutional draft, Beffroy de Reigny directly rejects the representatives' immunity (Beffroy de Reigny, *La Constitution de la Lune*, 96).

[54] *Declaration*, Article 31.

[55] Comité de Constitution, *Projet de Constitution*, VII.I, Articles 13–15 e Comité de Salut Public, *Projet de Constitution*, VII, Articles 5–6. Furthermore, for example, Anonymous H, Daunou, Debry, and Saint-Just explicitly mention the representatives' substantive immunity (respectively, Anonymous H, *Vœu d'un Citoyen sur la Nouvelle Constitution Présentée par la Convention [Chez Frouillé, Imprimeur-Librarie, 1793]*, Archives Nationales, Series Lb41, n. 702, Article 43; Daunou, *Essai sur la Constitution*, II, Article 19; Jean-Antoine Debry (Baron), *Projet de Déclaration des Droits de l'Homme et de Constitution Française* (AP, t. LXIII (April 24, 1793)), Article 10; e Saint-Just, *Projet de Constitution*, Article 17).

[56] See Boissy d'Anglas, *Constitution*, V.I, Articles 14, 16–17; Cappin, *Projet de Constitution*, VII, Articles 17–19; Pénières, *Plan et Projet de Constitution*, *Assemblée nationale*, Article 8);

There are, however, some variations on this topic. Two proposals seem to mitigate this substantive immunity, but for very different reasons. Beffroy de Reigny states that a representative could not be held accountable for an opinion shared by at least two-thirds of the Legislative body.[57] Poultier declares that the representative of the people who proposed a change in the constitution was to answer for the crime of "*lèse*-nation" and be tried by the Legislative body itself.[58]

Even though in both cases we have a decrease in the representatives' freedom of opinion and expression, the reasons are plainly different. Beffroy de Reigny is trying to reinforce the uniformization of the Legislative body's positions, while Poultier is concerned with preserving the sovereignty of the people by preventing changes in one of the Republic's fundamental laws from being proposed by illegitimate actors. The representatives of the people were not considered legitimate for such proposals, as the right to change the constitution belonged only to the people.[59] In stark opposition to Poultier, we have Boissy d'Anglas, who proposed that any attack on a representative was a crime of "*lèse*-nation."[60]

There is, therefore, a link between substantive immunity and holding representatives accountable. This correlation is evident during the June 15, 1793, debates. The members were discussing the question of substantive immunity, but we can find in their speeches a summary of the main controversies regarding the oversight of the Legislative body.

At the occasion, they were debating the wording of article 5, chapter VII, of the draft presented by the Committee of Public Safety—which would later become article 43 of the final text. The first four interventions repeat the same general idea already present in Poultier's aforementioned position. Raffron de Trouillet, the third to speak, affirms that substantive immunity was a license to impunity because the representatives could promote anti-civic sentiment and then be forced later to retract their words. Rühl, Thuriot, and Basire, in the same vein, claim that opinions that try to reestablish monarchical rule or destroy the unity and indivisibility of the

Poultier, *Constitution Populaire*, IV, Article 23; and Saint-Just, *Projet de Constitution*, Article 17).

[57] Beffroy de Reigny, *La Constitution de la Lune*, 98.

[58] Poultier, *Constitution Populaire*, IV, Articles 17 and 20.

[59] Poultier, *Constitution Populaire*, IV, Article 19.

[60] Boissy d'Anglais, *Constitution*, Article 15.

Republic may be promoted by a corrupt majority, which could even lead to nominating a tyrant.[61]

The answer comes, according to the parliamentary archives, from "*many members*": "*the people are there.*"[62] After Basire's reply, affirming that such a position would needlessly drive the people to insurrection, Robespierre develops the topic in great length. His introductory paragraph perfectly illustrates what was at stake:

> It is not possible not to honor the patriotic motives that inspired the venerable old man who preceded me at this tribune; every citizen would be painfully affected by the thought that part of the people's representatives could violate their rights with impunity, and conspire, while at the tribune, with insidious eloquence without being subjected to any punishment. It would be desirable that any such crime be punished and no impunity be found in relation to the role of representative through which he could become unworthy and the freedom of opinion could be abused; but the difficulty lies in the means to be employed in order to punish him and that is why we should defend the committee's principle.[63]

During this speech, Robespierre also mentions another speech he gave on May 10 that same year, in which he proposed a series of institutional mechanisms precisely to ensure that representatives be held accountable. He had said that creating a court was not the best possible solution, because the only possible tribune was the people itself.[64]

He mentions a set of proposals that were circulating during the constitutional debates regarding the creation of a court specifically to try the people's representatives' actions or, more broadly, all public officials. The drafts presented by both committees provide for such a body and also exemplify its two main variants.

Title X of the Constitution Committee proposal focuses on the administration of justice and its Section V is titled "On the national jury." Its

[61] AP, t. LXVI, 542.

[62] AP, t. LXVI, 542. A small remark regarding the translation should be made. The original French wording is *le peuple est là*. The word *là* is generally translated as "there," in opposition to *ici*, which stands for "here." But it can also mean the place where one is or where something is located. So, the phrase could also be translated as "the people are here." In a sense, the phrase can be read as stating that the people ar here and there, both meaning spatial locations and situations.

[63] AP, t. LXVI, 542.

[64] Robespierre, *Discours sur le Governement Représentatif*, 11.

role was solely trying crimes of high treason. Three jurors from different departments were to be chosen by the primary assemblies to sit on the jury.[65]

Chapter XV of the Committee of Public Safety text is titled "On the grand national jury," whose only role was to guarantee rights against any possible oppression by the Legislative body or the Executive council. This institution would comprise one citizen from each department, also to be chosen by the primary assemblies. It would be able not to impose penalties, but only to refer the case to the competent court.[66]

Whereas the national jury is inserted in the first text within the topic of the administration of justice, following the regulation of Judiciary censors,[67] the grand national jury of the second proposal is outside of the stricter field of Judiciary action—after the institutional design for both the Legislative body and the Executive council. The Constitution Committee's choice to create a kind of high court for more serious offenses appears in a few proposals.

The choice for a national jury dedicated only to crimes of high treason is not common.[68] In general, when this issue arises, the proposals combine ruling such matters (including "*lèse*-nation" crimes) with oversight of the representatives' and public officials' conducts. This is an important distinction in comparison with the oversight mechanisms proposed for other governmental bodies. Whereas the control over the Executive council and

[65] Comité de Constitution, *Projet de Constitution*, X.V, Articles 1–3.

[66] Comité de Salut Public, *Projet de Constitution*, XV, Articles 1–3.

[67] The judicial censors appear in many different proposals. As a general rule, they serve as appellate courts or courts of cassation. For example, in the Constitution Committee text, they fit the latter role, as they are not allowed to decide on the merits (Comité de Constitution, Projet de Constitution, X.IV, Article 4). Faure, however, expressly speaks against censors and defends the continuation of the previous model of courts of cassation (Faure, *Observations sur le Gouvernement de France*, 287). This continuity with 1791 was adopted in the final 1793 text (*Constitution*, Articles 98–100). Also providing for a court of cassation we have, among others, Lambert (Lambert, *Plan de Constitution Républicaine*, IX.IV) and Saint-Just (Saint-Just, *Projet de Constitution*, II.VI). What we should keep in mind is that, in both cases, be it a court of cassation or Judiciary censors, they have a purely judicial role. They review cases involving only private citizens. We should not mix them with the other censors analyzed further below, who are closer to the idea of oversight of the Legislative body and public officials. The fact that the revolutionaries used the same term—"censors"—should not lead us to conflate both institutions.

[68] Crimes of high treason appear in other constitutional drafts, but their trial is not necessarily delegated to a separate body. For example, Anonymous E states that the Legislative body should rule on such matters (Anonymous E, *Quelques Idées*, Article 65).

administrative bodies generally involves some kind of direct oversight by the Legislative body, oversight of the Legislative itself tends to be conceived as an oversight of the government as a whole.

For example, Debry proposed a national jury for crimes against the nation and crimes committed while performing public functions. This jury would be summoned by the Legislative body.[69] The oversight of the Legislative body being intermediated, in some way, by the Legislature is not uncommon. We have already seen that the prosecution of its members for common crimes required the Legislature's authorization. Debry's proposal simply extends the same logic to this matter.[70]

Pressavin also proposed a national court for crimes of "*lèse*-nation" or crimes against the constitutional freedoms that were committed by the members of the Executive council or the Legislative body, including abuse of authority cases. The difference is that the Legislative body did not take part in the adjudication itself.[71]

The revolutionaries' proposals, however, tend to prefer not a proper court for such crimes, as in the Constitution Committee text, but a less judicial-like oversight mechanism, even if they sometimes use the term "court" or "tribunal" when describing this institution. Lanthenas, for example, dedicates one of his texts exclusively to the topic of censorship.

According to the revolutionary, censorship emanates from the people and it should be the one to enforce it. In order to do so, he proposed two parallel mechanisms: an internal control and an external control.

For the internal control, each assembly and each department would choose censors to monitor its own activities.[72] For the external oversight, there would be a national tribunal of public censorship to try public officials that had been reported by a competent body. In the case of members

[69] Debry, *Projet de Constitution*, Article 16.

[70] Lambert follows the same model. A national higher court would be responsible for trying "*lèse*-nation" and abuse of authority cases, and the Legislature would act as the jury (Lambert, *Plan de Constitution Républicaine*, IX.V). Hazard also keeps the oversight of the Legislative as an internal matter. The only difference is that it is the subsequent Legislature who is to judge the precedent one (Hazard, *Vues d'un Patriote*, 10).

[71] Pressavin, *Projet de Constitution*, 389. The same thing appears in Lagrange and Dupin's text. They propose a so-called Court of Seven, responsible for ruling on abuse of authority cases involving members of the Executive council or the Legislative body (Lagrange et Dupin, *Projet de Constitution*, Articles 67–69).

[72] François-Xavier Lanthenas, *Censure Publique, Ou Nécessité de Confier a Un Certain Nombre de Citoyens Instruits et Vertueux, Choisis et Périodiquement Renouvellés, la Surveillance de Mœurs* (Archives Nationales, Series AD/XVIIIC/291, n. 3), II, Articles 1–2.

of the Executive council or the Legislative body, a decree by latter was also required.[73] Analogous institutions appear in other drafts. For example, Beffroy de Reigny's text describes a censorship tribunal to which each legislator would account for his expenses and also to report to the people any plot by the Legislature.[74]

Different texts proposed many forms of accountability that were not exactly judicial in nature.[75] Their role sometimes can be restricted to surveillance without any actual power. For instance, in Barailon's draft, the censors are called the eyes and watchmen of the city, but their role is limited to reporting on officials accused of malfeasance and they pay special attention to public life and the morality of public officials.[76]

Beffroy de Reigny's aforementioned proposal points to yet another underexplored but important issue: the role of the people. The idea of adding another institution, a tribunal or court, is criticized by some revolutionaries. Salle states that the grand national jury would be detrimental to freedom, paralyze the powers, and potentially rule over them.[77]

[73] Lanthenas, *Censure Publique*, III.

[74] Beffroy de Reigny, *La Constitution de la Lune*, 141. Another example is found in Anonymous E, whose draft proposes the idea of the keepers of the constitution. They could exclude up to ten representatives from a given session of the Legislative body and would act as prosecutors in high treason cases (Anonymous E, *Quelques Idées*, Articles 81 and 83).

[75] Mellinet proposed a censorship committee capable of issuing censorship decrees against members of the Legislative body and each administrations' directory should form a list of the censored persons (François Mellinet, *Sur le Comité Censorial* (AP, t. LVI (January 8, 1793)), Articles 4 and 7). Picque provides for an assembly of censors to be organized by the primary assemblies (Jean-Pierre Picqué, *Nécessité d'Établir une Censure Publique* (AP, t. LXIV (May 10, 1793) 513–519)), Article 1). Wandelaincourt describes the censors as protectors of the weak, responsible for bringing matters to the courts in order to guarantee the enforcement of the law (Wandelaincourt, *Observations sur le Plan de Constitution*, 417). In Pressavin's text, each commune would choose one censor and they all would form a censorship tribunal for each *arrondissement*, being responsible for overseeing public officials, with the expressly mentioned possibility that private citizens present their complaints to the tribunal (Pressavin, *Projet de Constitution*, 388).

[76] Barailon, *Projet de Constitution*, II.VII, Articles 1–2. This interest in moral conduct reaches its peak in Duplantiert's text, in which the censors would judge on the behavior of the citizens in general, and not only that of the public officials (Duplantier, *Réflexions sur le Scrutin*, XIII). This is the sole exception. In all other texts, the control is limited to citizens exercising some kind of public role.

[77] Salle, *Examen Critique de la Constitution*, 396. Anonymous I features a similar logic. A national jury would paralyze the powers. The general will, according to him, never errs. Legal censorship would suffice.

Cloots makes a similar criticism when claiming that officials were already under the immediate oversight of the sovereign, therefore it would be absurd to create a higher court, as ordinary courts would suffice to try cases of abuse of authority, "*lèse*-society," and "*lèse*-nation."[78]

The creation of a national jury was rejected by the National Convention during the June 16, 1793, debates, against Hérault de Séchelles' insistence. Thirion and Thuriot voice the initial criticism: "a tribunal of this kind already exists; it is the public opinion. Such a tribunal would be detrimental to the freedom of opinion of the members of the Legislature" and "you have decreed that the Legislature would exercise sovereignty: it is ridiculous to try to erect a superior authority next to it."[79]

Even if we acknowledge that their criticism has different grounds,[80] the concern is similar. But the issue was not easily solved. Billaud-Varenne reiterates that "the Convention should establish a measure to protect the people against attacks on its liberty that come from the national representatives." He is seconded by Robespierre.[81]

Following this trend, but still believing in the need to institutionalize this control, we can find four solutions, proposed by Daunou, Boissel, Saint-Just, and Robespierre. Daunou is closer to Cloots' criticism and limits himself to state that every citizen can initiate the proceedings against a public official that allegedly committed an act of malfeasance by simply reporting said official.[82]

Boissel states that a people are already constituted as a republican jury to judge mandataries and that popular societies—which play a central role in the organization of society, as we will see in the next chapter—supervise, receive complaints, and discuss the representatives' conducts.[83] Saint-Just goes along similar lines. As each commune had elected one representative or member of the Executive council, it could also decide

[78] Cloots, *Bases Constitutionnelles*, 395. The term "sovereign" is used by the revolutionaries, and I will do the same when referring to the people.

[79] AP, LXIV:576 and 577.

[80] Thirion seems to defend the people's sovereignty to decide over the destiny of their representatives, while Thuriot claims that sovereignty is exercised by the representatives themselves.

[81] Robespierre states: "the Legislature should not commit acts of oppression with impunity. If there is no tribunal similar to those proposed by you, the people will be the one to scrutinize the conduct of the mandataries" (AP, t. LXVI, 577).

[82] Daunou, *Essai sur la Constitution*, I.IV, Article 1.

[83] Boissel, *Les Entretiens du Père Gérard*, III.I, Articles 4–5.

that such a person betrayed its confidence. Upon a first complaint, the official needed only to explain himself. If a second complaint occurs, the case would be referred to the courts.[84]

Robespierre, in his May 10, 1793, text, claims there are two different kinds of accountability for the representatives: moral and personal.[85] The former would comprise the publicity of their actions and their regular accounting, both potentially subjected to the censorship of the people. As for personal accountability, Robespierre proposes that each member of the Legislative body and other public officials, in general, be subjected to a trial by the people after its mandate. If the people declared its confidence to have been lost, the individual would be declared unfit to hold any public office. Other sanctions, in case the official had committed a crime, would be imposed by ordinary courts.[86]

A similar proposal appeared once the June 16, 1793, debate continued on June 24. Hérault de Séchelles introduced the debate stating that there were two ways through which the people could protect itself from oppression, given the rejection of the national jury. Firstly, through insurrection, but this could not be institutionalized. Secondly, through censorship by the people.

Hérault de Séchelles proposed five articles that were very similar to Robespierre's May 10 text. The people would exercise its censorship powers at the end of each Legislature through the primary assemblies. The former representative, if denied confidence by the people, would be prevented from holding any public office until his conduct was approved.[87]

This proposal, however, was rejected. The main argument against it was presented by Thuriot and Levasseur. Each representative belonged to the nation in its entirety. No section of the people could, on its own, rule on a representative and limit the people's choice.[88] In this line of reasoning, censoring the representatives would be close to establishing revocable mandates—what nowadays we would call a recall.

[84] Saint-Just, *Projet de Constitution*, I.XIV, Article 17.

[85] Robespierre is against using the word "representative," preferring the term "mandatary." For simplicity's sake, I will maintain the former until the next chapter, in which I will discuss the issue further.

[86] Robespierre, *Discours sur le Governement Représentatif*, 2. Robespierre does not explain if such prohibition would expire after a certain amount of time, if there would be ways of rehabilitating the affected official or if it would be a definitive sanction.

[87] AP, t. LXVII, 139–140.

[88] AP, t. LXVII, 140.

The possibility of revoking a mandate is virtually absent from the conventional debates. It only appears in Robespierre's speech from May 10, 1793, and in Dufriche-Valazé's report presented on the 6th of that same month.[89] The former proposed that all public officials elected by the people could have their mandate revoked "without any other motive than the imprescriptible right that belongs to it to revoke its mandataries."[90]

In Dufriche-Valazé's report, when discussing the role to be attributed to the primary assemblies, the representative lists the three main functions that appear in the different drafts: to write the representative's mandates, to revoke the mandate of disloyal representatives, and sanction laws.[91]

According to Dufriche-Valazé, the right to revoke a mandate derived from the federative system and was, therefore, incompatible with the French Republic. It would be a covert form of imperative mandate—an instrument of federative governments. The imperative mandate had already been abolished by the 1791 Constitution and reinstating it would go against the sovereignty of the people. The proper solution was, the rapporteur claimed, to let the competent courts try the representative.[92]

The idea of delegating the matter of revoking mandates to the Justice system finds little support in other texts.[93] Among the drafts, 13 provide for revocable mandates.[94] They differ in regard to who is responsible for

[89] I should note that Robespierre's speech is extracted from the parliamentary archives, so the speech itself may have differed from this written version.

[90] AP, LXIV:432. The same proposal also appears in the print version of his speech (Robespierre, *Discours sur le Gouvernement Représentatif*).

[91] Dufriche-Valazé also lists which authors backed which proposals. For the first one, only Gleizal and Varlet. For the recall, Daunou, Lambert, Cusset, Pénières, Saint-Just, Poultier, and Barlow. Finally, Bourgois, Poultier, Daunou, Dalzan, Ragonneau, and Keiffer defended the people's sanction and veto powers. This latter topic will be explored in greater detail in this chapter's final section. Dalzan's and Keiffer's drafts could not be located. They also do not appear in Ollivier's list of available proposals (Ollivier, *Les Projets Constitutionnels de 1793*, 531), which seems to indicate they were lost.

[92] AP, LXIV:206. Dufriche-Valazé is also opposed to giving the people the power to veto laws, as it would allegedly paralyze the Legislative body. The right to petition and to censor would be enough (AP, LXIV:206).

[93] One of the few examples are: Anonymous D, restricting it to "*lèse*-nation" crimes (Anonymous D, *La France Heureuse*, 11); and Debry, for whom a public official elected by the people could only be suspended by a jury (Debry, *Projet de Constitution*, Article 22).

[94] Barailon, *Projet de Constitution*, II.VIII, Articles 15, 17–18); Barlow, *Lettre a la Convention Nationale*, 294–295; Cappin, *Projet de Constitution*, XVI; Coupé, *Idée Simples de Constitution*, 269; Cusset, *Projet de Décret sur la Constitution*, III.II, Articles 3–4; Daunou, *Essai sur la Constitution*, I.IV, Articles 2ff; Florent Guiot, *Essais sur les Droits dont*

revoking and who can suffer such an action. Part of the texts limit themselves to state that there should be a revocation procedure, but do not explain how this could be done. That is the case of Robespierre, Coupé, and Thirion, as well as Poultier, who declare that this was the best way to avoid an insurrection and that it created the less risk of social convulsion.[95]

As for who would be responsible for initiating the recall procedure, as a general rule it was the primary assemblies, with different territorial extensions required for revoking the mandate. Only Cusset demands that, prior to calling the primary assembly to decide on the matter, the issue go through a governmental body.[96] In all other instances, the initiative is not under the control of a governmental body.[97]

For instance, Barlow lets the department decide on the revocation, while Pénières gives each *arrondissement* the right to recall the representative it had elected.[98] This pattern is broadly repeated in the other drafts. Those responsible for electing the representative were also responsible for the revocation. In some texts, although this is less common, we have a more detailed procedure.[99] Only Guiot defends the right to recall but states that it did not belong to the section responsible for the election.

le Peuple a Confié l'Exercice a la Convention Nationale, et sur les Devoirs que l'Exercice de ces Mêmes Droits Lui Impose (Archives Nationales, Series Lb41, n. 89), 17; Lambert, *Plan de Constitution Républicaine*, III.V, Article 3; Pénières, *Plan et Projet de Constitution*, *Des élections*, Articles 12–15; Poultier, *Sur la Constitution Présentée par le* Comité de Salut Public, 380; Robespierre, *Discours sur le Governement Représentatif*, 20; Saint-Just, *Projet de Constitution*, I.XIV, Article 7; and Thirion, *La Pierre Angulaire*, Article 11.

[95] Robespierre, *Discours sur le Governement Représentatif*, 20; Coupé, *Idée Simples de Constitution*, 269; Thirion, *La Pierre Angulaire*, Article 11; and François-Martin Poultier [Poultier d'Elmotte], *Sur la Constitution Présentée par le* Comité de Salut Public (AP, t. LXVII (June 24, 1793)), 380.

[96] More precisely, the municipality would be responsible for checking if the proof of incivility presented provided sufficient grounds for, in theory, revocation (Cusset, *Projet de Décret sur la Constitution*, III.II, Article 3).

[97] The primary assemblies are, of course, part of the organizational structure of the government, but I do not believe we should simply equate them with other bodies such as the municipalities, departmental administrations, and the like when analyzing this topic, as the assemblies are not elected, but directly constituted by the people.

[98] Barlow, *Lettre a la Convention Nationale*, 294; Pénières, *Plan et Projet de Constitution*, *Des élections*, Article 12. Saint-Just also follows the same logic (Saint-Just, *Projet de Constitution*, IXIV, Article 7).

[99] Cappin, for example, established that 20 *arrondissements* could call the departmental assembly to decide on the revocation (Cappin, *Projet de Constitution*, XVI).

Another kind of revocation appears in proposals by Barailon, Daunou, and Lambert. They provide for the dissolution and renovation of the whole Legislative body if it loses the confidence of the people.[100] The only difference between them is that Daunou and Lambert propose a phased procedure—the primary assemblies would initiate the deliberation of the immediate larger territorial unity and so on—while Barailon proposes that primary assemblies meet periodically (once a year) to decide if they approved or disapproved the conduct of the Legislature and other representative bodies.[101]

Although a good number of texts proposed the revocation of mandates, the topic was not openly discussed at the National Convention at the time. Nor is the proposal for imperative mandates, which also appeared in a few drafts.

Boissy d'Anglas, in his draft, states explicitly that no representative could be subject to a mandate or *cahier*. Conversely, Varlet and Barlow propose the creation of imperative mandates—the former declares such a mandate would ensure the people's sovereignty, and the latter leaves the task of writing the mandates to each department. Gleizal provides for a kind of national imperative mandate, instead of confining its writing to a single subnational body.[102]

In the end, none of these propositions is incorporated, but their appearance in a noticeable number of drafts attests to the revolutionaries' concern with the risks involved in having an overgrown and overpowered Legislative body. We should take Robespierre's speech on the June 15, 1793, session seriously, in which he reflected on his May 10 proposition and hesitated to endorse the trial of the representatives at the end of each Legislature.

[100] Barailon, *Projet de Constitution*, II.VIII, Articles 17–18; Daunou, *Essai sur la Constitution*, I.IV, Article 2; Lambert, *Plan de Constitution Républicaine*, III.V, Article 3. In Daunou's case, the possibility of renovation is extended to the administrative body, Judiciary courts, and the Executive council.

[101] The term "representative bodies" is Barailon's own words. It includes bodies like the Executive council, which, as he has already seen, is not considered representative in nature by the other revolutionaries.

[102] Barlow, *Lettre à la Convention Nationale*, 294–295. Gleizal proposed each primary assembly to write its own mandate or *cahier* expressing its vision for the Legislative body (Gleizal, *Projet de Décret*, II, Article 12). The texts would be compiled into a single document and the mandate would be imperative in regard to all Articles expressing the nation's view, while the others would be considered mere petitions (Gleizal, *Projet de Décret*, III, Articles 3 and 4).

The proposition's principle seems to be in accordance with the natural rights of man, but the practical difficulties involved in coming up with a proper procedure without creating new problems—such as establishing a parallel power beside the Legislative, violating the people's sovereignty, and undermining the representatives' freedom of opinion and expression—offer no solution in sight at that moment.

This realization, however, does not give rise to a blind trust in the Legislative. In the next chapter, I will discuss the importance of the debates over popular insurrection. The stance assumed by some revolutionaries—notably Robespierre—that the people should always suspect those in positions of power, be it the Executive council, the Legislative body, or any other public official does not change.

On the contrary, the constant and different attempts to curb the Legislature's power show us how pressing the issue was to the representatives and to the French and foreign citizens who presented their propositions for the new constitution. It is clear that the corruption of the Legislative body was a real threat. Its closer proximity with the general will, in comparison with other governmental bodies, was not enough to prevent such risk.

One form of control that did end up in the final text was the people's power to veto or sanction a law. Although this did not act upon the persons or the conduct of the representatives, either individually or collectively considered, such right was nonetheless one of the most important mechanisms of popular oversight of the Legislature.

6.4 Constitutional Change, Legislative Procedure, and Sanction

Before analyzing the issue of the legislative procedure and popular veto, I will offer some brief remarks on the topic of constitutional change as it appears in the drafts. While the first two present great diversity among the presented drafts, including some who oppose the very idea of popular veto, the regulation of constitutional change gets a more uniform treatment.

The topic was not expressly present in the 1789 Declaration, but the 1791 Constitution dealt with the revision of constitutional decrees under Title VII. The text appears to express a concern with restricting as much as possible any constitutional revision by creating a long and laborious procedure. To sum it up, three consecutive Legislatures had to present a uniform vision on any given revision. A fourth Legislature would then elect a separate revision assembly to decide on the matter. Also, the two Legislatures that followed could not propose any kind of reform.

In 1793, the matter was brought to the Convention's attention on two occasions: on April 22, when discussing the Declaration, and on June 18, during the debates over Chapter XXIV of the constitutional text. The first occurrence is short and with few interventions. The article is approved as initially proposed, with almost no changes, and only a minor objection regarding its phrasing is raised and rejected.[103]

The possibility of constitutional change by the people appears in a great number of drafts, pointing to a relative consensus over its adequacy. For example, the drafts of Chevret, Harmand, the Constitution Committee, and Committee of Public Safety all share this same broad statement.[104]

The June debates are limited to two articles of the Committee of Public Safety text. One determined that the Convention should convene at a minimum distance from the Legislative body and the other regulated the scope of the Convention's work.[105] There is no open debate over how the Convention was to be called or formed,[106] but the drafts show us the multiplicity of alternatives being conceived.

The debate starts over the minimum distance issue. The crux of the matter was not the distance itself, but the coexistence of a Convention and a Legislative body. This issue was first raised by Thuriot. He affirms that such coexistence would lead to political chaos and the Legislative should stop its works.[107] Robespierre agrees and adds that double representation is the seed of federalism and civil war.[108]

[103] The text submitted to the discussion was "A people always has the right to review, to reform and to change its Constitution. No future generation can submit the following generations to its laws and all hereditary function is absurd and tyrannical" (*Declaration*, Article 28). The disagreement was over the need for the second part, as any future generation is itself the people, so it has equal power over its own present (AP, t. LXIII, 116).

[104] Chevret, *Principes de Sociabilité*, XXIV; Jean-Baptiste Harmand, *Opinion* (AP, t. LXII (April 17, 1793)), Article 26; Comité de Constitution, *Projet de Déclaration* (AP, t. LVIII (February 15, 1793)), Article 33; Comité de Salut Public, *Déclaration des Droits de l'Homme* (AP, t. LXVI (June 10, 1793)), Article 30.

[105] Comité de Salut Public, *Projet de Constitution*, XXIV, Articles 2 and 4.

[106] Comité de Salut Public, *Projet de Constitution*, XXIV, Articles 1 and 3.

[107] AP, t. LXVI, 674.

[108] AP, t. LXVI, 674.

The opposite side of the debate—as expressed by Ramel-Nogaret, an unidentified member, and Albouys—claims that the Legislative would act to preserve the Constitution. On the contrary, the concentration of powers would create risks. Any risk of political turmoil would be prevented if the power of each body was defined by the Constitution.[109] The final solution was changing the proposed article so that the Convention concentrated also the Legislature's powers.[110]

The only other debated point was the provision that would eventually become article 117 of the final text—limiting the Convention's scope to "the subject that had motivated its calling"—but the discussion itself was around the possibility of limiting the duration of the Convention. The final version opts for the Committee of Public Safety's position not to establish any time limit. Even though the proposition was not in the presented text, this option was proposed by Levasseur with the support of Garran-Coulon.[111]

Other representatives also support the motion and propose different terms. Philippeaux, Oudot, Méaulle, and an unnamed member suggest one year—also proposed in the Constitution Committee text.[112] Méaulle references roman dictatorial power as an example of a limited-term institution and an unnamed member mentions the roman *decemvir* with their one-year terms.[113]

The temporal question is one of the main points of variation among the drafts. It included not only the duration of the Convention itself, but also its minimum and maximum periodicity. On the first topic, for instance, Cappin suggests a six-month period, but, in general, the drafts do not present an explicit time frame.[114]

[109] AP, t. LXVI, 674.

[110] *Constitution*, Article 116.

[111] AP, t. LXVI, 675.

[112] Comité de Constitution, *Projet de Constitution*, IX, Article 16.

[113] The Roman dictator was nominated, initially, for a six-month period in order to perform a specific task (Harry Thurston Peck, *Harper's Dictionary of Classical Antiquities* (New York: Trustees of Tufts University, 1898), 509). He could, therefore, renounce before the end of his term once his job was done (see also *decemviri* entry in William Smith, *A Dictionary of Greek and Roman Antiquities* (London: John Murry, 1890)). The *decemvir* were ten commissioners nominated to write a code of laws for the Roman state, but after their first one-year term, the commissioners elected for the second term refused to step down (Peck, *Harper's Dictionary*, 475).

[114] Cappin, *Projet de Constitution*, VIII, Article 4.

During the conventional debates, Robespierre claimed that the enemies of the people would try to stall the Convention in order to prevent it from accomplishing its task. In the end, he states that they should trust the sovereignty of the people and let it strip the Convention of its powers itself if it no longer fulfilled its role.[115]

On the other hand, the question of when to call a convention was a matter of great contention. Besides other ways of establishing a new convention—as we will see later on—a good number of drafts propose some kind of limit or constraint to the new Convention. Out of 24 drafts expressly dealing with national conventions, half of those reference the temporal issue.[116]

Bacon-Tacon, Barailon, Boissy d'Anglas, Cappin, Debry, Lambert, Pénières, Ruault, Thorillon, and the Constitution Committee's proposals all provide for a periodic revision of the constitution—proposing time frames between 5 and 25 years.[117]

Curiously, we can find two temporal limitations that apparently contradict the people's sovereignty and their right to change their own constitution as expressed in the 1793 Declaration of Rights. Bourgois establishes that no new convention could meet in less than ten years after the ratification of the previous one and Isnard proposes a 30-year minimum interval.[118] Their concern seems to be maintaining stability and preventing social convulsion, and we can find echoes of this idea in other texts. Isnard expresses the same concern, but he does not propose a specific time frame, and Faure seems to deny that a constitutional review procedure should be

[115] Along the same lines, Amar states that the power to set an expiration date for the convention's power should reside only with the people (AP, t. LXVI, 673).

[116] These are: Bacon-Tacon, Barailon, Barlow, Boissel, Bourgois, Cappin, Chabot, Daunou, Debry, Faure, George Edwards, Guiot, Isnard, Lambert, Montgilbert, Pénières, Poultier, Ruault, Saint-Just, Thirion, Thorillon, Wandelaincourt, and the Constitution Committee's and Committee of Public Safety's drafts.

[117] Respectively Pénières (Pénières, *Plan et Projet de Constitution*, *Assemblée nationale*, Article 3) and Barailon (Barailon, *Projet de Constitution*, II.VIII, Article 12). The most common duration is ten years, as proposed in three different texts: Bacon, Pierre-Jean-Jacques (Comte de), *Plan Patriotique*, IX), Cappin (Cappin, *Projet de Constitution*, VIII, Article 1) and Thorillon (Thorillon, *Idées ou Bases d'un Nouvelle Déclaration*, 590). Wandelaincourt is the only one who proposes a periodic review based on the occurrence, or not, of specific facts (more precisely if a war or a revolution broke out, the government should be revised—Wandelaincourt, *Suite des Observations sur le Plan de Constitution*, 418).

[118] Bourgois, *Plan de Constitution*, VIII, Article 3.

written in the constitution when he claims that the constitutional text should not be open to change at all times.[119]

Most revolutionaries, however, are committed to keeping the possibility of constitutional change open. Only Bacon-Tacon provides for a substantial limitation: the new convention would only examine the three powers (in his words), their limits, and balance.[120] All the other drafts in which the topic appears seem to give unlimited powers to the Convention.[121] This power should not, however, be read as an arbitrary or indiscriminate power. As I have already pointed out on the topic of temporal limitation, the Convention would always be under the scrutiny of the people and submitted to its sovereignty.

In some cases, limitations on the matter addressed are what distinguish statutory reform from constitutional change. For instance, Daunou defends that the Legislative body could not deliberate over the rights of man and citizen, civil or political status, the territorial partition of the republic, or the constitution of the powers without a petition from at least 50,000 citizens.[122] In such a case, a substantive limitation is what triggers the possibility of constitutional change or, in other words, what triggers the calling of a new convention.[123]

It is precisely this issue, of how to call the convention, that presents the greatest diversity among the proposals.[124] The general trend is to establish the people as the main agent in calling the convention. But there are exceptions. Barlow determines that the Legislative body may propose a

[119] Henri-Maximin Isnard, *Déclaration des Droits de l'Homme [et] Projet de Pacte Social* (AP, t. LXIV (May 10, 1793)), Article 17 and Faure, *Observations sur le Gouvernement de France*, 28.

[120] Bacon-Tacon, *Plan Patriotique*, IX.

[121] For instance, Barailon states that the Convention would revise the whole Constitution (Barailon, *Projet de Constitution*, I.I, Article 78).

[122] Daunou, *Essai sur la Constitution*, II, Article 4. The final text would still need to be sanctioned by the people.

[123] Apparently, Daunou does not provide for the calling of a new convention, leaving the task to the Legislative body. This proposal, albeit not completely absent from other texts, is uncommon.

[124] Only Barailon, Pénières, and Thorillon—all of which, as explained before, provide for a periodic revision of the constitutional text—do not establish the procedure to call the Convention, and so they limit the occurrence of constitutional reform to predetermined moments. Barailon, however, proposes an exception: the territorial division of the Republic could be revised by the primary assemblies held in January (Barailon, *Projet de Constitution*, II.VIII, Article 12).

constitutional revision for the next Legislature. However, even in this case, the people occupies a central role, as it was responsible for discussing any possible changes during the interval between the Legislatures.[125]

In all the other proposals, the authority for calling a convention is either shared between the people and the Legislative or attributed exclusively to the former. Boissy d'Anglas, for example, demands that two consecutive Legislatures propose the establishment of a convention so that a third Legislature converts into a National Convention.[126] In a few drafts, the Legislative body is to take the imitative of proposing to the people the formation of a new convention, leaving the final decision to them.[127]

In most cases, the people is directly responsible for establishing a new convention. The Constitution Committee's and Committee of Public Safety's drafts both follow this trend, although they come up with different procedures. The former extends the rules that had already been proposed for censoring new laws, while the latter demands at least 50% plus one of the departments and at least one primary assembly demand the revision of the constitutional text. The Legislative body would then call all primary assemblies to deliberate on the matter.[128]

In some drafts, no specific procedure is established, and they simply state that the people was responsible for accepting any constitutional revision or change.[129] What is absent in almost all proposals is how the people would participate in the new convention's deliberations. Only Thorillon mentions this issue when asserting that the primary assemblies may

[125] Barlow, *Lettre a la Convention Nationale*, 297. Lambert also allows for the Legislative body to call a new convention when it is deemed convenient but establishes two other possibilities: periodic revision each 20 years and by motion of the majority of voters in each commune (Lambert, *Plan de Constitution Républicaine*, VIII.I, Article 4).

[126] Boissy d'Anglas, XVIII, Article 6. Boissy d'Anglas also provides for the calling by order of half the primary assemblies (Boissy d'Anglas, XVIII, Article 7).

[127] This proposition appears in two texts: Constitution Committee's draft (Comité de Constitution, *Projet de Constitution*, IX, Article 7); and George Edwards' proposal (Edwards, *Idées pour Former une Nouvelle Constitution*, 495).

[128] Respectively Comité de Constitution, *Projet de Constitution*, IX, Article 5, and Comité de Salut Public, *Projet de Constitution*, XXIV, Article 1. The Committee of Public Safety's proposal was approved during the June 22, 1793, session, but the minimum number of primary assemblies required to trigger the procedure was raised from one to one-tenth for each department (AP, t. LXVI, 675).

[129] See Saint-Just, *Projet de Constitution*, XIV, Article 1; Poultier, *Constitution Populaire*, IV, Article 2; Montgilbert, *Projet des Lois Constitutionnel*, XIX, Articles 1–2; and Thirion, *La Pierre Angulaire*, Article 13.

propose changes, article by article, during the vote regarding the proposal submitted by the new Convention.[130]

However, considering the experience of the 1793 Convention, this does not seem to indicate that the people would be excluded from the constitutional revision procedure, but only that it would be guided by a group of elected representatives and submitted to the popular vote after deliberation.

As for the power of popular veto, the drafts go into more detail and the topic can be divided in two: the popular veto itself, and auxiliary oversight mechanisms of the legislative work (something that, as we will see, can be linked but not equated to contemporary constitutional review).

The second topic is underdeveloped in comparison with the veto question, as it appears in a small number of texts. Some, like Boissel, limit themselves to defend that the Legislative be prohibited from taking any action, either individually or collectively, that could compromise the rights of man, liberty, equality, fraternity, unity, and indivisibility.[131] Gleizal proposed that no law should contain provisions that contradict the rights of man or the Constitution.[132]

But we should not take the lack of a specific procedure to deal with such contradiction for a lack of control in general. Most of these proposals also provide for popular veto or some kind of *a posteriori* popular censorship, such as, for instance, Boissel and Gleizal, respectively. These kinds of proposals seem to serve as a guidance to the Legislative body and to the primary assemblies responsible for vetoing or censoring new laws. This reading seems to be reinforced by the Constitution Committee's statement that any law or act that contradicts the Constitution was to be censored.[133]

In other instances, the draft assigns to a body (not necessarily a new institution) the responsibility for this kind of oversight. Beffroy de Reigny, for instance, tasks the Executive council with the job of reporting to the assemblies any decree deemed contrary to the rights of man. If the claim was considered unfounded, the council would answer for defamation and

[130] Thorillon, *Idées ou Bases d'un Nouvelle Déclaration*, 589.

[131] Boissel, *Les Entretiens du Père Gérard*, IV.II, Article 10.

[132] Gleizal, *Projet de Décret*, III, Article 8. This generic ban on contradicting the Constitution, Declaration, rights of man, or social pact (the words vary among the authors) also appears in Chabot, *Projet d'Acte Constitutif*, III, Article 1; and Isnard, *Déclaration des Droits de l'Homme [et] Projet de Pacte Social*, Article 5.

[133] Comité de Constitution, *Projet de Constitution*, VIII, Article 27.

be interdicted. Pressavin also assigns a similar role to the Executive council—to report on everything it deemed contrary or dangerous to public affairs or contrary to the constitutional principles—but it was to address the Legislative body, not the primary assemblies.[134]

Six drafts assign some kind of control to a body that is not the Executive council, among which four should be highlighted: Kersaint, Lagrange and Dupin, Rouzet and Ruault.[135] The names and powers vary greatly. In Rouzet's text, there are no actual rules on how the oversight would work. He simply states that the *éphores* would be responsible for monitoring the rights of the people.[136]

For example, Kersaint and Lagrange and Dupin propose a group of censors who could not take part in deliberations. In Kersaint's text, their role is to examine the decrees issued by the Legislative body and the political conduct of the constituted bodies in comparison with existing

[134] Respectively, Beffroy de Reigny, *La Constitution de la Lune*, 98, and Pressavin, *Projet de Constitution*, 385. We should not mix this role assumed by the Executive council with its possibility of checking with the Legislature if any doubt or unforeseen case arose, as in Poultier (*Poultier, Constitution Populaire*, V, Article 28), or a generic duty of the Legislature to explain the laws and interpret the obscure ones, as in Bourgois (Bourgois, *Plan de Constitution*, II.V.IV.1, Article 3). Anonymous E proposed a hybrid system in which the Executive council could bring before the primary assemblies a decree by the Legislature if the council disagreed with it (Anonymous E, *Quelques Idées*, Articles 72–73). This is an isolated case and no other draft presents a similar proposal.

[135] In Williams' text we find an institution called the constitutional council. Its name can be deceiving, as its role was to deal with conflicts between administrations and to monitor governmental transactions (David Williams, *Observations sur la Dernière Constitution de la France avec des Vues pour la Formation de la Nouvelle Constitution* (AP, t. LXIII (April 29, 1793)), 589). Another isolated proposal can be found in Beffroy de Reigny. His draft states that the people could delegate the power to ratify the law since it could delegate the power to make it. The difference would be the recipient of such delegation. For the law's final approval, the role would be performed by the committee of each *ressort*, a kind of popular assembly from an intermediary administrative unity (Beffroy de Reigny, *La Constitution de la Lune*, 142–143).

[136] Rouzet, *Projet de Constitution Française*, Article 67 [footnote]. *Éphores* is the name given by Rouzet to some governmental authorities in his proposal. Their main role is to receive petitions and the final result of deliberations, including by the Legislature, as well as to travel across the territory to receive complaints and instructions (Rouzet, *Projet de Constitution Française*, Articles 59–61 and 67). The name is taken from ancient Greece and refers to one of five Spartan magistrates responsible for somewhat limiting the king's power (SMITH, 1890). Beffroy de Reigny also creates an institution that runs parallel to the Legislative body, the national orators. They could be summoned by the Legislature to express their view on a proposed law (Beffroy de Reigny, *La Constitution de la Lune*, 138). This role seems closer to a legislative advisor than to some kind of oversight of legislative work, therefore it is not included among the other examples.

constitution and laws, but he does not explain what such a body could actually do. Lagrange and Dupin, on the other hand, state that the censors could delay up to two times the entry into force of a decision made by the Legislature for up to 48 hours, suspending its execution. The final decision would still rest with the Legislative body.[137]

In all these cases, the separate body acts only by supervising the legislative work. It does not take part in the legislative work itself. Only Prunelle proposes a hybrid institution called the tribunal of public conscience. The institution could not act, annul, or suspend decrees, but only issue what the revolutionary calls testimonies. At first, the Legislature is free to debate the matter or not. If the testimony is ignored or disregarded, the tribunal may make a second request, but this time the Legislature is obliged to debate and vote on the matter. In a third round, the primary assemblies are called to decide on their support to the tribunal's motion. If they deny it, the matter could not be brought back for ten years.[138]

Such institutions, however, are the exception. As a rule, the revolutionaries' proposals do not include a separate body to deal with such issues. The criticism they had presented against the national jury can be extended to such proposals. Creating a parallel institution to the Legislative body would pose a risk to the unity of government, as they would compete with each other. Safeguarding against possible incompatibilities and violations of rights present in laws and decrees was found in the issues of popular sovereignty and the popular veto, as these were present in most drafts.

A quote by Merry sums up this strong version of the people's sovereignty that seems to be the general trend of most constitutional drafts:

> it is certain that no man can delegate to another the right to think for himself; it is, therefore, impossible for a nation to be free unless all the individuals who compose it maintain the right to think for themselves; unless the whole is not governed if not by the whole.[139]

[137] Kersaint, *De la Constitution*, 426; Lagrange et Dupin, *Projet de Constitution*, Article 11 and Lagrange et Dupin, *Projet de Constitution*, Articles 12–13. Ruault takes a different path and leaves the final call to the additional body. The revolutionary proposed a Revisory Body responsible for analyzing if the decrees by the Legislative were compatible with the social pact (Ruault, *Projet de Constitution*, VI.III, Article 1).

[138] Prunelle, *Observations et Projet de Décret sur l'Établissement d'un Tribunal de la Conscience du Peuple*, Articles 7, 15–17, and 19.

[139] Robert Merry, *Réflexions Politiques sur la Nouvelle Constitution qui se Prépare en France* (Archives Nationales, Series Lb41, n. 125), 8. A small but interesting translation note is required. Merry writes *le tout* and not *tous*. The latter would be translated as "all," in the

In a few cases, there is a relative equality between sanctioning the law and changing the constitution. For instance, in Ducastellier's text, the only difference is the quorum required for the approval by the primary assemblies.[140] In almost all drafts, the two matters are kept distinct. There are two broad proposals that take different shapes in the individual texts. The first is restricted to a small group of revolutionaries and simply denies the possibility of popular sanction.[141] This is Bonnemain's case. Although there is no explicit prohibition, his text states that the Legislative body writes reglementary laws from a constitutional foundation, which seems to indicate there would be no need for popular approval.[142]

Robert and Faure also deny the popular sanction procedure, but for practical reasons. The people's constant gatherings would mean "the abandonment of commerce and agriculture, and, by consequence, the ruin of the State."[143] Faure goes one step further. The possibility of a law being censored by the people was in itself negative, as it would create a convulsive people and troublesome citizens who would constantly try to change the laws. It would be enough that the right to petition be ensured to a group of the interested parties.[144]

sense of all the people, but translating the former as "all" would rob the sentence of its meaning, even though the *tout* also means "all."

[140] M. Ducastellier, *Le Drapeau de l'Indépendance sous lequel les Français Doivent se Réunir à l'Assemblée Conventionnelle* (AP, t. LXIII (April 24, 1793)), pp. 242 and 244. In Beffroy de Reigny's text, the only difference is that of which citizens' assembly is responsible for approving (as he opts for a larger administrative sphere) and raises the necessary majority to three-quarters (Beffroy de Reigny, *La Constitution de la Lune*, 144).

[141] Sometimes it is possible to pinpoint what the author's intention was. For example, in Wandelaincourt's text, the revolutionary states that only the people could sanction the law, but, if it was not able to do it by itself, it could nominate representatives to do so, since long and frequent assemblies would be bad (Wandelaincourt, *Observations sur le Plan de Constitution*, 411). The text seems to imply that popular sanction would not be applicable to the French context, but the author does not enunciate it as such. We have a similar case in Beaulieu's draft, in which the author simply states that the legislative function would be delegated to representatives (Beaulieu, *Nouvelle Rédaction*, II, Article 3).

[142] Bonnemain, *Instituts Républicains*, 25. Cappin goes along similar lines when he claims that the Legislative body should decide by itself the ratification of the laws. The only difference would be the quorum: absolute majority for laws of general interest (Cappin, *Projet de Constitution*, VIII, Article 13). See also George Edwards, who dismisses the need for popular sanction to non-constitutional laws (Edwards, *Idées pour Former une Nouvelle Constitution*, 495).

[143] Robert, *Discours*, 231.

[144] It is worth reading a direct quotation from Faure's text: "There is no need to mobilize the primary assemblies to change decrees or to issue new ones on agriculture, manufacturing

This trust in the Legislative body and mistrust in relation to the continuous exercise of sovereignty by the people, however, is the exception. In most texts, the popular sanction appears as the main instrument for exercising and guaranteeing the people's sovereignty. Even Ruault, who expressly denies that sanctioning is an act of sovereignty, includes this as part of his constitutional draft.[145] The only major difference between the proposals is the option for popular sanction or a censorship procedure.[146]

Both committee's drafts propose a censorship mechanism, albeit with different shapes. In the Constitution Committee text, citizens could call their primary assembly in order to propose a reform or the repeal of a law or to propose a new one. At least 50 citizens were required to sign this call and, if the motion was approved, it was submitted to the commune, then the department and, lastly, to the republic itself.[147]

In the Committee of Public Safety draft, the project is to be sent to the communes. In the following 30 days, if at least one assembly of at least ten departments objected to the text, all the primary assemblies in the country would be called. After the deadline, if those conditions were not met, the law was considered to have been tacitly sanctioned, but the same procedure could be triggered to repeal it afterward.[148] In comparison to the Constitution Committee proposal, this one makes it easier for the people to reject a bill, although it does not demand an explicit manifestation of the will of the people. In other words, it is not a popular sanction properly speaking, but a kind of censorship or mere ratification.

Once we look into the constituent debates that took place on June 15, 1793, we can see that the proposal was further restricted. The discussion

or trade. Farmers, manufacturers and traders will present their petitions to the Legislative body, who, in its wisdom, will take it into consideration" (Faure, *Observations sur le Gouvernement de France*, 285).

[145] For Ruault, the only act of sovereignty of the people is accepting the social pact—according to him the declaration of rights and a preamble to the constitutional text itself (Ruault, *Projet de Constitution*, 30).

[146] I am using the word "sanction" when the draft demands the express manifestation of the will of at least part of the people for a law or decree to come into force, while "censorship" is a procedure initiated by the people after a law has already been ratified by the Legislative body in order to strike it down. In some cases, as in Mont-Réal (Mont-Réal, *Projet de Constitution, De la sanction.*), the word "sanction" is also used to mean tacit approval. I will treat his proposal under the label of "censorship," against the author's wording, as it best describes the general naming practices of the other texts.

[147] Comité de Constitution, *Projet de Constitution*, VIII, Articles 1, 3–4, 10, 11, and 13.

[148] Comité de Salut Public, *Projet de Constitution*, XI, Articles 4–6.

is centered in what would become article 59 of the final text. The proposed, and accepted, change in the text is the same I have presented above regarding calling a new National Convention: a tenth of the primary assemblies, instead of only one assembly.[149] The article providing for later repeal following the same procedure is rejected under the argument that this would already be covered by the tacit ratification or express sanction by the people,[150] but the connection does not seem to hold water.

The notion that tactic ratification by the people was enough is also present in some drafts, but they do not make the majority of the proposals. The idea of later censorship only appears in a handful of texts.[151] Even if we do not count the texts in which there is only a generic affirmation of the people's right to sanction, without explaining its procedure,[152] we still get a large number of proposals defending people's sanction instead of mere censorship.

Before going into those texts, we should keep in mind that in the Constitution Committee's and the Committee of Public Safety's drafts, as well as in many other drafts, censorship is applicable only to laws—not to decrees. Articles 54 and 55 of the final text make this distinction: laws are more general in scope or deal with matters of greater importance, while decrees handled urgent, exceptional, and related matters.[153] Only the former would be under the peoples' censorship powers, while the decrees would come into force directly by legislative approval.

[149] On the other hand, the waiting period is increased from 30 to 40 days, as proposed by an unnamed representative (AP, t. LXVII, 139).

[150] AP, t. LXVII, 139.

[151] Barthélémy Albouys, *Principes Constitutionnels Présentés a la Convention Nationale [En Trois Parties]*, AP, t. LXVII (June 24, 1793):176–186, Articles 12 and 14)—who claims it is impossible for the people to directly exercise its power (Albouys, *Principes Constitutionnels*, Article 4). See also Debry, *Projet de Déclaration*, Articles 39–40 and 43; and Gleizal, *Projet de Décret*, III, Article 8) and Lambert (Lambert, *Plan de Constitution Républicaine*, 434).

[152] See Pénières, *Plan et Projet de Constitution*, *Droits du citoyen*, Article 6).

[153] This theoretical distinction does not necessarily correspond to present-day legal classifications and we should not conflate the two. For example, in the final text, a declaration of war, as we have already seen, is considered to be a law. Although it is not a general matter, it is considered a matter of greater importance, as well as public honors to the memory of great men. However, the annual distribution of public works is considered to be a decree, as well as changes in the partial distribution of the French territory. We can see then how the classification made in each draft is more important than the general distinction between law and decree.

The distinction also appears in many drafts and, in general, they use emergency as a criterion.[154] For example, Anonymous P states that laws in general are submitted to sanction by the people, but emergency laws are not. The same idea appears in Daunou and Dupont, among others.[155] Only one draft creates a separate body to analyze emergency laws.[156] In all other cases, emergency decrees dispense with popular sanction, or this distinction is simply not made.

Even when popular sanction is required, some texts suggest the laws should be provisionally enforced while the sovereign's will has not yet expressed itself.[157] The same provision appears in the Constitution Committee text when discussing people's censorship powers: "the provisional enforcement of the law will always come into effect."[158]

On the other hand, almost no draft explicitly denies the possibility of provisional enforcement.[159] The lack of an explicit treatment seems to indicate that laws were not to be enforced prior to people's sanction. This conclusion is reinforced by the Committee of Public Safety's original draft

[154] Calés is the only one who expressly claims it is useless to distinguish between law and decree (Calés, *Notes*, VII.I, Article 4).

[155] Respectively, Anonymous P, *Essai sur la Constitution Française*, 38; Daunou, *Essai sur la Constitution*, I.III, Article 1 and Pierre-Charles-François Dupont [de Bigorre], *Bases de la Constitution Française* (AP, t. LXVII (June 24, 1793)), VII, Article 2. For other texts in the same vein, see, for instance, Boissel, *Les Entretiens du Père Gérard*, IV.II, Article 13; Bourgois, *Plan de Constitution*, II.V.IV.1, Article 2; and Ruault, *Projet de Constitution*, IV, Article 4). In some cases, it is not possible to determine the author's position. For example, Anonymous D states that all definitive decrees (they do not use the word "law") should be subjected to the sanction procedure, which seems to take into account an implicit distinction between laws of a general and definitive character and urgent or temporary decrees. This kind of explanatory void is not uncommon.

[156] Anonymous P suggests creating a national intermediary council responsible for sanctioning any urgent law with a six-month term (Anonymous P, *Essai sur la Constitution Française*, 35).

[157] For example, Bacon-Tacon, *Examen Impartial des Bases de la Nouvelle Constitution*, 603); Harmand, *Opinion*, Article 4; François-Agnes Montgilbert, *Suite de l'Avis au Peuple sur la Liberté et L'exercice des Droits, Contenu dans un Projet de Constitution Républicaine* (AP, t. LXVII (June 24, 1793)), 346); and Poultier, *Constitution Populaire*, III, Article 14).

[158] Comité de Constitution, *Projet de Constitution*, VIII, Article 29.

[159] The two exceptions are Daunou (*Essai sur la Constitution*, I.III, Article 2) and Lefebure, who claims that a law may not come into force before the people's veto (*Constitution du Gouvernement*, *Du Corps législatif*, Article 3). Guiot states that fundamental laws (to be defined by the constitutional text) could not be provisionally enforced (*Essais sur les Droits*, 14). This seems to be more closely related to the material limitations to constitutional change and less to the sanctioning power.

in which the matter of provisional enforcement appears only once: if, after the 30-day period without any opposing view presented by the primary assemblies, they decided to repeal the law, the law would still be enforced while all primary assemblies were called. Since this article was rejected, it is reasonable to conclude that provisional enforcement was also excluded from the final text.

With that in mind, I can now analyze the 28 drafts that provide for an expansive view on popular sanction.[160] The only limitation I can find in them regards the ban on the deliberation of law projects by primary assemblies, but this prohibition only appears in two texts. The general rule is to guarantee the freedom to debate.[161]

Even though most drafts do not forbid deliberation, they also do not care to detail how this deliberative procedure would occur. This seems to leave room for the primary assemblies to organize their own discussions.[162] But some minimum rules are suggested. Some revolutionaries are apparently worried with criticisms of the excesses of assemblies and establish a specific moment for when ratification should take place.[163] For example,

160 They are: Anonymous A, Anonymous D, Anonymous O, Bancal, Barailon, Blaviel, Boissel, Bourgois, Chabot, Coupé, Daunou, Dupont, Guiot, Le Suer, Léfebure, Merry, Momoro, Montgilbert, Oswald, Ragonneau, Rouzet, Ruault, Sade, Saint-Just, Thirion, Thorillon, Varlet, and Wlriot. This list includes the proposals that assert the peoples' right to sanction, but do not provide for a specific procedure. For some of the related dispositions, see: Anonymous A, *Réfléxions sur les Bases d'une Constitution*, 68–69; Anonymous D, *La France Heureuse*, 11–12; Anonymous O [Par Cosmopolite], *Discours Fraternel et Instructions*, Article 22; Bancal, Jean Henri (Bancal des Issarts), *Du Nouvel Ordre Social*, (AP, t. LV (December 24, 1792), 416; Antoine-Innocent Blaviel, *Réflexions Préliminaires sur la Constitution Française et sur l'organisation d'un Gouvernement Populaire* (AP, t. LXVII (June 24, 1793)), 248 and 250; Antoine-François Momoro, *Déclaration des Droits* (Archives Nationales, Series Lb41, n. 2978), Article 10; Rouzet, *Projet de Constitution Française*, Article 59; Ruault, *Projet de Constitution*, IV, Article 2; and Thirion, *La Pierre Angulaire*, Article 11).

161 Anonymous D and Sade are two examples of texts that expressly provide for deliberation by the assemblies, although they do not give much detail on procedural matters (Anonymous D, *La France Heureuse*, 11–12; Sade, *Idée sur le Mode de la Sanction des Loix*, 14). Regarding the other proposals, the lack of an explicit prohibition seems to indicate it would be permissible.

162 See Blaviel, Chabot, Guiot, Lesuer, Lefebure, Montgilbert, Ragonneau, Sade, Saint-Just, Thorillon, and Varlet.

163 For a limitation of the scope, see Anonymous A, *Réfléxions sur les Bases d'une Constitution*, 68, and Wlriot, *Hommage à la Convention*, 569). This does not mean such concern was widespread. For instance, Wlriot says that sanction would take place the first Sunday of each month (Wriot, *Hommage à la Convention*, 579) and other drafts, as we will

Montgilbert, Bourgois, and Ragonneau determine that peoples' sanction would happen once a year. Only the first one talks about provisional enforcement of the laws and it is not possible to conclude if this is also implicit in the last two revolutionaries' proposals.[164]

One of the reasons why I can make such a claim when the text is not explicit on the matter lies in the fact that, in some proposals, the elongated deliberative period does imply a ban on the provisional enforcement of the law. For instance, Coupé does not speak of provisional enforcement and his proposal is that of a semestral bulletin to be sent to all primary assemblies, covering the current state of the Republic and any laws to be proposed or pending sanction. The primary assemblies would then discuss and send their orders to the Legislative body, which, in turn, would have six months to assess these mandates. Otherwise, the following bulletin would deal with the body's renewal.[165]

Considering the degree of public engagement demanded by Coupé, it would not be reasonable to assume that the laws would be provisionally enforced. The mandated empowerment of primary assemblies appears in many other drafts. Barailon, for example, defends that law projects be sent to the primary assemblies for discussion. If they are rejected, the matter could not be presented again in the next four years—except if the difference between votes was small or non-existent.[166]

The concern with guaranteeing the primary assemblies' deliberative space manifests its stronger form in Boissel's and Oswald's drafts.

see later on, give more detailed instructions for more prolonged debates. Therefore, it seems safe to claim that the more frequent position is that a longer period for debates over the law projects is a necessary part of respecting the people's sovereignty. Generic claims over the need for previous sanction also corroborate such hypothesis—as in Guiot, to whom silence is not to be considered a ratification (Guiot, *Essais sur les Droits*, 11–12), and Lefebure, to whom the law would not come into force prior to the people's sanction (Léfebure, *Constitution du Gouvernement*, *Du Corps législatif*, Article 3).

[164] Respectively Montgilbert, *Suite de l'Avis au Peuple*, 347; Nicolas Bourgois, *Plan de Constitution Proposée a la République Française* (AP, t. LXIII (April 24, 1793)), II.IV, Article 15; Ragonneau, *Plan d'une Nouvelle Constitution* (AP, t. LXIV (May 6, 1793)), IV, Article 1.

[165] Coupé, *Idée Simples de Constitution*, 269. Coupé does not use the word "mandate," but, considering its meaning, its use seems adequate.

[166] Barailon, *Projet de Constitution*, II.VIII, Articles 9 and 11. Other examples are: Merry (if a tie occurred, deliberation was suspended until the following year—Merry, *Réflexions Politiques*, Articles 6–8); and Daunou (during a two-month long session, each primary assembly would discuss it Article by Article—Daunou, *Essai sur la Constitution*, 353 and I.III, Articles 4–6).

According to Galy, the latter's proposal was an isolated case in which "the sovereign's approval is the rumbling of the rabble."[167]

In Boissel's text, popular societies served as intermediaries between the people and the government. The term "intermediary" may not be the best option, but it seems appropriate in this context, as it occupies the place in which the general will is gathered and manifests itself.[168] They would then send inputs to the Legislature and even the representatives themselves would have to present their proposals through these means. Sanctions were also assigned to popular societies, together with discussions on how to improve the rights of man.[169]

In Oswald's proposal, we also have primary assemblies with central roles in the production of laws. The significant difference is that this is one of the few texts that theorize about the limits of representation. According to him, representation had perverted the mind of men and the people were no longer able to see the truth of things. Everything was seen through representational lenses: representation of the nation's sovereignty; representation of the nation's nobility; representation of commercial interests. In his words, "a metaphysical Ark of Noah in which every animal and even every ideal world has its own representative."[170]

Oswald divides legislative work in two acts. An act of comprehension (to be done through the primary assemblies' deliberation) and an act of power (exerted by the nation through the primary assemblies). For a proposal to be definitely approved or rejected, he required a nine-tenths majority. As long as such a proportion was not met, the debates would continue.

[167] Galy, *La Notion de Constitution dans les Projets de 1793*, 105.

[168] In the next chapter, I will discuss Boissel's proposal in greater detail. For now, it is sufficient to know that popular societies would act as primary assemblies in regard to legislative matters, although, in general terms, they are the people itself in the exercise of its sovereignty.

[169] See Boissel, *Les Entretiens du Père Gérard*, IV.I, Articles 8 and 14; and Boissel, *Les Entretiens du Père Gérard*, IV.II, Article 12). This idea of primary assemblies as the place for discussing how to improve the law also appears, for instance, in Dupont. He proposed a kind of feedback process through which the primary assemblies would send their observations to the Legislature, who would then analyze them and send a formalized proposal back to the former (Dupont, *Bases de la Constitution Française*, VII, Article 4).

[170] John Oswald, *The Government of the People; or, a Sketch of a Constitution For the Univesal Common-Wealth* (Archives Nationales, Series Lb41, n. 2983), 8.

Although this ratio seems to be too high,[171] his tone does not differ significantly from the others. However, there is an important disagreement. If the proposed institutional arrangements are similar, the place reserved for representation and, by consequence, to peoples' sovereignty is not the same.

Robespierre sums up what is at stake in his June 16, 1793, speech to the National Convention:

> I observe next that the word 'representative' cannot be applied to any mandatary of the people, because the will cannot be represented. The Legislature's members are mandataries to whom the people entrusted the first power; but, in its true meaning, we cannot say that they represent the people.[172]

In order to understand this relationship, we need to grasp what the revolutionaries meant by citizenship and its limits, as we will see in our next chapter.

Appendix

Historical References for the 1792–1793 Debates

Explanatory Notes

1. Whenever possible, the drafts are cited by article or chapter and article, not by page.
2. I reference the anonymous texts' authors as "Anonymous A" to "Anonymous U" to more easily reference them in the main text of this book.
3. Since this is an abridged version of the original thesis, not all of the texts listed below are mentioned throughout the main text. I chose to include them in the references for fellow researchers interested in the topic.

[171] Only Le Suer requires something similar: five-sixths of the votes (Le Sueur, *Idées*, V, Article 2).

[172] AP, t. LXVII, 141.

4. The final and approved text of the Declaration and Constitution of the Year 1 of the Republic are cited as *Declaration* and *Constitution*. The other primary texts are listed below.

Parliamentary Notes, Newspapers, and Legal Texts

Archives parlementaires de 1787 à 1869 (First series). Paris: Paul Dupont, 1867–2021. [cited as "AP," followed by tome number, page, and the document's date, when available].

Drafts

Albouys, Barthélémy. *Principes Constitutionnels Présentés a la Convention Nationale [En Trois Parties]*. AP, t. LXVII (June 24, 1793):176–186.

Anonymous A. *Cit.* ***. *Réflexions sur les Bases D'une Constitution…Présentées par Bresson*. Archives Nationales, Series AD/XVIIIC/257, n° 20.

Anonymous D. la *France Heureuse ou Tout le Monde Content*. Archives Nationales, Series AD/XVIIIC/262, n. 15.

Anonymous E. *Quelques Idées sur une Constitution Populaire pour un Grand État*. AP, t. LXIII (April 24, 1793), 296–302.

Anonymous H. *Vœu d'un Citoyen sur la Nouvelle Constitution Présentée par la Convention [Chez Frouillé, Imprimeur-Librarie, 1793]*. Archives Nationales, Series Lb41, n. 702.

Anonymous O [Par Cosmopolite]. *Discours Fraternel et Instructions a mês Citoyens pour les Mettre a la Hateur des Républicains: Ouvragre Nouveau sur les Droits de l'Homme et du Citoyen, d'Après des Principes Physiques et Moraux*. Archives Nationales, Series Lb41, n. 2982.

Anonymous P. *Essai sur la Constitution Française par un Citoyen du District de Montivilliers, Départment de la Seine Inférieure*. Archives Nationales, Series Lb41, n. 2993.

Bacon-Tacon, Pierre Jean Jacques (Comte de). *Examen Impartial des Bases de la Nouvelle Constitution*. AP, t. LXIII (April 29, 1793), 601–604.

Bancal, Jean Henri (Bancal des Issarts). *Du Nouvel Ordre Social*. AP, t. LV (December 24, 1792), 409–423.

Barailon, Jean-François. *Projet de Constitution Présenté a la Convetion Nationale*. AP, t. LXVII (June 24, 1793):187–220.

Barlow, Joël. *Lettre a la Convention Nationale sur les Vices de la Constitution de 1791 et sur l'Étendue des Amendements a y Porter, pour Lesquelles cette Convention a Eté Convoquée.* AP, t. LIII (November 7, 1792), 286–297.

Beaulieu, Claude François. *Nouvelle Rédaction de la Déclaration ses Droits et des Deux Premier Titres de la Constitution.* Archives Nationales, Series Lb41, n. 80.

Beffroy de Reigny, Louis-Abel. *La Constitution de la Lune, Rêve Politique et Moral, par le Cousin-Jacques.* Archives Nationales, Series Lb41, n. 706.

Blaviel, Antoine-Innocent. *Réflexions Préliminaires sur la Constitution Française et sur l'organisation d'un Gouvernement Populaire.* AP, t. LXVII (June 24, 1793), 248–251.

Boissel, François. *Les Entretiens du Père Gérard.* AP, t. LXVI (June 17, 1793), 613–642.

Boissy d'Anglais, François-Antoine (Comte de). *Constitution.* AP, t. LXII (April 17, 1793), 291–315.

Bonnemain, Antoine-Jean-Thomas. *Instituts Républicains, ou Développement Analytique des Facultés Naturelles, Civiles et Politiques de L'homme.* Archives Nationales, Series Lb41, n. 2385.

Bourgois, Nicolas. *Plan de Constitution Proposée a la République Française.* AP, t. LXIII (April 24, 1793) 259–279.

Cappin [or Capin], Joseph. *Projet de Constitution.* AP, t. LXIV (May 6, 1793) 235–243.

Chabot, François. *Projet d'Acte Constitutif des Français.* AP, t. LXVII (June 24, 1793) 261–266.

Chevret, Jean. *Principes de Sociabilité, ou Nouvel Exposé des Droits et des Devoirs de l'Homme et du Citoyen, Suivies d'Observations Importantes, Relatives aux Propriétés, a la Liberté du Commerce & a la Proportion du Prix des Subsistances avec les Facultés des Citoyens.* Archives Nationales, Series Lb41, n. 2883.

Cloots, Anacharsis. *Bases Constitutionnelles de la République du Genre Humain.* AP, t. LXIII (April 26, 1793) 389–403.

Comité de Constitution. *Projet de Déclaration.* AP, t. LVIII (February 15, 1793) 601.

Comité de Constitution. *Projet de Constitution.* AP, t. LVIII (February 15, 1793) 602–609.

Comité de Salut Public. *Projet de Constitution du Peuple Français.* AP, t. LXVI (June 10, 1793) 260–264.

Comité de Salut Public. *Déclaration des Droits de l'Homme.* AP, t. LXVI (June 10, 1793) 259–260.

Coupé, Jacques-Marie (Abbé). *Idée Simples de Constitution*. AP, t. LXVII (June 24, 1793) 266–279.

Cusset, Joseph-Marie. *Projet de Décret sur la Constitution*. AP, t. LXIII (April 29, 1793) 599–601.

Daunou, Pierre-Claude-François. *Essai sur la Constitution*. AP, t. LXII (April 17, 1793) 350–370.[173]

Debry, Jean-Antoine (Baron). *Projet de Constitution*. AP, t. LXIII (April 24, 1793) 238–241.

Desacy, Claude Louis Michel. *Additions Au Plan de Constitution, Présentées a la Convention Nationale*. AP, t. LXII (April 17, 1793) 370–374.

Ducastellier, M. *Le Drapeau de l'Indépendance sous lequel les Français Doivent se Réunir à l'Assemblée Conventionnelle*. AP, t. LXIII (April 24, 1793) 241–259.

Duplantier, Jacques-Antoine-Paul. *Réflexions sur le Scrutin a Etablir pour l'Élection des Représentants et des Magistrats du Peuple Français*. AP, t. LXVII (June 24, 1793) 309–310.

Edwards, George. *Idées Pour Former une Nouvelle Constitution, et Pour Assurer la Prospérité et le Bonheur de la France et d'autres Nations* AP, t. LIX (February 28, 1793) 482–498.

Faure, Pierre-Joseph-Denis-Gauillaume. *Observations sur le Gouvernement de France, Relativement Au Plan du Comité de Constitution*. AP, t. LXIII (April 24, 1793) 279–292.

Garnier [de Saintes], Jacques. *Aperçu de Réflexions sur la Constitution*. Archives Nationales, Series Le38, n. 2302.

Gleizal, Claude. *Projet de Décret sur les Elections, les Assemblées Primaires, le Corps Législatif, le Conseil Exécutif, l'Administration de Département, les Municipalités, les Tribunaux, l'Arbitrage et les Bureaux de Pacification*. AP, t. LXII (April 17, 1793) 411–420.

Guiot, Florent. *Essais sur les Droits dont le Peuple a Confié L'exercice a la Convention Nationale, et sur les Devoirs que l'Exercice de ces Mêmes Droits lui Impose*. Archives Nationales, Series Lb41, n. 89.

Harmand, Jean-Baptiste. *Opinion*. AP, t. LXII (April 17, 1793) 275–276.

Hazard. *Vues d'un Patriote Présentées à la Convention Nationale*. Archives Nationales, Series Lb41, n. 2391.

[173] The document is subdivided as follows: *Projet de Déclaration, Bases de l'Établissement en France, Constitution ou Définition et Distribution des Pouvoirs dans la République Française* and *Principes de la Législation en France*.

Isnard, Henri-Maximin. *Déclaration des Droits de l'Homme [et] Projet de Pacte Social* AP, t. LXIV (May 10, 1793) 421–423.

Kersaint, Armand Guy Simon Coetnempren (Comte). *De la Constitution et du Gouvernement Qui Pourraient Convenir a la République Française.* AP, t. LXII (April 17, 1793) 420–429.

Lafont. *Nouveau Mode de Nomination aux Emplois de la République.* AP, t. LXIV (May 6, 1793) 245–246.

Lagrange et Dupin. *Projet de Constitution.* AP, t, LXIV (May 6, 1793) 248–252.

Lambert, Charles. *Plan de Constitution Républicaine, Précédé de Quelques Observations sur Celui que le Comité de Constitution a Présenté a la Convetion les 15 et 16 Février.* AP, t. LXII (April 17, 1793) 434–466.

Lanthenas, François-Xavier. *Censure Publique, Ou Nécessité de Confier a Un Certain Nombre de Citoyens Instruits et Vertueux, Choisis et Périodiquement Renouvellés, la Surveillance de Mœurs.* Archives Nationales, Series AD/XVIIIC/291, n. 3.

Lanthenas, François-Xavier. *Des Elections et du Mode a Elire par Listes Epuratoires.* AP, t. LXIV (May 10, 1793) 510–513.

Le Sueur, Theodore. *Idées sur l'Espèce de Gouvernement Populaire qui Pourrait Convenir à un Pays de l'Étendue et de la Population Présumée de la France. Essai Présenté a la Convention Nationale par un Citoyen.* AP, t. LXII (April 17, 1793) 548–570.

Léfebure, Louis. *Constitution du Gouvernement pour la Nation Française.* Archives Nationales, Series Lb41, n. 2391.[174]

Mellinet, François. *Sur le Comité Censorial.* AP, t. LVI (January 8, 1793) 241–242.

Merry, Robert. *Réflexions Politiques sur la Nouvelle Constitution qui se Prépare en France.* Archives Nationales, Series Lb41, n. 125.

Momoro, Antoine-François. *Déclaration des Droits.* Archives Nationales, Series Lb41, n. 2978.

Mont-Réal, Louis-François. *Projet de Constitution.* AP, t. LX (March 2, 1793) 615–620.

Montgilbert, François-Agnes. *Projet des Lois Constitutionnel.* AP, t. LXVII (June 24, 1793) 352–362.

[174] A shorter version was published in the *Ancien Moniteur* on April 24, 1793 (AM, t. XVI, 202).

Montgilbert, François-Agnes. *Suite de l'Avis au Peuple sur la Liberté et L'exercice des Droits, Contenu dans un Projet de Constitution Républicaine*. AP, t. LXVII (June 24, 1793) 339–362.
Oswald, John. *The Government of the People; or, a Sketch of a Constitution For the Univesal Common-Wealth*. Archives Nationales, Series Lb41, n. 2983.
Oudot, Charles-François *Règles Générales Pour les Elections dans les Assemblées Primaires*. AP, t. LXVII (June 24, 1793) 364–368.
Pénières, Jean-Agustin. *Plan et Projet de Constitution Pour la République Française*. AP, t. LXII (April 17, 1793) 477–482.
Picqué, Jean-Pierre. *Nécessité d'Établir une Censure Publique*. AP, t. LXIV (May 10, 1793) 513–519.
Pressavin, Jean-Baptiste. *Projet de Constitution*. AP, t. LXVII (June 24, 1793) 380–390.
Prunelle, Léonard Joseph. *Observations et Projet de Décret sur l'Établissement d'un Tribunal de la Conscience du Peuple*. Archives Nationales, Series AD/XVIIIC/261, n. 13.
Poultier, François-Martin [Poultier d'Elmotte]. *Constitution Populaire*. AP, t. LXII (April 17, 1793) 482–492.
Ragonneau. *Plan d'une Nouvelle Constitution*. AP, t. LXIV (May 6, 1793) 252–259.
Réal, Guillaume-André. *Réflexions sur le Meilleur Mode d'Élection*. Archives Nationales, Series AD/XVIIIC/261, n. 14.
Robert, Pierre-François-Joseph. *Discours*. AM, t. 16 (April 27, 1793) 230–231.
Robespierre, Maximilien Marie Isidore de. *Discours sur le Gouvernement Représentatif par Maximilien Robespierre Prononcé à la Tribune de l'Assemblée Nationale*. Archives Nationales, Series Le38, n. 245.
Rouzet, Jacques-Marie. *Projet de Constitution Française*. AP, t. LXII (April 17, 1793) 496–513.
Ruault, Alexandre-Jean, *Projet de Constitution de la République Française*. Portiez de l'Oise Collection, t. 176, n. 15.
Sade, Donatien Alphonse François (Comte de). *Idée sur le Mode de la Sanction des Loix*. Archives Nationales, Series Lb41, n. 2400.
Salle, Jean-Baptiste. *Examen Critique de la Constitution*. AP, t. LXVII (June 24, 1793) 391–400.
Saint-Just, Antoine-Louis-Léon de. *Projet de Constitution*. AP, t. LXIII (April 24, 1793) 200–215.

Seconds, Jean-Louis. *Art Rationnel Politique. De l'Art Social ou des Vrais Principes de la Société Politique (Quatrième Cahier)*. AP, t. LXII (April 17, 1793) 533–548.

Thirion, Didier. *La Pierre Angulaire de l'Édifice Constitutionnel*. AP, t. LXVII (June 24, 1793) 403–409.

Thorillon, Antoine-Joseph. *Idées ou Bases d'une Nouvelle Déclaration des Droits de l'Homme, de cette de ses Devoirs et d'une Nouvelle Constitution pour la République Française, où l'on Traite, entre Autres Choses, de la Liberté, de l'Égalité, des Insurrections, de l'éducation Nationale, du Code Civil, et Notamment des Enfants Naturels, de l'Adoption, d'une Seule Substitution Officieuse, de l'Organisation d'un Nouvel Ordre Judiciaire, etc.* AP, t. LXII (April 17, 1793) 582–598.

Wandelaincourt, Antoine-Hubert. *Observations sur le Plan de Constitution*. AP, t. LXVII (June 24, 1793) 409–415.

Williams, David. *Observations sur la Dernière Constitution de la France avec des Vues pour la Formation de la Nouvelle Constitution*. AP, t. LXIII (April 29, 1793) 583–591.

Wlriot (de Tours). *Hommage a la Convention d'un Projet de Gouvernement Républicain a Donner a la France*. AP, t. LXII (April 17, 1793) 574–582.

References

Galy, François. *La Notion de Constitution dans les Projets de 1793*. Paris: Editions Albert Mechelinck, 1932.

Ganzin, Michel (ed.). *Le Concept de Représentation Dans la Pensée Politique*. Aix-En-Provence: Presses Universitaires d'Aix-Marseille, 2003.

Ollivier, Nathalie. "Les Projets Constitutionnels de 1793." PhD Diss. Université Panthéon-Assas, 2002.

Peck, Harry Thurston. *Harper's Dictionary of Classical Antiquities*. New York: Trustees of Tufts University, 1898.

Smith, William. *A Dictionary of Greek and Roman Antiquities*. London: John Murry, 1890. http://www.perseus.tufts.edu/hopper/text?doc=Perseus%3atext%3a1999.04.0063

CHAPTER 7

Republic and Citizenship

un état permanent de délibération populaire
—Robert Merry

Up until now, I have analyzed the organization of different parts of the government, their internal relations, and oversight mechanisms, including how the people could take part in its workings. In the first chapter, we saw how certain legal literature (e.g., Moyn) presented the French Revolution by way of some key notions. Nationalism, abstraction, and legiscentrism were some of the main interpretative guidelines proposed by such authors, as they were inspired by François Furet and his followers.

In the previous chapters, we saw the revolutionaries' concern with creating a government based on the rights of man when presenting their propositions for an institutional design. Although the dispute between the debaters over natural rights and rights under the social state was not resolved—we will see part of this discussion in this chapter—the preoccupation with guaranteeing the rights of man was present in the most disparate proposals, by revolutionaries from the most diverse affiliations. The organization of government is the organization of the safeguard of rights.

Defending these rights is a common denominator among the drafts, even if the texts do not agree on their content and formalization. This

E. Baker, *Human Rights and Humanity's Rights During Year Three of the French Revolution*,
https://doi.org/10.1007/978-3-030-99508-9_7

does not mean, however, that rights were seen as empty receptacles that could be filled with any content. The primacy of the rights of man sets some boundaries to the proposals and discourses, as we can see in the relative homogeneity found in some matters, such as the popular ratification or censorship powers.

Two other issues are almost ubiquitous: citizenship and the Republic. So far, I have presented a view of the proposed structural organization of the government. In this chapter, my challenge is to comprehend which notion of the Republic was at play, where the idea of citizenship fit, and to what purpose—a debate that includes the revolutionaries' view on representation that I have started to examine in the last chapter. As we will see, these two notions can serve as a tool to bring together the different topics regarding the rights of man discussed in the previous chapters.

7.1 The Republic

There is an important link between the rights of man and the organization of governmental bodies that traverses the notions of Republic and citizenship. Only a few isolated voices claimed that France would be incompatible with the Republican regime due to its size or that the choice between a Republic or Monarchy was indifferent.[1] The almost unanimous position among the drafts is to end the monarchical rule and create a French Republic.

The Republic, however, is not exactly well defined in the drafts. Besides the general opposition to the monarchy, we saw how this Republic was able to accommodate a plurality of different institutional arrangements, and some of the elements of each arrangement were part of what the drafters understood as a Republic. For example, Bancal defines the republican government as direct elections to the Legislature and the Executive; frequent change of public officials; the individuals' right to petition; and the regulation by the sovereign to prevent convulsion.[2]

This list already shows us the impossibility of establishing a full consensus on the definition of the Republic among the drafts. The ratified constitutional text did not provide for direct election to the Executive and the themes of petition and "convulsion," to use Bancal's words, were very

[1] Respectively, Anonymous U, *Lettre sur la Prétendue République Française, a un Membre de la Prétendue Convention Nationale* (Archives Nationales, Series Lb41, n. 698) and DUC, 241–2.

[2] Bancal, *Du Nouvel Ordre Social*, 415.

diversely treated in the drafts. This, however, did not prevent the affirmation of the republican regime in each proposal.

Among the documents sent to the Convention, we find a "republican pledge" listing the precepts a true republican should follow, such as defending the country, persecuting tyrants, upholding the laws and virtues, sympathizing with one's compatriot and expelling schemers, helping the destitute *sans-culottes*.[3] Another anonymous text gives one of the few definitions of a Republic: a society in which peace is upheld, politics is the government of the many, and the public good is that which belongs to all in general and to each and every one in particular.[4]

These brief definitions present us with two facets of the Republic that I can explore in further detail. On the one hand, the government of the many and its relation to democracy and representation. On the other hand, virtue and the public good, and its relationship with the general will and the social contract. In between those, we can place the unity of the Republic and of the law as theorized by the constituent representatives.

I will not delve into the question if or how the republican thought as expressed in the drafts is inspired by classical republicanism. As I have already stated, my main *corpus* of analysis is limited to the sources and interpretations from the revolutionary period, so as to extract as much as possible from these primary sources, instead of taking the Revolution's interpreters or inspirations as the truth of the Revolution. But I should also point out that the revolutionaries were perfectly aware that there was a correlation between what they were trying to explain and create and the Classical Period. This realization, however, does not mean that they were trying to simply restore some supposed republican glory from a lost past.

Though aware of their inspirations, the revolutionaries were trying to come up with something new, as we can see in Rudel's text on a constitution for the French Republic:

> The idea of free republics was not unknown [...] this type of government was undoubtedly sweeter, more moderate; but those who established it kept part of the vices from monarchies and from tyranny, it was entrusted to the

[3] Anonymous M, *Le Dix Commandemens du Vrai Républicain* (Archives Nationales, Series Lb41, n. 2393). Palloy presents another version of a republican pledge (Pierre François Palloy, *Serment Républicain* (Archives Nationales, Series Lb41, n. 292.A)).

[4] Anonymous L, *Le Vétéran, en Civisme comme en Service Militaire, a ses Concitoyens: Observations Politico-Morales, sur l'Étymologie & la Définition des Mots Patrie, République, Citoyen, Liberté, Égalité, Etc. –par un Propriétaire-Agriculteur, Appellé Philosophe, Philantrope* (Archives Nationales, Series Lb41, n. 2388), 4–5.

most opulent or the most educated ones, that is to schemers that kept the peoples under the yoke of a servile dependency: oppression followed.[5]

Rudel continues to explicitly mention Greece and Rome as examples of corrupted republics. But more important for our purposes here than identifying the classical or neoclassical roots of the proposals is to understand these proposals by themselves and through the lens of their immediate context.

7.1.1 Government of the Many, Social Contract, and the Law

The government of the many can be summed up in the tension seen in Harmand's portrayal of two possible Republics: if part of the people exercises sovereignty, we have an aristocracy; if the people is the one exercising the sovereign power, we have a democracy. In a similar vein, Barailon talks about adopting a purely democratic republican government.[6]

As we have seen in the previous chapter, this does not mean that for Harmand or Barailon the people should be directly responsible for all governmental functions. If we look for a straightforward commentary on such a possibility, we can only find those who reject it. Calès, for example, denounces the Constitution Committee text for trying to implement what he calls an "absolute Republic" instead of the more adequate representative republic.[7]

In other drafts, the Republic is characterized mainly by the elective character of representation. For Saint-Just, the fundamental principle of the Republic was "that national representation should be elected by the people as a whole."[8] Wlriot expresses a similar notion by claiming "one will never believe there is a Republic unless the people choose all its magistrates."[9]

[5] Claude-Antoine Rudel, *Discours sur l'Éducation Publique Précédé de Notions Préliminaires sur la Constitution de la République Française* (Archives Nationales, Series AD/XVIIIC/240, n. 15), 4.

[6] Barailon, *Projet de Constitution*, I, Articles 1–2. See also Jean-Baptiste Harmand, *Préliminaire et Ordre de la Discussion sur la Constitution* (AP, t. LXVII (June 24, 1793), Article 1, and Article 2.

[7] Jean-Marie Calés, *Suite des Notes* (AP, t. LXII (April 17, 1793)), 333.

[8] Saint-Just, *Projet de Constitution*, 204.

[9] Wriot, *Hommage à la Convention*, 577.

In other instances, democracy and representation appear together, as in Beaulieu's distinction between a representative constitution and a democratic government, or in the famous quote from Hérault de Séchelles, when introducing the Committee of Public Safety's draft: "the French Constitution cannot be exclusively representative, for it cannot be less democratic than representative."[10]

This passage from the Committee of Public Safety's statement of intent for the constitutional draft deals with the distinction between a law (prepared by the Legislative body and ratified by the people) and a decree (directly approved by the Legislature). Or, in other words, between democracy and representation. In the previous chapters, we have seen how democracy can be characterized as the people exercising the sovereign power without intermediaries, but we still need to better define what the revolutionaries meant by representation.

Some authors limit themselves to state the representative character of government. For instance, Kersaint claims that, because of the extension of the territory, the Republic should be representative, and Thirion states that the government is representative, and all public authorities are temporary and elected.[11] These general remarks may be complemented with some further clues on how to better define representation.

Chabot claims the actual government can only be representative, delegating everything that does not hinder happiness.[12] Chabot's assertion sounds out of place, considering what we saw in the previous chapters. The idea that the people would leave all its powers in the hands of its representatives unless it caused loss or harm does not sit well with the different institutional arrangements studied above. On the contrary, the general tone seemed to be to keep the people a part of the political process, even though many factors may, in practice, mitigate its participation. Tensions are present in all the proposed arrangements. Chabot seems to point to the neutralization of popular power through the expansion of representation as a solution.

This problem is also identified in other texts. Some limit themselves to assert the irrepresentable aspect of the will, or that sovereignty or the

[10] Comité de Salut Public, *Exposition des Motifs* (AP, t. LXVI (June 10, 1793)), 258.

[11] Respectively, Kersaint, *De la Constitution*, 423 and Didier Thirion, *La Pierre Angulaire de l'Édifice Constitutionnel* (AP, t. LXVII (June 24, 1793)), Article 1.

[12] Chabot, *Projet d'Acte Constitutif*, *Des droits politiques*, Articles 2 and 6.

general will cannot be represented.[13] The common notion is that sovereignty belongs to the people. I will tackle the sovereignty problem in this chapter's second half, but two of the revolutionaries go a little more into detail when discussing representation: Merry and Oswald.

Merry takes his country of origin, England, as an example to illustrate the danger of submitting the protection of a nation's freedom to a representative body such as the Legislature. The only solution was to keep the general will in permanent activity: "a permanent state of popular deliberation."[14]

According to Merry, the problem of representation is that of how the will is formed. As the people are the only holders of sovereignty, representation is not possible. Only the whole can govern itself:

> it is certain that no man can delegate to another the right to think for himself; therefore, it is impossible for a nation to be free unless all individuals who make the nation keep the right to think for themselves; unless the whole is governed by the whole.[15]

The absence of representation does not mean the absence of public officials. Merry proposes an elected Executive council and even representatives, but the latter are seen as officials bound to the will of the people.[16]

Robespierre's quote presented in the closing section of the last chapter expresses the same idea. The word "representative" is inadequate because the will cannot be represented. The members of the Legislature are granted mandates, but they do not represent the people.

The quarrel over names makes a brief appearance during the constituent debates. When discussing article 21 of the Declaration, Charlier suggests the use of the word "delegates" instead of "representatives," and he is seconded by Danton, who claims "there are thousands of ways to preserve liberty without appealing to a representative government."[17]

The position adopted in the final text is the one defended by Buzot and Garran-Coulon. The former asserts that the will that is being expressed is

[13] Respectively Bourgois, *Plan de Constitution*, II, Article 6 and Ruault, *Projet de Constitution*, II, Articles 1 and 2 and 29.

[14] Merry, *Réflexions Politiques*, 7.

[15] Merry, *Réflexions Politiques*, 8.

[16] As we saw in the last chapter, for Merry, the "representatives" can only present decrees by way of the popular assemblies (Merry, *Réflexions Politiques*, 7).

[17] AP, t. LXIII, 108.

the will of the representative and not that of the people. The representatives are distinguished from other public officials in that they have a will of their own and are not limited to acting in accordance with the law. Garran-Coulon describes the distinction between a delegate and a representative by the following words: "a delegate is only the bearer of an expressed will, while the representative expresses the will."[18]

There seems to be no middle ground or reconciliation between these two positions. However, we should keep in mind that these revolutionaries are not claiming that the people are deprived of will. This is not the case of a full delegation of the Legislative power to the Legislative body. What is at stake is the nature of the Legislature's role and, therefore, what is meant by "people" and "sovereignty."

Buzot and Garran-Coulon's opinion is also expressed by Boissel. The latter states that "all the powers reside essentially in the people, but the people declares that it cannot exercise these powers if not through delegation."[19] Boissel's example is especially interesting since we have seen how his institutional design proposition is closer to a democratic radicalization, even though his take on representation seems to be closer to a restrictive notion of popular sovereignty. Fluidity and amalgamation of positions are common traits among the drafts. This can make a broader analysis harder, but not impossible.

John Oswald, a Scottish revolutionary who joined the Jacobin Club, presents a similarly critical view of the issue of representation. He claims that if the nation can deliberate by delegation, then it may also decide by delegation and the people's sovereignty would become "a vote to choose its masters."[20] In the last chapter, we have seen the centrality of the primary assemblies to Oswald's proposals. The justification of his position and its relation to the representational problem is thus expressed:

> Were a man to seriously propose that the nation should piss by proxy, he would doubtless be regarded as a madman; and yet to think by proxy is a proposition which we hear not only without astonishment but even with approbation. (…) it is by the habit of delegating to others the task of thinking for us that we insensibly unlearn to think altogether.[21]

[18] AP, t. LXIII, 109.
[19] Boissy d'Anglais, *Constitution*, III, Article 2.
[20] Oswald, *The Government of the People*, 5.
[21] Oswald, *The Government of the People*, 5.

A similar notion, albeit in less eloquent prose, appears in Varlet—the only one to explicitly propose an imperative mandate, as we saw in the preceding chapter. To the French revolutionaries, representation was the hallmark of monarchy. In a Republic, the delegates must be subordinated. They are only to collect the voices of their constituents because it is from the latter that the general will is born.[22]

The general tone of Oswald and Varlet is fundamentally the same as that of Merry. The government of the many (or of the people, in Oswald's words) implies the permanent mobilization of the people and the constant exercise of sovereignty through direct deliberation by the people. That is why it is understandable that other revolutionaries expressed some concern in this regard, as this notion seems to imply that the primary assemblies would be gathered at all times, thus removing, at least potentially, men and women from their work or homes.

However, there is no direct connection between having a large number of assembly meetings and rejecting the notion of representation. Merry, for example, proposed the decrees to be voted only once a year.[23] Oswald and Varlet do not define how often the primary assemblies should meet, but is not hard to understand that the popular mindset proposed here is rather a political and epistemological stance on how the will is formed than a requirement for a given number of in-person meetings.

This relationship with representation should not be confused with the dichotomy lying within the notion of the Republic. For Debbash, founding a Republic in 1793 could mean two different things. On the one hand, in a position he ascribes to Condorcet, it means "installing the institutions of liberty and equality [...] the establishment of a Republic coincides with that of a constitution."[24] Therefore, enacting the constitution would put an end to factionalism. On the other hand, we had the position adopted by Robespierre and others, to whom it was not possible to found a Republic before putting an end to the conflicting factions: "Liberty would be the fruit of this new society and not its author. It is the rejection of that political foundation of freedom."[25]

[22] Jean-François Varlet, *Déclaration Solennelle des Droits de l'Homme dans l'État Social*, http://gallica.bnf.fr/ark:/12148/bpt6k6699x, 267.

[23] Merry, *Réflexions Politiques*, 8.

[24] Roland Debbbash, "L'Accusation de Fédéralisme dans le Processus Politique de 1793," in *La Constitution du 24 Juin 1793*, coord. Naudin-Patriat, 68.

[25] Debbash in *La Constitution du 24 Juin 1793*, coord. Naudin-Patriat, 71.

This dichotomy posited by Debbash is not without its problems. Before examining it further, it is important to point out that the proposed distinction helps us better understand the nature of representation as discussed in the drafts. Adopting Debbash's distinction between legalism and virtue, it is not possible to equate the former, the idea of the Republic as institutionalization, with a defense of representation. Saint-Just, for instance, considers representation a centerpiece of his proposed Republic, and, at the same time, his draft is one of the few where virtue plays a major role. Representation assumes a moral and institutional dimension only as a derivation. This does not mean that representation can be understood in the other drafts as completely deprived of moral value, but we cannot understand it either simply as an attempt to placate the sovereign in permanent activity.

Conversely, the division Debbash tries to establish between freedom grounded in politics and the moralism of virtue seems anachronistic, as the importance of unity is not only stressed by the Jacobins. On the contrary, the unity of the Republic is one of the few features that are common to (almost) all proposals.[26] The sole exception is Anonymous F, who claims that the republican spirit is characterized by division. The Republic would thus be doomed to have two opposing factions, while unity would be an object of affection solely for the *royaliste*.[27] As we have seen above, some isolated defenses of monarchy are found in the drafts, but the dominant tone is that of the unity of the Republic.

As for the other issue, considerations over law and politics are filled with moral connotations for the revolutionaries. Even if we consider Robespierre somewhat distinct in this regard, this position cannot be ascribed only to a restricted group of Jacobin revolutionaries. The idea that freedom would be an effect of society and not its prerequisite is evidently contrary to Robespierre's take on natural law. His defense of the Declaration as a prior and necessary path to any Constitution demonstrates that freedom, equality, and reciprocity are starting points in

[26] Comité de Constitution, *Projet de Constitution*, I, Article 1; Comité de Salut Public, *Projet de Constitution*, I, Article 1; *Constitution*, I, Article 1; Bacon-Tacon, *Plan Patriotique*, I, Article 1; Barailon, *Projet de Constitution*, I.1, Article 3; Bourgois, *Plan de Constitution*, II.I, Article 1; Ruault, *Projet de Constitution*, 34; and Durand-Maillane, *Examen Critique du Projet de Constitution* (AP, t. LXII (April 17, 1793)), I. Article 2).

[27] Anonymous F, *La France Déchirée par ses Enfants, sa Plainte au Tribunal du Genre Humain et Autres Textes [Imprimé A Londres]*, Archives Nationales, Series AD/XVIIIC/262, n. 19, 53–54.

constituting a society and government. They are not something to be achieved only after institutions are already put in place.

Robespierre's rejection of representation is not, therefore, a rejection of institutionalization *per se*. None of these revolutionaries proposed a pure or absolute democracy, as they called it. The impossibility of representing the will does not suppress the practical difficulties of organizing a country with the size of France. On this topic, there seems to be no disagreement among the revolutionaries. The territorial extension and the populational size hindered any classical type of democracy.

Will and unity go together in the drafts' descriptions of the Republic. According to Durand-Maillane, "the economy of your republican institutions should rest entirely on the citizens' attachment to their homeland and to the laws."[28] Only in Anonymous O can we find an interpretation of the will that is close to the opinion in regard to the Republic that Debbash ascribes to Condorcet. The unnamed revolutionary states that individuals are to leave their particular interests aside for the common cause, which is the Law and the Constitution.[29]

The issue of the equation of particular and general interests also shows up during the debates over the Declaration. One of the few instances where the topic is directly addressed, in the discussion of article 19, dealt with the forfeiture of property by an act of government. I am not discussing here the revolutionaries' view on property, but the exchange between Mallarmé and Thirion helps us understand the link between private and general interest.

The debate centers around the notion of "necessity." After Dupont's suggestion to replace it with "utility," Mallarmé defends the initial choice of words, because, on the contrary, "at every moment our property would be claimed under the pretext of public utility."[30] Thirion responds by claiming that Mallarmé is mixing private interest with general interest because in all cases the latter must prevail. For Thirion, "all property is protected under the law, but we should not forget that it emanates from the social pact."[31]

[28] Durand-Maillane, *Examen Critique du Projet de Constitution*, 376.

[29] Anonymous O [Par Cosmopolite], *Discours Fraternel et Instructions*, 18. Below in this chapter, we will see that the very idea of adherence to the law and legalism, or legiscentrism, to use Gauchet and Jaume's wording, can be understood in different ways, including against these authors' thesis that legiscentrism and abstraction go hand in hand.

[30] AP, t. LXIII, 117.

[31] AP, LXt. VIII, 117.

Thirion's opinion is not necessarily shared among the revolutionaries as a whole—Ducos retorts that property is a sacred right of man, as are equality and freedom[32]—and this contrast points to the issue of how to think about the general will.

The expression "general will" does not appear in Mallarmé, Thirion, or Ducos. In fact, the expression is almost absent from the constituent debates, at least in a straightforward formulation. One of few exceptions is on April 26, one of the first days in which the Convention debated the Declaration. In a long speech by Michel-Edme Petit, the revolutionary talks about the role of the general will in then-contemporary France as "giving to each one necessarily the love for the republican government."[33] Michel-Edme was discussing the need to include duties in the Declaration, but more important than his proposal is his justification highlighting the intrinsic reciprocity of natural rights: "our rights are always born from the duties others have in relation to us."[34]

The debate between Mallermé and Thirion seems to indicate that the general will works differently if the rights in question are natural rights or rights deriving from the social pact. The general will act as a mediator and regulator between private and general interests. But this does not solve one important issue—that of the extent of the general will itself.

In most cases, we see the idea defended by Thirion that the relationship between private interest and general interest is applied to the general will. For example, Montgilbert claims that "it is always the club of the general will that knocks down private resistances."[35] However, this should not be read as merely subjecting the individual citizen to an abstract general will. The consequence of this realization, according to Montgilbert, is that the citizens should fight not only for their own rights but also for the rights of other members of society.

[32] AP, LXt. VIII, 117.

[33] AP, LXt. VIII, 407.

[34] AP, LXt. VIII, 407. A similar idea appears in Anonymous A's draft. The author speaks of how the influence of general interest on private interests depends on the citizens' reflection, which leads to the perception that men are connected to the general interest by their properties and commerce (*Anonymous A, Réfléxions sur les Bases d'une Constitution*, 15). Prior cognition and reflection make citizens realize their interdependence in relation to each other and to the whole. This is facilitated and promoted by the action of the general will.

[35] Montgilbert, *Avis au Peuple*, 330. See also Barailon, who states that the particular should be sacrificed in benefit of the will of the majority (Barailon, *Projet de Constitution*, I, Article 6).

The general will is a uniting factor. It does not imply erasing the individual will, as the Analysis Committee highlights when declaring that "every citizen, from one or the other sex, has a will that is free and independent from the general will in everything that does not concern the interest of the others or the public interest."[36]

Neither the will of the individual citizen nor the will of the people itself is alienated. According to Bonnemain, the sovereign's interest is its own preservation. This justifies the need for an absolute authority but it does not imply the alienation of the will.[37] The general will structures society and, at the same time, it is structured by it. The general will depends on the institution of the social contract to emerge and to make itself manifest. If the law is the act of the general will *par excellence*, the social contract is the condition of possibility for it to manifest itself and, at the same time, the main path through which its form and limits are established.

I have examined here one of the main points of contention among the drafts. Bacon-Tacon claims that rights are only a convention and not the result of natural faculties.[38] The social contract thus creates society and rights. In this case, as the general will is the main outcome of such an act, one may argue for a boundless general will, since no prior rights exist.

But even this negating stance on rights as the basis for the social contract is more complex than that. Barailon states that no arrangement stemming from the state of nature is binding except for physical needs and preservation. Rights are not the foundation for the pact, but they aren't either a simple product that is freely created by the parties: rights are the result of the relationships between the individuals and their consequences. Therefore, even when negating natural rights, the general will is shaped by a social proto-structure that is not the result but the boundary for its own action.[39]

This interdependence also shows up in Barlow's text. According to the US-born Barlow, the social contract aims to guarantee the exercise of a

[36] Comité de Analyse, *Projet du Comité de l'Analyse ou Commission des Six* (AP, t. LXII (April 17, 1793)), II, Article 2.

[37] Bonnemain, *Instituts Républicains*, 10.

[38] Bacon-Tacon, *Plan Patriotique*, 3.

[39] Barailon, *Projet de Constitution*, II, Articles 2, 3, and 10. This position appears in other revolutionaries' texts. Blaviel, for example, claims that men have rights only insofar as the pact grants them so. Therefore, the principles of the social contract should not be in the Declaration, as the latter comes after the former (Antoine-Innocent Blaviel, *Opinion* (AP, t. LXII (April 17, 1793)), 287).

certain kind of equality and a specific kind of liberty. The former consists in equally enjoying the fruition of all kinds of rights in so far as they are in accordance with the good order, industry, and reward for due merit. The latter means each individual's independence in relation to the others and, at the same time, the greatest possible dependence in relation to the whole community.[40]

This way of thinking about the general will and the social contract takes different shapes as the revolutionaries fully embrace the philosophy of natural law. Boissel, for instance, tries to define the relationship between the natural constitution and the moral and political constitution of a people:

> We shall understand the natural Constitution of a people as nothing other than its way of existing within the natural or physical order; that, in this sense, the natural Constitution of a nation is nothing other than the qualities its population and its territory have by nature. (...) We shall understand the moral and political Constitution of a people as nothing other than its way of existing within the moral and political order to which it is subjected.[41]

The issue of the basis for the social contract is entangled with the different positions on the primacy, or absence of primacy, of rights in face of the constitution of society, even though the revolutionaries themselves did not necessarily discuss the two at the same time. Those who, like Boissel, defend the existence of some kind of prior normativity to the creation of society tend to place natural rights as the starting point for the Declaration and, therefore, for the social pact. This opinion is not limited to the Jacobins. Boissy d'Anglas, for example, asserts that the purpose of association is preserving and guaranteeing previous and inalienable rights. Only the general good and the preservation of other people's rights serve as a limitation to one's rights. In this case, natural rights serve as a limit to regulation.[42]

To some revolutionaries, however, the mere acknowledgment and declaration of the existence of natural rights were not enough to constitute a

[40] Barlow, *Lettre a la Convention Nationale*, 291.

[41] Boissel, *Les Entretiens du Père Gérard*, 625.

[42] Boissy d'Anglas, *Déclaration des Droits de l'Homme*, Article 6. In a similar vein, Beaulieu says that natural rights derive from natural needs (Beaulieu, *Nouvelle Rédaction*, Article 1). According to Daunou, they admit no oppression, restriction, or exception (Daunou, *Essai sur la Constitution*.1, Article 11).

society. France was under a process of refounding. This meant establishing a new and explicit social contract that broke with the previous regime of oppression. That is what we see, for example, in Bancal. According to him, men had three possible states: the state of nature (in relation to which we could only speculate, as all the peoples found by travelers were already beyond such a state); against nature (the state previously found in France and characterized by the great revolution against oppression and the violation of the laws of nature); and the civil state. In light of this, Bancal presents his bases for the social contract: the desires of the soul and the body, striving for their conservation and improvement; and considering that there are no rights without duties since both are common and reciprocal.[43]

Something similar is to be found in Isnard. When talking about the need for a social pact intermediating the relationship between the declaration and the constitution, he defends "an authentic and reciprocal contract (…) tracing the limits that the future law and will of the society won't be allowed to cross."[44] Through this act, society was to be created.

The two propositions are distinct, but they present an important common element: the need for some kind of intermediary between the written and formal Constitution of the French nation and its constitution as a society, or societal constitution. In both cases, natural rights appear as the structuring element for such intermediation. Isnard is explicit in claiming that this social pact would be the guarantee for natural rights.[45]

The idea of making the social contract explicit has a few consequences and conditions. Isnard asserts that the social pact requires the unanimous consent of all its articles. Durand-Maillane states that every citizen has the right to withdraw from society and return to the first natural rights—which also meant society would no longer be required to offer any social guarantee to this citizen.[46] For Ruault, the social pact had equality as its fundamental principle and the conservation of rights as its purpose, and it

[43] Bancal, *Du Nouvel Ordre Social*, 409–410 and 415.

[44] Henri-Maximin Isnard, *Discours et Présentation* (AP, t. LXIV (May 10, 1793)), 418.

[45] Isnard, *Discours et Présentation*, 419.

[46] Durand-Maillane, *Examen Critique du Projet de Constitution, Droit civils et politiques du citoyen ou de l'homme en société*, Article 9.

required a unanimous and periodical consent.[47] Such a pact was to ground all laws: "this social pact of humankind, as applied to the French nation."[48]

However, if we examine Ruault's pact, we can find an important difference in comparison with Bancal's bases or Isnard's pact. Ruault's text is a declaration of rights, albeit under a different name.[49] This terminological and conceptual fluidity can be interpreted as signaling the revolutionaries' efforts to come to terms with a reality still under construction that went beyond their contemporary intellectual framework. This issue of the moment when a social contract "happens" illustrates such difficulty.

Only Isnard appears to propose an actual social contract. Even those who speak of the conditions for a social pact (as Jollivet, who stresses the importance of mutual aid in the preservation of life, does)[50] do not require a concrete moment of adherence. We can reasonably interpret this as an extension of an implicit acceptance. However, it seems more fruitful to go back to Boissel's idea of connecting the natural, and the moral and political constitutions that were prior to the establishment of a formalized government.

The same notion appears in other texts. One of the first is Cloot's contribution. He speaks of a primitive contract uniting all men: "this eternal condition is the only stamp of sovereignty."[51] However, the universalistic philosophical approach assumed by Cloots distinguishes this idea of a primitive contract from other pacts since it does not depend on the mutual recognition of its adherents as members of the same society.

We can find at least two other revolutionaries who express a position similar to Boissel's: Coupé and Saint-Just. According to Coupé, the political constitution is an exterior regime aiming to organize a large gathering of men, but before it, "the intimate sense of their rights, of reason, of eternal rectitude; and of that physical and moral constitution, superior to

[47] Ruault, *Projet de Constitution*, 1–2. Isnard also states that the social pact needs unanimous approval for all its Articles, but he does not talk of periodic renewal. The revolutionary himself, however, admits to consent through lack of explicit protest. Silence would be proof of adherence.

[48] Ruault, *Projet de Constitution*, 6.

[49] Ollivier brings us a list of other authors who presented a similar position, thus equating the Declaration with the social pact (Ollivier, *Les Projets Constitutionnels de 1793*, 138).

[50] Jean-Baptiste-Moïse Jollivet, *Principes Fondamentaux du Régime Social Comparés avec le Plan de Constitution* (AP, t. LXI (April 12, 1793)), 647.

[51] Cloots, *Bases Constitutionnelles*, 390.

all political institutions" already existed.[52] Saint-Just speaks of a social state (defined as the relationship among men) prior to the political order. This state would not be spontaneously abandoned by men, but only, as in Bancal, "through a long alteration do they arrive at this polite savagery invented by tyrants."[53]

The constitution is understood, in those texts, as something that goes beyond the organization of government. Ollivier highlights the word's polysemy but gives special emphasis to two meanings: as a synonym for government; as the organization of constituted authorities.[54] For Boissel, Coupé, and Saint-Just, the idea of a constitution seems to point to a third direction: the form of the organization of men before the creation of a formalized government. This is a constitution that is prior to both meanings stressed by Ollivier.

Seconds declares that man is necessary to man and society is prior to all conventions, since it was in man's nature. However, there is an important distinction in comparison to the other revolutionaries. According to Seconds, this meant that reason was the basis for a political society and not will. In other words, there was no contract. The result is an apparent theory of the legitimacy of government since its authority was a natural need as well. Political society and government were both the products of nature.[55]

But Seconds seems to be somewhat isolated in this regard. By removing the will from the act that establishes an organized society under a government, Seconds removes the natural freedom men have to transform themselves into citizens through their mutual accord. The dividing line, as we have repeatedly seen, is not that clear.

Boissel, Coupé, and Saint-Just expressly declare the existence of a natural constitution and a moral constitution, both prior to its organization by law. Both these constitutions would pose limits to the political society to come. As in Seconds, the transition to the political state appears to be a natural development. But, for the three revolutionaries, the expressed will of man is a structuring condition in the formation of the political society.

[52] Coupé, *Idée Simples de Constitution*, 270.

[53] Saint-Just, *Projet de Constitution*, 200.

[54] Ollivier, *Les Projets Constitutionnels de 1793*, 132.

[55] Jean-Louis Seconds, *De l'Art Social ou des Vrais Principes de la Société Politique* (AP, t. LVI (January 7, 1793)), 579–581.

The seemingly natural aspect of the transition does not do away with the need for its members to be present and to express their will.

Reason alone is not enough, as Seconds defends. Different constitutions are mutually conditioned, but they are not mutually exhaustive. The natural constitution acts upon the moral constitution, but it does not fully determine it. Both act upon the constitution of the political society, but they do not fully determine it either. The social contract establishing the political society is not fictional, it is an act of will, even if it is informed by reason and by prior constitutions.

There is a similarity here with the proposals of Ruault, Bancal, and Isnard. In all these cases, there is something prior to the establishment of the constitution, and this is understood as the document that organizes the government. However, while for these three, this "something prior" is the social contract itself, for Saint-Just, Boissel, and Coupé, it is another constitution (natural and/or moral) that is prior to that constitution. We must be careful not to define the latter as a political constitution in contrast to the former since the preceding state is already a social state and not the state of nature.

According to Ollivier, Saint-Just's opinion is better interpreted as a rejection of the very idea of a social contract. The author understands, following Gueiniffey and Jaume, that Saint-Just and Robespierre share a refusal in accepting Rousseau's social contract theory while embracing his hypothesis of the natural goodness of man.[56] Ollivier claims that the social contract would be an instrument of submission in their view.[57]

In my view, however, Ollivier's reading does not seem to be the most appropriate interpretation of the available material. Maybe stemming from the fact that the author's reading is based on two authors whose take on the Jacobin revolutionaries is not exactly sympathetic (as I will address when analyzing Jaume's position further below), her reading is based on the idea that the revolutionaries had Rousseau's work as a model to which they compared themselves. In rejecting the social contract as presented by the Genevan philosopher, they rejected the very idea of a social contract. I have already criticized such an approach to the revolutionary sources.

[56] More precisely, she cites Patrice Gueniffey's 1997 text *La "Grande Terreur". La formation et la chute d'une dictature idéologique* and Jaume's *L'État Jacobin et le Constitutionnalisme en Procès*. Ollivier's position is not very clear in regard to Robespierre, but I think the generalization holds, considering other instances where she analyzes Robespierre and her inspirations for this passage.

[57] Ollivier, *Les Projets Constitutionnels de 1793*, 146–147.

This is not to deny the influence of Rousseau, Montesquieu, and other thinkers, but to point out that we should not believe the revolutionaries were trying to directly apply their political theories to the French reality.

If that is the case, what social contract exactly is to be understood when reading proposals such as those of Saint-Just, Coupé, Robespierre, and Boissel? One way to answer this is to analyze another instance in which the relationship between reason and will is also questioned: that of the law, as it is the main new tool made possible by the establishment of the social contract, that is, of the politically structured society.

Before examining how the drafts treat the subject, it is important to briefly go back to a notion presented in the first chapter—that of legiscentrism, as named by Jaume, that is very close to the way Gauchet interprets the French Revolution's philosophy of law.

In Jaume's interpretation, legiscentrism has characterized the originality of the French conception of human rights since the 1789 debates. The centrality of the law in France contrasts with the US or Anglo-Saxon models. While the latter two guaranteed individual rights, through the action of a judge or through the idea of due process, respectively, in France, the law itself was the guarantor of individual rights. Jaume's reading stems from his conception of citizenship during the revolutionary period. I will tackle the topic directly later in this chapter. For now, it is sufficient to point out that, for Jaume, 1789 innovates by putting the citizen as an element of the nation, from which civic rights derived. At the same time, the Declaration did not define the boundary between man and citizen, allowing for the progressive expansion of the space reserved for citizenship to the detriment of individual rights.[58]

Gauchet presents a similar vision when he states that the notion of natural rights advanced by the revolutionaries created the implicit risk of individual rights being assimilated by the sharing of social power.[59] Law would be the only arbiter between coexistence and freedom, defining their limits and transgression: "the guarantee of rights is under threat by their pure and simple absorption by the sphere of law."[60]

From what I have presented so far, it should already be possible to see Jaume and Gauchet's reading as selective. Their interpretation seems to be an extrapolation from the contribution of only a few revolutionaries. For

[58] Jaume, Les déclarations des droits de l'homme, 55–58.

[59] Gauchet, *La Révolution des Droits de l'Homme*, 78.

[60] Gauchet, *La Révolution des Droits de l'Homme*, 120.

example, Mont-Réal claims that the government is a tool to preserve the social contract and Montgilbert states that only a popular government is legitimate, that is, the government where the people is the only sovereign, obeying its own laws and recognizing only its own authority.[61] If we limit our interpretation to this kind of manifestation, we may be led to believe that Jaume and Gauchet's position holds, but only at the expense of leaving aside a large portion of the revolutionary *corpus*.

There are two interdependent problems in the legiscentrism hypothesis: the relationship between the government, the sovereign, and the law; and the notion of law itself. On the first issue, legiscentrism presupposes a government and representatives standing above the citizens, since the reunion of the latter would form the abstract people or nation that manifested itself only through the former two. This vision does seem to be shared among the revolutionaries.

Schreiber states that the main duty of those who govern a State is to put into practice the respect of natural law all across the State.[62] Robespierre affirms that "this undeniable maxim that the people is good, and that its delegates are corruptible; that is in virtue and in people's sovereignty that we should look for a safeguard against the vices and the despotism of government."[63] In other words, the preservation and guarantee of natural rights rest, ultimately, not in the government, but in the people. It does not lie in law, but in popular sovereignty, since the term "delegates," as used by Robespierre, includes the Legislature.[64]

This interpretation also derives from the analyses, developed in the previous chapters, on the formation of law and popular control over governmental activities. We have seen that there were indeed those who defended a government that operated more independently from and above the popular will, but that was neither the only nor the prevalent view present

[61] Respectively, Mont-Réal, *Projet de Constitution*, *Exécution du contrat social du gouvernement*, Article 1 and Montgilbert, *Suite de l'Avis au Peuple*, 341.

[62] Jacques Schreiber, *Exposé des Principes sur l'Instruction Publique de la Jeunesse pour Consolider leurs Amês a l'Amour de Dieu, a la Vertu et aux Bonnes Mœurs, et de Former au bon Citoyen de la République du Genre Humain* (Archives Nationales, F/17/1001, n. 83bis), 139.

[63] AP, LXIV:430.

[64] This does not mean that the Legislature is the main enemy of the people. We have seen in the previous chapters on external relations and on the Executive how Robespierre sees the latter as the main foe and as a risk to the people's freedom. However, to identify this part of the governmental apparatus as the main source of concern and an object of control does not preclude Robespierre's general distrust in relation to all those who hold delegated powers.

among the proposals. If a legiscentrism as defined by Jaume and Gauchet is to be found in 1793, it is a philosophy of law of minor expression in comparison to the defense of popular sovereignty against governmental arbitrariness.

Furthermore, there is a second point that ties this matter to the problem of law: Jaume and Gauchet's emphasis on individual rights. According to Gauthier, "the politics of natural right is that of the reciprocity of law."[65] There is a necessary intersubjective dimension to natural rights such as freedom, equality, and resistance to oppression. For Gauthier, these are all complemented by citizenship. In a similar vein, Bosc states that "the words liberty-equality-fraternity do not constitute separate stages or unconnected and juxtaposed times [...] the three terms say the same thing under three forms."[66]

Jaume and Gauchet seem to read this interdependence as a subordination of individual rights to an abstract people. But the category of individual rights is not so easily applied to the revolutionary context. This difficulty does not stem from their subsumption to an abstract law but is due to the intersubjective aspect of each and every natural right by way of fraternity and reciprocity. We have already seen this at play in the chapter on external relations, especially in Robespierre's opposition to the war by grounding his position on precisely those two elements of natural rights, which does not seem to fit into the legiscentrism hypothesis.

Going back to Mont-Réal's text, which characterized the government as the way of preserving the contract, we can see that he had defined the law as resulting from the rights and duties of man. It was then the expression of a presumed will that, if unjust, would lose its character of law, turning this expression into oppression and having as its response the general duty to resist.[67]

[65] Gauthier, *Triomphe et Mort*, 41.

[66] Yannick Bosc, "Sur le principe de fraternité," Révolution Française.net, last modified January 19, 2010, https://revolution-francaise.net/2010/01/19/359-sur-le-principe-de-fraternite.

[67] Mont-Réal, *Projet de Constitution*, *Des droits de l'homme en société ou du citoyen*, Articles 1 and 11. For other similar cases, see Ducastellier or Coupé. The former describes the law as a pact, a social contract, therefore, if unjust, it would be void (Ducastellier, *Le Drapeau de l'Indépendance*, 246). Coupé highlights the reciprocity of rights and duties and this can be interpreted as the constitutive reciprocity of the law intermingled with the constitutive reciprocity of natural rights (Coupé, *Idée Simples de Constitution*, *Droits de l'homme*, Article 5).

This characterization of the law as the free and solemn expression of the general will, as the final text of the 1793 Declaration reads,[68] does not limit the interpretative frameworks present in the debates and preparatory drafts. In a related topic, Sophie Wahnich presents an interesting interpretation of what she calls a civil religion of the rights of man and citizen.[69]

Wahnich starts by identifying a certain kind of historiography which defends that the French Revolution operates "a simple change in *imago*, where abstract law replaces the figure of the king."[70] This is Gauchet's interpretation, for whom, in the pre-revolutionary model, "the kingdom was, in this sense, symbolically identified with the King. The King concentrated the nation in himself."[71] The French Revolution was then responsible for promoting a symbolic transformation through which the Nation is no longer the king but takes his place: "the representatives become the visible, fallible and mortal body of the invisible and perpetual body of the Nation, a mystical person having no voice and no hands but that of the elected, who lend it a tangible figure."[72] Even though Gauchet privileges the beginning of the Revolution in his analysis (here, specifically, he is discussing a 1789 writing by Sieyès), he intends for his reading to encompass all the revolutionary period.

Wahnich sums up the problem with this position in the following way: "such an affirmation leads us to renounce the idea that the Revolutionaries understood that which they loved and defended."[73] In other words, it presupposes that the acceptance of the supremacy of law meant, for the revolutionaries, uncritical adherence to the cold and simple legality of the enacted laws. Considering the role played by natural law in their thinking, this reading only makes sense in two scenarios: if natural law is subordinated to or subsumed by legislated law; or if legislated law is necessarily equal to natural law.

Neither of those two hypotheses is embraced by the revolutionaries. Something close to the first idea can be found in those few authors who

[68] *Declaration*, Article 4.

[69] Bosc gives us a similar reading, albeit focused on Robespierre's contributions more specifically (Yannick Bosc, "Robespierre et l'Amour des Lois," *Jus Politicum* 10 (2013)).

[70] Sophie Wahnich, "Une Religion Civile des Droits de l'Homme et du Citoyen en 1792," in *Républicanismes et Droit Naturel: Des Humanistes aux Révolutions des Droits de l'Homme et du Citoyen*, ed. Marc Belissa, Yannick Bosc, Florence Gauthier (Paris: Kimé, 2009), 73.

[71] Gauchet, *La Révolution des Droits de l'Homme*, 24.

[72] Gauchet, *La Révolution des Droits de l'Homme*, 26.

[73] Wahnick, 'Une religion civile', 73.

deny the existence of natural rights. But, as we have already seen, at this point in the Revolution they are very few in number.[74]

Other revolutionaries come close to denial of natural rights but cannot be considered exactly as defending said position. For instance, Carnot claims that the Declaration is a declaration of the rights of man in society, since in the state of nature the rights are undefined and, at most times, illusory.[75] But elusiveness is not the same as non-existence and this illusory aspect can reasonably be interpreted as the inherent insecurity of the state of nature, instead of meaning that these illusory rights are false rights. This reading seems to be reinforced by Carnot's statement that the goal of the association of men is not to restrict rights but to enhance them.

Wahnich analyzes the opinions of revolutionaries in relation to the 1791 Constitution—considering the fact they upheld the censitary suffrage, in opposition to the Declaration of 1789, which affirmed equality among citizens. Two main answers were put forward. The first, represented by Isnard's position, was that of a "religion of patriotism" understood as the religion of law and equality, and prohibiting the critique of the enacted constitution. The other was expressed by Robespierre. To him, the Constituent Assembly had indeed violated the principles of justice and reason proclaimed by the Declaration of 1789 by maintaining a divided citizenship regime. This realization, however, did not remove the need to defend the constitution against the Executive, the factions, and, more broadly, those who claimed it to be unenforceable.

> For Robespierre, the Constitution is the political tool that, once inscribed in history, permits men to act in history. Contrary to Isnard, he does not take the letter of the Constitution to be a sacred object, but a historical and perishable object of political and civil life, while the spirit of its principles are atemporal and sacred.[76]

Wahnich exemplifies these two different notions of love for the law by way of the Simoneau episode. To briefly summarize the affair, Jacques Guillaume Simoneau owned a leather tanning factory and was mayor of Étampes. Because of the depreciation in the *assignats*, the price of essential

[74] I can cite Lasource's speech during the April 17, 1793, session of the National Convention, but the claim is quickly refuted by the other deputies (AP, LXII:280).

[75] Lazare-Nicolas-Marguerite Carnot, *Déclaration des Droits de l'Homme* (AP, t. LXII (April 17, 1793)).

[76] Wahnick, 'Une Religion Civile', 78.

products was rising more rapidly than the wages. On March 3, 1792, a group of people announced that they were going to Étampes to impose the taxation of butter. Simoneau refused to impose a limit on the price of butter and bread, and he was killed by the insurgents.[77] Simoneau is praised as a martyr who defended the law.

Wahnich poses the following question: "Is a martyr of law a martyr of principles or a martyr of the adopted public policies?"[78] The question poses two different ways to interpret the notion of law, or, in other words, the term "law" may designate two very distinct things: defending the law as a defense of the free exchange of grain or defending the law as a defense of taxation and as a limit and rejection of domination.

> Freedom and its definition are, therefore, that which allows for the distinction between laws. The only freedom accepted by the taxcollectors is one that does not harm the others and one that acknowledges the reciprocity of limits [...] The only freedoms that are valid to the law of the market are those of the absence of regulatory constraints to pricing, as well as the free exchange of goods, putting human lives at risk and, therefore, the sacrality of life itself. [...] this is the freedom to dominate.[79]

It is in this sense that we can interpret opinions such as that of Bourgois, who claims that the purpose of all law is to preserve rights and that sovereignty only acts through the law. Or Varlet, for whom the purpose of the law is upholding the rights of man in the social state.[80]The finality of the law is mixed with that of the government itself. It is the fruition of the natural and imprescriptible rights of man (using the terms used in the Declaration of 1793)[81] or, in Robespierre's words, the happiness of men, which, in turn, demands the preservation of natural rights.[82]

[77]The episode can be reconstructed by a reading of the *Ancien Moniteur* published at the time of the facts (AM, XI:557) and the debates that followed (AM, XI:563, 573, 578), including a letter by the municipality describing the facts (AM, XI:566).

[78]Wahnick, 'Une Religion Civile', 78.

[79]Wahnick, 'Une Religion Civile', 78–79.

[80]Respectively, Bourgois, *Plan de Constitution*, II.IV, Articles 1 and 3 and Varlet, *Déclaration Solennelle*, Article 7.

[81]*Declaration*, Article 1.

[82]Maximilien Marie Isidore de Robespierre, *Discours sur la Nécessité de Commencer la Discussion du Projet de Constitution Présenté par le Comité des Six, par une Discussion Générale sur les Droits de l'Homme et du Citoyen* (AP, t. LXII (April 15, 1793)), 158.

Therefore, Gauchet and Jaume are right in identifying the centrality of law in revolutionary thought, but they are wrong in exactly how to characterize the "law" and the relationship between the enacted law and the citizens, the people, public officials and, above all, with the Legislature.

It is this law of revolutionary republicanism that is expressed in Montgilbert's discussion of the republican constitution:

> The Republic is understood as a society of voluntarily united free men and it does not recognize any authority among men other than that of the laws they gave themselves. [...] A republican Constitution has, therefore, as its purpose bringing men closer to nature, creating in them a pure and enlightened morality by exterminating their prejudices, by making them happy among themselves, and by closely uniting them through the bonds of equality and fraternity.[83]

Or lastly, in Mont-Réal's definition, the Republic is a great family in which each individual is the object of its love and that this love equals virtue.[84]

7.2 The Many and Citizenship

If we have already had a grasp of what the revolutionaries meant when they used the term Republicanism, we still need to understand who is a part of such a Republic and who are the many that govern. The main notion at play is citizenship and the requirements and demands for the exercise of political rights.

To better understand the context of 1793, it is important to know how the previous regime was defined by the Constitution of 1791. Under Title II, articles 2 and 3, we find a definition of the French citizen, and article 6 lists the conditions for losing French citizenship. There were many ways of becoming a French citizen, such as: being born to a French father on French soil; being born outside France, to foreign parents, but establishing residence inside the kingdom, by acquiring a house; marrying a French woman; or establishing a commercial or agricultural business—the latter included the requirement to take a civic oath.[85]

[83] Montgilbert, *Suite de l'Avis au Peuple*, 339–340.

[84] Mont-Réal, *Projet de Constitution, Application du contrat social au peuple français*, Articles 2 and 3.

[85] The other available means to acquire French citizenship were: being born in France to a foreign father, but settling residence in the country; being born outside France to French

Nationality was lost in case of naturalization in a foreign country; being convicted to penalties that included civic degradation, until rehabilitation; being judged *in absentia*, until an annulment; and being part of a chivalric order or foreign corporation that implied proof of nobility.

However, the Constitution of 1791 divided the citizens into two different groups. There were passive citizens and active citizens. Only the latter could legitimately participate in the primary assemblies. To be an active citizen, besides the general requirements of citizenship listed above, article 2 of the section on primary assemblies also required the following: having at least 25 years of age; residing in the village or canton corresponding to that primary assembly; paying a direct contribution equal or greater than three days' worth of work; not being in a state of domesticity; being registered with the national guard; and having taken the civic oath.

7.2.1 Restricted Citizenships

The topic of the requirements for French citizenship acquisition was not debated during the conventional sessions. The chapter "On the state of citizens" was approved with only a minor amendment by Thuriot: changing the verb from "residing" to "domiciled." But if we look into Lanjuinais' report of April 29, 1793, analyzing the conditions for acquiring citizenship and the exercise of rights, we can see that the main points of disagreement were over some of the requirements previously laid down in the Constitution of 1791.[86] Lanjuinais uses the term "active citizen"—something that is repeated only in a small number of proposals,[87] but, even so, there is a fundamental difference in comparison to 1791: the almost unanimous rejection of monetary contribution as a requirement for citizenship.

Lanjuinais declares that voting is a right not only for those who pay taxes, because "it is by virtue of being a person and not by external goods that one is a citizen; it is the person who consents to the social pact; it is

parents and settling in France; or being born to foreign parents, but descending from at least one French person who was been expatriated for religious reasons. The last two also required a civic oath.

[86] AP, t. LXIII, 561–567.

[87] According to Ollivier, only Ragonneau, Barlow, and Rubigny use this term (Ollivier, *Les Projets Constitutionnels de 1793*, 214) and, as we will see, even so, the meaning is not the same as in 1791, and Barlow's inclusion in the list is questionable.

by the person and through the person that society is established."[88] The contribution requirement for exercising citizenship rights had already been harshly criticized by Robespierre in his famous *marc d'argent* speech on January 25, 1790,[89] and had been revoked after the insurrection of August 10, 1792, in the same decree that regulated how the primary assemblies were to be assembled in order to form the National Convention.[90] This decree, however, did not reject the discrimination against domestic workers, and these workers were still formally banned from taking part in political life.

Lanjuinais starts his report by giving a general definition of the citizen as the "member of the city, of the civil society, of the nation."[91] He reinstates the notion of active citizenship as a requirement to vote and be voted, but he does not use the term "passive citizen." Instead, he talks about "citizens in the sense of the most ordinary language,"[92] including all those who exercise civil rights.

In the remaining proposals, when the term "active citizen" is used, it means not being a domestic worker.[93] Ollivier seems to misinterpret Barlow's proposition. According to the researcher, Barlow also excluded domestic workers from active citizenship.[94] Barlow did define the active citizen as the "independent man, every man not placed under the guardianship of another by law, for being a minor or because of one's domesticity." However, as the text continues, Barlow states that "I am, likewise, completely convinced that the Assembly was mistaken in supposing that the state of domesticity must deprive a man of the rights of a free man. It is still a remnant of the ideas of the old regime that inspired it."[95]

[88] AP, t. LXIII, 565.

[89] AP, XI: 320–325. The original title of Robespierre's speech was "On the need to revoke the decrees that bind the exercise of the rights of the citizen to the contribution of a *marc d'argent* or a certain number of work days." *Marc d'argent* could be roughly translated as a silver mark. It was a kind of monetary coin and unit of measure.

[90] Baudoin, ed., *Collection générale des décrets rendus par l'Assemblée nationale* (Paris: Baudouin, 1789–1795), v. 31: 93–97.

[91] AP, t. LXIII, 562.

[92] AP, t. LXIII, 562.

[93] Ragonneau imposed as a condition for active citizenship not being a domestic worker, and added other requirements, such as registration in the national guard, at least 21 years of age and taking a civic oath (Ragonneau, *Plan d'une Nouvelle Constitution*, II, Article 6). Besides him, only Cusset bars domestic workers from voting, but he does not use the term "active citizen" (Cusset, *Projet de Décret sur la Constitution*, II, Article 4).

[94] Ollivier, *Les Projets Constitutionnels de 1793*, 213.

[95] Barlow, *Lettre à la Convention Nationale*, 291.

Barlow then affirms that even considering the argument that domestic workers would vote under the influence of their employers [96] is not without merit, every man is

> absolutely free to adopt any profession, any kind of industry is equally encouraged and rewarded, and particularly as long as all men are well instructed on their duties and rights.[97]

This is the same argument presented by Lanjuinais to refute the ban on the domestic workers' right to vote. The relation of dependence was "voluntary and instantaneous," since, albeit unequal in properties, the domestic workers and their employers "can be [equal] in liberty and in virtue," due to public education. Barlow and Lanjuinais share the same idea, summarized by the latter as: "Every place where the domestic worker is less free than the employer, there is abuse in government."[98]

Domestic workers are workers just like the rest. The secret ballot would have also helped prevent any risks. Outside of this brief discussion, the question of domestic workers did not show up again.[99] But this issue points to one of the two most important elements regarding the notion of citizenship, as presented by the revolutionaries: the citizen's independence from domination by others.[100] We can see this in the discussion over the loss or suspension of citizenship, or the incapacity to vote—the terminology varies among the drafts.

[96] The word used in French is *maître*, which may be translated as "master," considering the Old Regime's heritage that Barlow claims to have tainted the previous Constituent Assembly. However, Barlow precisely indicates that such a moment of subordination had already been overcome, or it was in the process of being overcome. That is why I have translated it as "employer."

[97] Barlow, *Lettre à la Convention Nationale*, 292.

[98] AP, t. LXIII, 565. Lanjuinais makes a direct reference to Barlow's text in a footnote to this passage, reinforcing our reading that Ollivier misinterpreted Barlow by including him with the proponents of barring the access of domestic workers to active citizenship.

[99] Saint-Just claims that the law does not recognize domesticity as a master relation among citizens, but only as "an equal and sacred engagement between the man who works and the man who pays" (Saint-Just, *Projet de Constitution*, I.III, Article 3). Thorillon goes along the same lines, as shown in my previous discussion over the possible influence of employers on their subordinates' votes.

[100] The second central issue is the connection with the French people or nation. This will be analyzed later on when I discuss the demands imposed on foreigners.

The Constitution Committee's proposal, for example, lists attested imbecility as a reason for incapacity to exercise the right to vote.[101] The same interdiction appears in many texts.[102] In his commentaries to the Constitution Committee's draft, Anonymous H lists imbecility or dementia, both to be attested by court,[103] as motives for suspension, instead of loss, of the rights of the citizen. The author explains the rationale behind this rule: the impossibility to exercise that which is required to use reason.[104]

The reasoning is related to the question of dependence raised in the debate on domestic workers. They—for those in favor of not allowing their voting—were prevented from freely exercising their reason because of a relation of dependence and domination. Whereas domestic workers had an external barrier to the use of reason, citizens with dementia had an internal barrier.

The lack of independence in relation to others also shows up when discussing female suffrage. The topic is not presented during the debates, but it is reported by Lanjuinais. According to him, although the committee's draft excludes women from exercising political rights, at least five drafts defended women's suffrage: those of Williams, Moriet, De Grawers, Guyomar, and Romme.[105]

Lanjuinais, however, does not agree with this expansion. Citizenship included both sexes, but active citizenship was barred for women.[106] He claims that then-current customs and vices in education seemed to preclude that possibility for months or years. Furthermore, "women's

[101] Comité de Constitution, *Projet de Constitution*, II, Article 5.

[102] Daunou, Debry, and Lambert also present similar hypotheses (see Daunou, *Essai sur la Constitution*. 2, II.III, Article 4; Debry, *Projet de Déclaration*, Article 2; and Lambert, *Plan de Constitution Républicaine*, II, Article 5), as well as Bourgois, who adds *fureur habituelle ou actuelle* as another motive for suspension (Bourgois, *Plan de Constitution*, I.I, Article 5).

[103] I will not delve into the juridical distinctions between dementia, imbecility, and other mental conditions, as it does not seem to be relevant to our debate.

[104] Anonymous H, *Vœu d'un Citoyen sur la Nouvelle Constitution*, *Acte constitutionnel*, Article 5.

[105] Moriet's and De Grawers' texts could not be located. In the footnote in the *Archive Parlementaire* notes these were handwritten proposals (AP, t. LXIII, 564, note 1, left column).

[106] Although outside the time frame for this book, De Gouges' text should be pointed out one of the most important contributions to this debate, see Olympe de Gouges, *Les Droits de Femme* (Paris: N.p., 1791), http://gallica.bnf.fr/ark:/12148/bpt6k426138.

physique, their destination, their use, alienates them from the exercise of a great number of political rights and duties."[107]

Before examining the debate in depth, I should point out that the debate is restricted to women's participation and vote in the primary assemblies responsible for deliberating on the matters established by constitutional or legal provisions. It was not about barring them from engaging in political life altogether. Gauthier alerts us of the fact that this formal exclusion did not prevent women's participation in political life through popular movements, popular societies, and assembly debates, be it in primary or popular assemblies.[108]

Ollivier analyses women's participation in the assemblies responsible for accepting the Constitution of June 24, 1793. Aberdam expands on the topic and presents the different kinds of primary assemblies (from those limited only to active citizens to more inclusive communitarian assemblies) and how women took part in them. Godineau has a detailed analysis of women's vote outside of the primary assemblies.[109]

Even so, the demand for women's suffrage is somewhat reduced. One notable exception is a speech by a female citizen from the Beaurepaire section. On July 4, 1793, after reading that section's statement on the acceptance of the Constitution of 1793, she declares

> Citizens-legislators, you have given men a Constitution, they now have all the rights of free men, but women are still very far from such heights. They are not taken into account in the political system. We require them from primary assemblies and, as the Constitution is founded on the Rights of men, we demand today their full exercise.[110]

Although this is an exception and placed outside of our previously set time frame, this passage shows the existence of a popular movement for women's voting rights, even if it was a minor mobilization.

[107] AP, t. LXIII, 564.

[108] Gauthier, *Triomphe et Mort*, 185–186.

[109] See: Ollivier, *Les Projets Constitutionnels de 1793*, 222; Serge Aberdam, "Soumettre la Constitution au Peuple," in *La Constitution du 24 Juin 1793*, coord. Naudin-Patriat, 149, and Dominique Godineau, "Privées par notre sexe du droit honorable de donner notre suffrage," last modified March 12, 2008. https://revolution-francaise.net/2008/03/12/215-privees-notre-sexe-droit-honorable-donner-suffrage.

[110] AP, LXt. VIII, 254.

Going back to the 1793 constitutional drafts, we can identify a small portion of proposals that are preoccupied with directly rejecting women's suffrage. Anonymous N and Daunou are two such examples. The former justifies the distinction by appealing to the protection of the weak (even though the author does not present any argument justifying this claim). The latter appeals to Sieyès' position in 1789: women do not have any intrinsic incapacity to vote, but the answer lies in contemporary customs which still prevented such expansion.[111]

Ollivier lists eight projects proposing female suffrage: Barailon, Chabot, Guyomar, Lanthenas, Pénières, Rouzet, Thorillon, and Williams. We can also add Anonymous E, Joubert, Ruault, and the Analysis Committee to reach a total of 12 proposals.[112]

The 12 projects' propositions for women's suffrage, however, are not uniform. Chabot, for example, recognizes the exercise of political rights only to married mothers and limits their right to be elected only for public positions relating to education and social assistance, civil jury, and criminal jury for crimes committed by other women.[113]

The general trend is to restrict women's right to vote. For example, Anonymous E postpones women's right to take part in deliberations until 30 years of age, while men are allowed at 21. Williams recognizes this right only to widows and single women.[114] Joubert's position is less

[111] Respectively, Anonymous N, *Déclaration des Droits et des Devoirs de l'Homme [1792–3 ?]* (Archives Nationales, Series Lb41, n. 2395), 6; and Pierre-Claude-François Daunou, *Vues Rapides sur L'organisation de la République Française* (AP, t. LXII (April 17, 1793)), 346. The opinion mentioned by Daunou is probably from Sieyès' speech on July 21, 1789, one week after the fall of the Bastille. That day, Sieyés summed up the category of passive citizens, including the issue of the *marc d'argent*, by stating that "Women, at least in the current state of affairs, children, foreigners, those that did not contribute anything to the public establishment, should not actively influence public affairs" (AP, t. VIII, 259).

[112] Beffroy de Reigny's text guarantees women's participation in what he calls civic association (Beffroy de Reigny, *La Constitution de la Lune*, 234)—a kind of primary assembly, but with ill-defined powers. However, since he does not directly mention the right to vote, including him in the list did not seem appropriate, considering the standard position was to not grant women voting rights.

[113] Chabot, *Projet d'Acte Constitutif, De la constitution du peuple français*, Article 5.

[114] Respectively: Anonymous E, *Quelques Idées*, Article 13; and Williams, *Observations sur la Dernière Constitution*, 586. See also: Barailon, only to widows (Barailon, *Projet de Constitution*, I, Article 17), and Rouzet, who creates a series of alternatives requirements—for instance, being a mother of citizens with five children or three children up to 14 years of age or 21 years and living with a husband that is also a citizen (Jacques-Marie Rouzet, *Projet de Constitution Française* (AP, t. LXII (April 17, 1793)), Articles 2 and 3).

clear. He accepts the exercise of political rights by women who run their households, because "a political body does not have sex, therefore women, in fact, are part of it," but seems to extend the same requirement for men.[115]

In the other cases, we have an apparently broader expansion of political rights to women. Ruault simply claims that the national body—the one responsible for the acts of political life—is composed of all members of the commune with no distinction of gender. He also expressly states that citizens of any sex can present complaints against a law they deem to be inadequate.[116]

This generic extension is repeated only in the Analysis Committee draft. Or at least its ambiguous language seems to leave room for such interpretation. The text limits itself to affirm that men and women have the right to consent to their belonging to the social body when they come of age, and so become citizens.[117]

In the three remaining cases, Guyomar, Lanthenas, and Thorillon, women have the right to vote, but, albeit the apparently universalistic language, they are not electable.[118] Even the most well-known text from the 1793 constituent debate on the political rights of women, that is, Guyomar's text, only deals with the right to vote. To justify it, Guyomar appeals to the notion of people's sovereignty and natural rights. The sexual difference would not affect the equality of rights. To deny women's

[115] Louis Joubert, *Essai sur la Force Publique Ou Recherches sur les Bases d'une Recensement Conforme aux Principe de la Justice, de la Liberté, de l'Égalité, de l'Humanité. Rapport Fait à l'Assemblé Permanente de la Section de Beaupaire Ci-Devant des Thermes de Julien* (Portiez de l'Oise Collection, t. 547, n. 7), 11.

[116] Ruault, *Projet de Constitution*, III.I, Article 1 and 51.

[117] Comité de Analyse, *Projet du Comité, Droits politiques*, Article 1. In reality, the text says "men, of both sexes," indicating that humanity, and, therefore also citizenship, would start with men.

[118] Thorillon declared: "*J'ignore si la philosophie républicaine ne doit point en ce moment faire justice de cette espèce d'esclavage, dans lequel nous tenons les femmes et les filles*" (Thorilon, *Idées ou Bases d'un Nouvelle Déclaration*, 589), but he speaks only of the right to vote, while "pour tout le rest, je les rapelle au gouvernement intérieur" (Thorilon, *Idées ou Bases d'un Nouvelle Déclaration*, 589)—that is, he leaves the question of electability or other aspects of women's political rights to future regulation. Lantenhas affirmed "le droit incontestable, qu'elles ont, de voter selon leur conscience, pour le bien commun" (François-Xavier Lanthenas, …*Sur la Constitution. Prononcé dans la Séance du Vendredi 10 Mai 1793* (Archives Nationales, Series AD/XVIIIC/258, n. 3), 14).

claim to the rights inscribed in the Declaration was to violate the principles of cosmopolitanism, equality, and liberty, creating a "formal aristocracy of men":[119]

> the superiority men have over women is as offensive to justice as it is to sovereignty. All or nothing, that is the alternative that the partisans of equality and freedom can and shall propose. In this great cause, compromises are as illusory as they are derisive. In fact, man and woman are independent of each other in the state of nature where meetings are fortuitous.[120]

Guyomar is the only one to directly connect this idea to the social contract. For him, if women cannot participate in political life, they are neither obliged to respect the laws, as they had not agreed with their imposition.[121] But Guyomar expressly rejects women the right to be voted, except for positions that do not include displacement, such as teaching. Using a reasoning that resembles Anonymous N's ban on extending any political rights to women, Guyomar claims that "maybe the day will come when the kingdom of customs will allow for individuals of both sexes to circulate with the same security."[122]

Before starting my next section on the general requirements for citizenship, I should make a brief note on the place of black people in the discussions over citizenship. During the 1793 constituent debates, the issue was simply not raised, neither in the proposals nor during the speeches. There is no explicit proposal to limit the access of black persons to citizenship and we should keep in mind that it had already been extended to all free black persons by the April 4, 1792, decree.[123] The debate over the colonies, presented in the previous chapter, can be read as a background, but that should not distract us from the fact that the color of the skin bears no direct relation to acquiring, or being prohibited from acquiring, citizenship.

The only direct mention is in Guyomar's text: "Either I am gravely mistaken, or a white or black skin no longer characterizes the exclusion

[119] Pierre-Marie-Augustin Guyomar, *Le Partisan de l'Égalité Politique entre les Individus ou Problème Très Important de l'Égalité en Droits et de l'Inégalité en Fait* (AP, t. LXIII (April 29, 1793)), 593.

[120] Guyomar, *Le Partisan de l'Égalité Politique*, 592.

[121] Guyomar, *Le Partisan de l'Égalité Politique*, 592.

[122] Guyomar, *Le Partisan de l'Égalité Politique*, 596.

[123] Baudoin, Collection générale des décrets, v. 28, 99–104.

from the sovereignty of humankind than does the male or female sex."[124] In other words, just as the color of the skin does not define the belonging or exclusion from taking part in sovereignty, neither is sex.[125]

Therefore, and considering the ban on selling oneself or being sold as stated by the Declaration and by a good number of drafts,[126] we can safely assume that the absence of a direct treatment of this matter can be read as the absence of any prohibition.[127]

7.2.2 Delineating Citizenship

Now that I have already presented the special cases of restrictions to citizenship, we can look into the general requirements for its exercise. As a starting point, we have the drafts by the two main committees and the

[124] Guyomar, *Le Partisan de l'Égalité Politique*, 592.

[125] For an excellent text on *des homme et des femmes "de couleur"*, although covering the years before the time period studied in this book, see Florence Gauthier, *L'Aristocratie de l'Épiderme: Le Combat de la Société des Citoyens de Couler, 1789–1791*. Paris: CNRS, 2007.

[126] *Declaration*, Article 18. See also the drafts by the Committee of Public Safety (Comité de Salut Public, *Déclaration des Droits de l'Homme*, Article 18), Constitution Committee (Comité de Constitution, *Projet de Déclaration*, Article 20), and Beffroy de Reigny (Beffroy de Reigny, *La Constitution de la Lune*, 81). Furthermore, we have already seen, in the chapter on external relations, that the preservation of slavery in the colonies depended on the non-application of the rules being developed in European France to its ultramarine territories.

[127] Another class of interdiction appears in a small number of drafts, but I have understood that it does not merit a separate treatment, is that of *célibetaires*. Anonymous E states that those over 30 years of age would lose the right to take part in the primary assemblies (Anonymous E, *Quelques Idées*, Article 13). Borel and Montgilbert remove only the right to hold a public office but do not prevent them from voting (Hyacinthe-Marcelin Borel (du Bez), *Opinion sur la Régénération des Mœurs* (Archives Nationales, Series Le38, n. 689), Article 2; Montgilbert, *Projet des Lois Constitutionnel* XIII.IV, Article 25). Others simply raise their contribution (Lagrange et Dupin, *Projet de Constitution*, Article 96). This last option had already been implemented through a decree from January 13, 1791 (Baudoin, Collection générale des décrets, v. 10, 72–84). The matter has not been examined much in depth, but two main hypotheses seem to be raised: the demographic angle (Anita Fage, "La révolution française et la population," *Population* 8, n. 2 (1953); and male homosexuality (Thierry Pastorello, "La sodomie masculine dans les pamphlets révolutionnaires," *Annales Historiques de la Révolution Française* 361 (July/September 2010)). Both fall outside our preoccupations in this book, reinforcing the choice not to delve into the topic.

final text. All of them present a minimum age of 21 years and a general residence rule of at least one year within the French territory.[128]

For foreigners, the system varies. The Constitution Committee proposed a unified model with the same requirements for those born inside or outside of the French territory. Besides the two conditions listed above, it also required a person to be registered in the civic table of a primary assembly. In the Committee of Public Safety's proposal and in the final version, foreigners had a separate procedure for acquiring French citizenship, with several options: living from their own work; acquiring property in France; marrying a French woman; adopting a child; or taking care of an elderly person. The two conditions listed above were also required. In any case, whether a foreigner or not, the person had to have lived for at least three months in the specific canton where the election was to be held—the required period was extended to six months in the final text of the Constitution.[129]

The most common age for acquiring citizenship in the drafts was 21 years of age.[130] A few drafts keep the minimum age of 25 from the Constitution of 1791.[131] Only Barlow and Le Sueur propose a lower requirement (respectively 20 and 18 years), but, for the latter, that applies only to voting. In order to occupy a public position the minimum age set by Lesueur is 30 years of age.[132]

The strategy of setting a higher minimum age for electability also appears in other texts. The most common proposition is that of 25 years of age, as it appears in the drafts of the Constitution Committee and

[128] *Constitution*, Article 4; Comité de Constitution, *Projet de Constitution*, II, Article 1; Comité de Salut Public, *Projet de Constitution*, III, Article 2.

[129] Comité de Salut Public, *Projet de Constitution*, III, Article 2; *Constitution*, Article 4 and Comité de Salut Public, *Projet de Constitution*, V, Article 2; *Constitution*, Article 11. Both proposals also present another possibility: to acquire French citizenship by an act of the Legislative body—when the person is considered to *avoir bien mérité de l'humanité* (*Constitution*, Article 4).

[130] That is the case of Bacon-Tacon, *Plan Patriotique*, VIII, Article 1; Bourgois, *Plan de Constitution*, I.I, Article 1; Cusset, *Projet de Décret sur la Constitution*, II, Article 1; Daunou, *Essai sur la Constitution*. 2, II.II, Article 1; Dupont, *Bases de la Constitution Française*, II, Article 3; Poultier, *Constitution Populaire*, III, Article 4; Saint-Just, *Projet de Constitution*, I.III, Article 1) and others.

[131] See Barailon (Barailon, *Projet de Constitution*, I, Article 15) and Lagrange and Dupin (Lagrange et Dupin, *Projet de Constitution*, Article 1).

[132] Respectively, Barlow, *Lettre à la Convention Nationale*, 291, and Le Sueur, *Idées*, I.I, Article 4.

Dupont, among others.[133] Dupont also proposes additional requirements for being a member of the Legislature: at least one year of service in a prior public position that is filled by the people's vote.[134] Other restrictions show up in other texts—such as Montgilbert's ban on priests and ministers holding office[135]—but these do not amount to a coherent trend.

I have already highlighted similar arguments in my discussion on voting and how the Legislature was formed, presenting some of the revolutionaries' proposals on improving the quality of votes and of representation. The restrictive approach is also minoritarian here and the notion of the sovereignty of the people prevails, giving them the freedom to choose any citizen they deem worthy of the position.

Two striking differences from the 1791 regime can be highlighted: the minimum time of residence; and the treatment of foreigners. While the previous constitution chose a regime mixing *jus sanguinis* and *jus solis, as* presented above, having a five-year rule for the residence of foreigners, the Constitution of 1793 set a general rule of one year for all persons born outside of France.[136] This reduced period appears in a reasonable number of the drafts in which a fixed period is set.[137]

[133] Other examples are Cusset, *Projet de Décret sur la Constitution*, II, Article 10; Pierre-Toussaint Durand-Maillane, *Suite de l'Examen Critique du Projet de Constitution* (AP, t. LXII (April 17, 1793)), II, Article 10; Lambert, *Plan de Constitution Républicaine*, II, Article 8).

[134] See Comité de Constitution, *Projet de Constitution*, II, Article 9 and Dupont, *Bases de la Constitution Française*, II, Articles 9–10. The provision appears in a limited number of texts. For instance, Lambert raises the minimum age to 30 years for holding a position within the Legislature, the National Convention, *cassation* judge, or member of the higher court (Lambert, *Plan de Constitution Républicaine*, II, Article 8). Thorillon proposes 30 years for judges and 40 years for members of the legislative or executive bodies, arguing that, by then, fortune and knowledge of the vices and virtues would have already been stabilized (Thorilon, *Idées ou Bases d'un Nouvelle Déclaration*, 593). Rouzet presents a similar limitation by demanding the previous exercise of the rights of the citizen for five years before holding any position in delegated offices (Rouzet, *Projet de Constitution Française*, Article 14).

[135] Montgilbert, *Projet des Lois Constitutionnel*, XIV, Article 1.

[136] Only one of the drafts mentioning a minimum age does not actually indicate one. Anonymous O's text limits itself to say "men of a certain age" (Anonymous O [Par Cosmopolite], *Discours Fraternel et Instructions*, Article 17).

[137] See Bacon-Tacon, *Plan Patriotique*, VIII, Article 1; Bourgois, *Plan de Constitution*, I.I, Article 1; Lagrange et Dupin, *Projet de Constitution*, Article 1; Cusset, *Projet de Décret sur la Constitution*, II, Article 1/ Ruault, *Projet de Constitution*, I.II, Article 2; Ragonneau, *Plan d'une Nouvelle Constitution*, II, Article 3; Lambert, *Plan de Constitution Républicaine*, II, Article 1; and Saint-Just, *Projet de Constitution*, I.III, Article 1. In the latter, to be more precise, the minimum period is one year and one day.

Some propose an extension for this period, but they rarely present a significant increase,[138] as the seven-year minimum period of residence required for foreigners by the Constitution of 1795. Although the draft of the Committee of Public Safety and the final text present alternative ways through which a foreigner was able to acquire French citizenship besides the one-year general rule, the issue of foreigners is further detailed in only four proposals: those of Masuyer, Ragonneau, Rouzet, and Ruault.[139] All the remaining cases are comprised within the general rules presented, like that of the Constitution Committee's text proposal for at least one year of residence.[140]

Ragonneau presents a mixed system close to that of the Constitution of 1791, combining criteria related to the parents' nationalities with the place of birth. Ruault has a similar proposition but adds the possibility of acquiring French citizenship by buying an establishment in France—similarly to the Committee of Public Safety's proposal. In both cases, it is also required that the foreigner take a civic oath, present in the Constitution of 1791 but absent from the 1793 final text. The issue is not even raised during the speeches regarding the relevant constitutional section.[141]

Rouzet and Masuyer, however, are more critical of the inclusion of foreigners. Rouzet requires them to exercise a recognized profession and increases the time of conscription to the national guard to three years (two, if both parents were French) and bars them from participating in the primary assemblies or the Legislature. Masuyer set a minimum of two

[138] Boissy d'Anglas and Dupont propose a two-year minimum period (Boissy d'Anglais, *Constitution*, I, Article 1; Dupont, *Bases de la Constitution Française*, II, Article 5), while Barailon opts for three years (Barailon, *Projet de Constitution*, I, Article 15). Only Anonymous E sets a significantly higher minimum period of residence for foreigners: ten years (Anonymous E, *Quelques Idées*, Article 4).

[139] The history of foreigners in the French Revolution goes way beyond the scope of my treatment here. For an extensive treatment, see Sophie Wahnich, *L'Impossible Citoyen. L'Étranger dans le Discours de la Révolution Française* (Paris: Albin Michel, 1997), as well as Godineau's review of her book (Dominique Godineau, review of *L'Impossible Citoyen. L'Étranger dans le Discours de la Révolution Français*, by Sophie Wahnich, *Annales Historiques de la Révolution Française*, 312 (1998)).

[140] Comité de Constitution, *Projet de Constitution*, II, Article 1.

[141] See Ragonneau, *Plan d'une Nouvelle Constitution*, II, Article 3; Ruault, *Projet de Constitution*, I.II, Article 1; and, for the speeches at the National Convention, AP, t. LXVI, 283. This does not mean the idea of an oath was absent from other texts. Palloy, for instance, presents a proposal for a republican oath (Palloy, *Serment Républicain*), but he himself points out that such an oath would not constitute a special requirement to be imposed on foreigners wanting to become French citizens.

years of residence and prevents foreigners from taking part in any assembly prior to 1795 and any public office before 1800.[142]

Rouzet does not justify his restriction, but Masuyer's reasoning may be extended to cover both propositions. On June 24, 1793, Masuyer delivered a speech criticizing the draft submitted by the Committee of Public Safety. On the topic of granting French citizenship to foreigners who adopt a child or take care of the elderly, Masuyer affirmed:

> I believe that they have let themselves go too far with this cosmopolitanism of the day, this puerile philanthropy (that may be good for Plato's Republic, but is false in practice) of granting the rights and the exercise of the rights of a French citizen indistinctly to every foreigner who had resided for one year in France and after three months of residence.[143]

For Masuyer, the access to citizenship should be limited to those that faithfully fulfill their duties in regard to society, including the payment of a minimum contribution, because "every man that exists in a society necessarily has properties, faculties or some kind of industry, even a beggar."[144]

Masuyer's stance highlights two issues. First, his rejection of revolutionary cosmopolitanism. Second, the role of the citizens' duties. The first point was already addressed in the chapter on external relations, but it is interesting to see how the issue reappears and impacts the discussion over citizenship. We can see this by looking at the discussion over a common cause for the loss of French nationality among the proposals: to accept or to acquire the nationality of another country.[145]

Even so, some drafts do not include naturalization in a foreign country as a cause for losing French citizenship. Barlow claims that such a possibility is wrong and represents a remainder of medieval ideas of loyalty

[142] Respectively, Rouzet, *Projet de Constitution Française*, Articles 1 and 9 and Claude-Laurent-Louis Masuyer, *Sur les Conditions Nécessaires Pour Acquérir la Qualité de Citoyen Français* (AP, t. LXVI (June 11, 1793)), 430 and 433.

[143] Masuyer, *Sur les Conditions Nécessaires*, 430.

[144] Masuyer, *Sur les Conditions Nécessaires*, 431.

[145] This motive for being stripped of French nationality is a common feature of the drafts and is also included in the final text (*Constitution*, Article 5). Both committees' texts also provide for this hypothesis (Comité de Constitution, *Projet de Constitution*, II, Article 2; Comité de Salut Public, *Projet de Constitution*, III, Article 2). We can find the same idea, for example, in Boissy d'Anglas (Boissy d'Anglais, *Constitution*, I, Article 3), Bourgois (Bourgois, *Plan de Constitution*, I.I, Article 4), Lambert (Lambert, *Plan de Constitution Républicaine*, II, Article 2), among others.

"founded on the supposition that the fidelity we own to a country is incompatible with the duties we have to another."[146]

Barlow's position highlights the suspicion the revolutionaries, or at least some of them, still have against foreigners, seen as a potential source for destabilization. However, considering the expansive view on granting citizenship, this concern seems to be somewhat mitigated. Greater emphasis is put on preserving republican virtue if we consider the number of proposals that include civic degradation as a cause for having one's citizenship suspended or lost.[147] The same can be said of another cause proposed by the Committee of Public Safety and incorporated in the final text: accepting favors or positions in a non-popular government.[148]

This leads us to the second question raised by our reading of Masuyer's text, that of duties. Apart from Masuyer, only Rouzet seems to directly link the right to vote to the fulfillment of civic duties—more specifically to the non-exercise of citizenship rights for five consecutive years.[149]

The debate over rights and duties had already taken place in 1789 with the defeat of those who demanded a declaration of duties in parallel to the

[146] Barlow, *Lettre à la Convention Nationale*, 292. Saint-Just does not even mention the issue of excluding the right to exercise citizen's rights. He includes only causes for suspension, such as religious ministers and off-duty military personnel (Saint-Just, *Projet de Constitution*, III, Article 4). This seems to indicate that the exclusion was connected to the general requirements for citizenship, like the minimum period of residence (Saint-Just, *Projet de Constitution*, III). Losing the right to exercise the rights of the citizen for being absent appears in some proposals. For instance, in the Constitution Committee's text, the right is lost after leaving France for six years (Comité de Constitution, *Projet de Constitution*, II, Article 6) and voting at the primary assembly is barred after being away from one's residence for one year (Comité de Constitution, *Projet de Constitution*, II, Article 7). Boissy d'Anglas and Bourgois also propose a six-Year interval (Boissy d'Anglais, *Constitution*, I, Article 7; Bourgois, *Plan de Constitution*, I.I, Article 4). Dupont speaks of a six-month residence in a foreign territory (Dupont, *Bases de la Constitution Française*, II, Article 4). Other drafts present similar intervals and measures. Only Cusset has an alternative proposition: requiring a stay inside the French territory equal to the time abroad (Cusset, *Projet de Décret sur la Constitution*, II, Article 8).

[147] For example, Comité de Constitution, *Projet de Constitution*, II, Article 2; Boissy d'Anglais, *Constitution*, I, Article 4; Bourgois, *Plan de Constitution*, I.I, Article 4; Daunou, *Essai sur la Constitution*. 2, II.III, Article 4; Dupont, *Bases de la Constitution Française*, II, Article 4; Durand-Maillane, *Suite de l'Examen Critique*, II, Article 3; Ragonneau, *Plan d'une Nouvelle Constitution*, II, Article 4; Lambert, *Plan de Constitution Républicaine*, II, Article 5; Debry, *Projet de Déclaration*, Article 2).

[148] Respectively, *Constitution*, Article 5 and Comité de Salut Public, *Projet de Constitution*, III, Article 2.

[149] Rouzet, *Projet de Constitution Française*, Article 7.

declaration of rights. Reading the 1793 text, the word "duty" only appears on three occasions: in the preamble; in article 30 of the Declaration, which states that a public office is a duty, not a reward; and article 35 of the same Declaration, which deals with the duty to rebel. Therefore, the only strictly speaking duty of the citizen is the duty to rebel, but I will discuss this in further detail later in this chapter.

This, however, does not mean that the issue was absent from the drafts. Eight proposals include the term "duty" in their titles[150] and seven other texts list the duties of the citizens, albeit not in a very uniform fashion.[151] The term also appears during the debates, but generally not with the same connotation as Masuyer's proposal. Oudot, for example, speaks of a "duty to contribute with what is superfluous for one citizen to the subsistence of fellow citizens for whom work is not enough to provide a livelihood."[152] Only Michel-Edme speaks of duties in the same manner as in the 1789 debates:

> I cannot help but notice the kind of danger that our Declaration of the rights of the citizen poses when separated from the formal recognition of our duties. This danger seems to me to bring fatal consequences to society, and I need to state it. By speaking so loudly of our rights, of the rights of the citizens, many lose themselves in the exaggeration of their ideas and imagine

[150] Anonymous N, *Déclaration des Droits et des Devoirs de l'Homme*; Marc-François Bonguoyd, *Essai d'un Catéchisme sur les Devoirs et les Droits de l'Homme* (Archives Nationales, Series AD/XVIIIC/259, n. 11); Chevret, *Principes de Sociabilité, ou Nouvel Exposé des Droits et des Devoirs de l'Homme et du Citoyen*, Guiot, *Essais sur les Droits* [...] *et sur les Devoirs que l'Exercice de ces Mêmes Droits lui Impose*, two texts by Lanthenas (François-Xavier Lanthenas, *Déclaration des Devoirs de l'Homme, des Principes et Maximes de la Morale Universelle* (Archives Nationales, Series Le38, n. 320; *Motifs de Fair de 10 Août un Jubile Fraternel, une Epoque Solennele de Reconciliation Génerale entre tous les Républicains, en Consacrant une Déclaration des Devoirs de l'Homme, des Principes & Maximes de la Morale Universelle. 1793* (Archives Nationales, Series Le38, n. 404)), Thorillon, *Idées ou Bases d'une Nouvelle Déclaration des Droits de l'Homme, de cette de ses Devoirs* [...], and Wandelaincourt (Antoine-Hubert Wandelaincourt, *Élements de Morale ou Devoirs de l'Homme et du Citoyen, d'après les Seuls Principes de la Raison & de la Conscience* (Archives Nationales, Series AD/XVIIIC/261, n. 20)).

[151] Barailon, *Projet de Constitution*, Barère, *Déclaration du Comité de Salud Public*, Beaulieu, *Nouvelle Rédaction*, Beffroy de Reigny, *La Constitution de la Lune*, Bourgois, *Plan de Constitution*, Coupé, *Idée Simples de Constitution*) and Pénières, *Plan et Projet de Constitution*.

[152] AP, t. LXIII, 120.

> themselves to owe nothing neither to the government nor to society. This exaggeration is the result of the Declaration of rights of 1789.[153]

Michel-Edme's opinion found no resonance in the Convention; his intervention was not even acknowledged during the subsequent debate on April 26, 1793. The topic was briefly mentioned by Raffron du Trouillet almost two months after this session, when the latter proposed the word "duties" to be added to the name of the recently ratified declaration of rights. The sole response comes from Robespierre:

> I remember that the Constituent Assembly, back when it was still worthy of the people, engaged in a three-day combat against the clergy so that the word 'duties' was not included in the Declaration of rights. One is to simply lay down the general principles of the rights of the people, from which their duties naturally derive; but the word 'duty' is not to be added to the declaration.[154]

The 1789 debate is, therefore, not repeated, but only mentioned and rejected.[155] It is important to note that Michel-Edme's criticism is focused precisely on the alleged excessively abstract and open character of the rights included in the Declaration of 1789, a model he wanted to prevent from being repeated in 1793. Abstraction emerges as a rhetorical device for the restriction of natural rights, and not an intrinsic flaw in the French revolutionary philosophy of law, as stated by Douzinas (explained in the first chapter).

Thorillon is the only one to propose a declaration of the duties of man next to the declaration of the rights of men and of the citizen. Even so, it does not appear that his concern is the same as that of Michel-Edme, as Thorillon does not set boundaries for the exercise of rights, but rather incentivizes the love for the Homeland and the observance of the laws.[156]

[153] AP, t. LXIII, 407.

[154] AP, t. LXVII, 108.

[155] For an extended analysis of the 1789 discussion on the topic, see Gauchet, *La Révolution des Droits de l'Homme*, 71 et seq., as well as Chap. 2, Sects. 2.1 and 2.2.1 of this book.

[156] Thorilon, *Idées ou Bases d'un Nouvelle Déclaration*, 597. The only draft that uses a language that is analogous to Michel-Edme is the one by Beffroy de Reigny, in which the revolutionary states that speaking of rights without speaking of duties is to preach anarchy (Beffroy de Reigny, *La Constitution de la Lune*, 39).

In the other proposals in which duties are mentioned, they appear as a way to define the immanent reciprocity of rights. For example, Beaulieu, when discussing the natural duties of the citizen, or Bourgois, when talking about the "reciprocal relations between the citizens and the nation."[157] Others equate duties with respecting the law, as Pénières and Barailon, even though they add other elements to the mix, such as that the citizen is to guide his ideas toward common utility and the love of the Homeland.[158]

As for the drafts which have the word "duties" in their titles, for the most part, they do not go into further details on this topic. Bonguoyd mentions the duty to preserve oneself and the duty to respect one's equals. Chevret has a text titled "new exposition of the rights and duties of man," but the only duties regarding the citizens are to make oneself useful through work, as well as the duties owners have due to their property.[159] In the remaining cases, the alleged duty is explained in even less detail or not at all, as in Guiot.

I can conclude that the concern over duties, understood as the need to set limits to the exercise of rights, was practically non-existent in 1793. Few texts brought up the matter explicitly and, when they did, their definition was connected rather to the consolidation of republican virtues than to the need to prevent the risks of alleged excessively abstract rights. A somewhat long quote by Billaud-Varenne on republicanism explains the heart of the matter:

> Therefore, in every civilized State, the first nuance we discover presents us with two very distinct classes of men: the citizens and the individuals. Citizens are those that, penetrated by social duties, relate everything to the public interest and mobilize their happiness and glory to consolidate the

[157] See Beaulieu, *Nouvelle Rédaction*, Article 20 and Bourgois, *Plan de Constitution*, I.II, Article 1.

[158] See: Pénières, *Plan et Projet de Constitution*, *Devoirs du citoyen*, Articles 1–2; and Barailon, *Projet de Constitution*, III, Articles 2 and 7. Regarding the other two drafts that explicitly deal with duties, Barère and Coupé, their point of view does not seem to differ from the general tone. Barère says that the preservation of freedom depends on submitting oneself to the law (Barailon, *Projet de Constitution*, Article 8) and Coupé states that the social duties are public order, defense, and communal charges (Coupé, *Idée Simples de Constitution*, *Droits de l'homme*, Article 6).

[159] See Bonguoyd, *Essai d'un Catéchisme*, IV and V; and Chevret, *Principes de Sociabilité*, Articles 18 and 15. Chevret also claims that it is the reciprocal love between men that informs reciprocal duties (Chevret, *Principes de Sociabilité*, Article 1), but he does not go any further than that.

> prosperity of their country. This noble devotion only becomes a universal sentiment in those empires where the people and the sovereign make one, which means every regime that guarantees the nation a direct influence over the government [...] Individuals, on the contrary, are those who isolate themselves or rather those who know less about working for the public good than calculating their private profit: in other words, these are the beings that strive to break the equilibrium of equality in order to increase their own personal well-being by usurping that of the others. The State ends up being populated by individuals once an order of things that separates the interest of the government from that of the nation exists.[160]

Citizenship in 1793 is above all citizenship as the actual possibility to exercise rights. It is the reciprocal achievement of freedom and equality through the establishment of a Republic. It is a potency that is open to the exercise of the persons who comprise the French people—which, as we have already seen, allows for restrictions, as in the case of women—and is not a restraint.

Citizenship will manifest itself in action by way of two main institutions: the citizens' assemblies and people's insurrection.

7.3 Assemblies, Natural Law, and Insurrection

If in 1791 the sole role of the primary assemblies was choosing the electors, by 1793 they were seen as one of the central pieces in the exercise of sovereignty by the people. The draft presented by the Committee of Public Safety reads: "the people exercise its sovereignty through the primary assemblies."[161] The expression does not appear in the Constitution Committee draft, nor in the final version, in which, after adopting a suggestion by Albouys during the June 11 session,[162] it is replaced by "the sovereign people is the universality of the French citizens."[163] The Constitution Committee draft limited itself to state that the primary assemblies were the place where the French exercised their rights as

[160] Jacques-Nicolas Billaud-Varenne, *Élements du Républicanisme* (AP, t. LXVII (June 24, 1793)), 224.

[161] Comité de Salut Public, *Projet de Constitution*, IV, Article 1.

[162] AP, t. LXVI, 284.

[163] *Constitution*, Article 7.

citizens.[164] The word "sovereignty" appears only in the preamble of the Committee's draft.

A cursory view of the proposals shows that a large number of texts espouse the notion of the primary assemblies as being the place where sovereignty is exercised by people.[165] In other instances, although the texts do not directly affirm the idea of the manifestation of sovereignty, a number of sovereign acts are attributed to the primary assemblies, such as deliberation over matters of general interest and changing the Legislature.[166] Only Beffroy de Reigny's text proposes the suppression of primary assemblies, as he denounces them as places of intrigue and indecency.[167] Some texts show a degree of distrust toward the assemblies, but do not directly denounce them.[168]

When discussing the Constitution Committee's proposals, Dufriche-Valazé presents a report on the title regarding the primary assemblies in which he compares the original draft by the committee with the proposals received up to that point.[169] More specifically, he deals with the roles to be fulfilled by the assemblies, general rules of elections, and how the assemblies are to deliberate on matters.

In the committee's draft, the role of primary assemblies was basically limited to the votes that were pre-determined by the constitution, and deliberation over matters of general interest.[170] The article on the subject of the latter presented a list of examples—such as ratifying a constitutional amendment and exercising the people's censorship rights—which comprise some roles that had been already assigned to the primary assemblies by the constitution. This provision appears to limit the primary assemblies' activities to the matters already listed by the constitutional text, thus repeating the Constitution of 1791, in which they were dissolved after the constitutionally mandated elections were finished.

[164] Comité de Constitution, *Projet de Constitution*, III.I, Article 1.

[165] Anonymous E, *Quelques Idées*, Article 1; Daunou, *Essai sur la Constitution*.3, I, Thirion, *La Pierre Angulaire*, Article 15; Dupont, *Bases de la Constitution Française*, I, Article 11, Debry, *Projet de Déclaration*, Article 4; and Montgilbert, *Suite de l'Avis au Peuple*, 349.

[166] Respectively: Comité de Constitution, *Projet de Constitution*, III.II, Article 2; Cusset, *Projet de Décret sur la Constitution*, III.I, Article 2 and Ragonneau, *Plan d'une Nouvelle Constitution*, IV, Article 1.

[167] Beffroy de Reigny, *La Constitution de la Lune*, 121.

[168] As Faure, who states it was futile and costly to allow the assemblies to be open for discussions (Faure, *Observations sur le Gouvernement de France*, 281).

[169] AP, t. LXIV: 203–210.

[170] Comité de Constitution, *Projet de Constitution*, III.II, Articles 1 and 2.

This hypothesis is reinforced by the fact that the same section of the text declares any act or deliberation by a primary assembly that does not conform to the constitution to be null and void.[171] Furthermore, the decision on any violation was to be made by the departmental administration, which could, in turn, send the matter to the Executive council or to the Legislature, if it was a matter of local or general interest, respectively. The power of self-oversight of the assemblies was limited to the validity of its votes.[172]

This control over acts by the primary assemblies gives us a glimpse of which notion of sovereignty was at stake. In drafts such as the one presented by the Constitution Committee, we can see the sovereignty of the people being subordinated to governmental authorities. The final call could even be made by the Executive.

In contrast, in the Committee of Public Safety's version and in the final text, the primary assemblies are not subordinated to the people's mandataries or delegates. The Constitution Committee draft did not even establish a procedure for members of the primary assembly to meet by their own initiative. This is pointed out by Dufriche-Valazé, whose report proposes including such possibility.[173] This hierarchical relationship between the primary assemblies and governmental authorities also appears in other texts, such as Faure's draft, in which the revolutionary expressly states that the assemblies should only meet by order of the department, and never upon any request presented by the citizens themselves.[174]

The Committee of Public Safety had suggested that half the members of the assembly should be able to request an extraordinary meeting and the final version is even more inclusive, requiring only a fifth of all citizens with voting rights.[175] But the restrictive approach of the Constitution Committee was also present in other propositions. Daunou and Dupont, for example, give the Legislative body the power of oversight on the acts

[171] Comité de Constitution, *Projet de Constitution*, III.II, Article 3.

[172] Comité de Constitution, *Projet de Constitution*, III.V, Articles 11–13.

[173] AP, LXIV:210.

[174] Faure, *Observations sur le Gouvernement de France*, 280.

[175] Respectively, Comité de Salut Public, *Projet de Constitution*, VI, Article 12 and *Constitution*, Article 34. We can find even broader proposals, like 1/6, proposed by Anonymous E, *Quelques Idées*, Article 17), and 1/20, suggested by Anonymous H, *Vœu d'un Citoyen sur la Nouvelle Constitution*, Article 34).

of the primary assemblies, such as the validity of their elections and the nullity of their acts.[176]

This restrictive tendency also manifests itself in different forms. Boissy d'Anglas states that all deliberation by the primary assemblies should take the form of yes or no questions, although he does recognize the possibility of internal debates. Lambert also adopts the procedure with yes or no questions, furthermore, he forbids any debates, except when the constitution or the Legislature directly authorizes it.[177]

However, the idea of imposing uniform rules of procedure to the assemblies—something equally defended by Pénières, even though he leaves this matter for the next Legislature[178]—is not majoritarian. Calès affirms that the content should not be subordinated to the form, since the primary assemblies are formed by well-intentioned citizens, even if they are not necessarily well-educated.[179]

Salle's interest in laying down constitutional rules on this matter aims to avoid the risk that the following Legislature may impose improper restrictions. He is concerned with guaranteeing the freedom of the assemblies, and not curtailing it. According to Coupé, the people are free and should be allowed to meet whenever they deem appropriate and as they see fit.[180]

This ample freedom of assembly is also highlighted in Edwards' text, in which he states that the primary assembly should be allowed to take into consideration any public matter that is considered relevant. Robespierre, in this text on the representative government, states that the people should be perfectly free in the assemblies. The Constitution should not go beyond

[176] See Daunou, *Essai sur la Constitution*.3, I.II, Article 14 and Dupont, *Bases de la Constitution Française*, III, Article 7. Boissy d'Anglas follows the same trend, as he leaves to the administration—that is, the executive agencies—the analysis of nullities regarding the formal aspects of the assembly's deliberations (Boissy d'Anglais, *Constitution*, Article 12).

[177] Respectively, Boissy d'Anglais, *Constitution*, IV.III, Article 1 and Lambert, *Plan de Constitution Républicaine*, III.V, Articles 1–2). Debry also speaks of limiting the primary assemblies to yes or no questions proposed in advance by the Legislature or the Convention (Debry, *Projet de Constitution*, Article 42). Ragonneau goes along similar lines, limiting the assemblies' affairs to what is expressly determined by the law and prohibiting them from meeting in any situation outside those determined by law (Ragonneau, *Plan d'une Nouvelle Constitution*, V, Article 3).

[178] Pénières, *Plan et Projet de Constitution*, *Des élections*, Article 19.

[179] Calés, *Notes*, II.V, Article 10.

[180] Salle, *Examen Critique de la Constitution*, 393 and Coupé, *Idée Simples de Constitution*, 267.

the general rules that are necessary to prevent intrigues and preserve freedom.[181]

In his declaration of rights, Robespierre formulates this freedom as such: "Each sovereign session, when gathered, should have the right to express its will with complete freedom: it is essentially independent of all established authorities and has the power to regulate its own police and its own deliberations."[182]

The only other declaration of rights with a similar provision is that of Thuriot, in which, after stating the "people's sovereignty can only be exercised by the people themselves when meeting in the primary assemblies," he affirms that:

> As long as the people are gathered in assemblies, no authority has the right to dissolve them, nor to impose any other rules or limits to their deliberation but those prescribed by reason itself, the interest of all and the general will.[183]

There are two clearly distinct notions regarding the content of people's sovereignty and how it is to be exercised. The same issue appears under a different guise when I examined how the right to petition was framed. When discussing the freedom of the primary assemblies, Faure had also included the right to pass on and communicate any matter considered useful or advantageous to all parts of the nation,[184] which seems to include freedom of correspondence and of petition. This position, however, is met with resistance in other drafts.

In many texts dealing directly with this issue, the right to petition is limited to individuals. Beffroy de Reigny, Bourgois, and Cappin use the term "individual petitions." In other cases, the wording is more ambiguous but the limitation seems to be the same. For example, Ruault speaks of individually signed petitions. In other authors, the meaning is even less transparent, and it is not possible to identify if petitions by more than one

[181] Respectively, Edwards, *Idées pour Former une Nouvelle Constitution*, 488, and Robespierre, *Discours sur le Governement Représentatif*, 24.

[182] Maximilien Marie Isidore de Robespierre, *Déclaration* (AP, t. LXIII (April 24, 1793)), Article 25.

[183] Thirion, *La Pierre Angulaire*, Article 15.

[184] Faure, *Observations sur le Gouvernement de France*, 488.

person are in fact prohibited. That is Saint-Just's case since he simply indicates that every man has a right to petition.[185]

However, the requirement of individual signatures does not imply that a petition is individual, only that it cannot be presented by a collective body. Lambert, for example, bans any kind of collective petitioning or a petition by a corporation, and, at the same time, he expressly allows for a petition to be presented by more than one petitioner.[186]

The concern over collective petitions is related to the discussion over representation and sovereignty. Lambert states that, even if a petition is signed by more than one citizen, the petitioners can never identify themselves as representatives of the sovereign.[187]

The right of petition was not a new concern.[188] The first decree on this matter, during the revolutionary period, dated back to December 22, 1789. It regulated primary assemblies and electors, and its article 34 read: "[the primary assemblies] may forward to the Legislative body any petitions and instructions they wish to be made available."[189]

The right to collective petitioning suffered a setback on May 9, 1791. On that day, Le Chapelier presents a report on the right to petition.[190] Presenting the same reasoning that became the foundation of what was to be known as the *Le Chapelier Law*,[191] the rapporteur identifies solely the individual as the unit of political action. The right to petition is reduced to the individual sphere in the final text approved the following day: "it

[185] Respectively, Beffroy de Reigny, *La Constitution de la Lune*, 142; Bourgois, *Plan de Constitution*, II.IV, Article 14; Joseph Cappin, *Projet de Constitution* (AP, t. LXIV (May 6, 1793)), I, Article 25; Ruault, *Projet de Constitution*, II, Article 6; and Saint-Just, *Projet de Constitution*, I.III, Article 5. The Constitution of 1791 also limited this right to individually signed petitions.

[186] Lambert, *Plan de Constitution Républicaine*, VIII.II, Articles 3–4.

[187] Lambert, *Plan de Constitution Républicaine*, VIII.II, Article 4. Daunou's ban on petitions sent by the primary assemblies seems to follow this justification (Daunou, *Essai sur la Constitution*, I.IV, Article 13).

[188] For an interesting analysis on the history of the right to petition, see Yann-Arzel Durelle-Marc, "Nature et Origines du Droit de Pétition," *Revue Administrative* (November 2008).

[189] Baudoin, Collection générale des décrets, v. 1, 243.

[190] AP, t. XXV, 678–682.

[191] *The Le Chapelier Law* was enacted on June 14, 1791, and extinguished corporations and forbade the establishment of any association of artisans or workers in general. It is interesting to note that, as in the more restrictive view presented above, the *Le Chapelier Law* also gave the executive agencies the power to annul communal deliberations that violated the required form (Baudoin, Collection générale des décrets, v. 15, 168–170).

cannot be exercised under a collective name by electoral, judicial, administrative, nor municipal bodies, by sections of the communes, nor by citizens' societies."[192] The decree also restricts the right only to active citizens.

In the first chapter, I have discussed Gauchet's and Habermas' approaches to the subjectification processes during the French Revolution. For both authors, to whom we can add Rosanvallon's reading of the constitution of the autonomous individual as the subject of politics during the event,[193] the French Revolution was characterized by the atomization of subjects. The social body was no longer seen as collective or composed of collectivities, and each individual component was isolated as a segregated unit. The instrument through which that was done, as well as the way through which the atomized being manifested itself, was the vote.

However, if we examine the debates at the National Assembly over the Constitution of 1791 we can see an opposite view was clearly articulated by Pétion de Villeneuve, Robespierre, and Grégoire. Pétion de Villeneuve's criticism was already relatively incorporated in 1793, as it dealt with the restriction of the right to petition solely to active citizens. His argument appeals to natural law. The right to petition is a "right that belongs naturally to every man, even to a foreigner that lives in our society, to petition."[194]

Robespierre goes along similar lines. He qualifies the right to petition as an ancient right, the "imprescriptible right of every man in a society [...] [before] any law had limited it." The only novelty would be establishing any limitations. On the topic of banning non-active citizens from petitioning, Robespierre states that those are the ones that precisely need to have such a right guaranteed, since "the more a man is feeble and unhappy, the more he needs, the more his prayers are necessary to him." According to Robespierre, "the Assembly, as legislators and representatives of the nation, is incompetent to strip from citizens that imprescriptible right of the man and of the citizen." Robespierre extends the same reasoning to collective petitions. It is also a natural right, no matter how the signing collective body names or constitutes itself. There is no usurpation of public authority.[195]

[192] Baudoin, Collection générale des décrets, v. 14, 220.

[193] Rosanvallon, *Le Sacre du Citoyen*, 69–88 and 135–143.

[194] AP, t. XXV, 682ff.

[195] AP, t. XXV, 685. The arguments by Grégoire do not add anything new and merely reinforce the issues already raised by Pétion de Villeneuve and Robespierre (AP, t. XXV, 689–690). [T.N.]: A note on the translation of Robespierre's speech. The word *prayers* is the

The criticisms are not endorsed by the National Assembly. According to Moreau, petitioning "is a political right that should only be exercised by those who are part of society and pay the duties."[196]

In 1793 we still find echoes of these 1789 debates. The project by the Analysis Committee treats the right to petition as the sacred right of every citizen and bars any kind of limitation.[197] Debry highlights the scope of the right to petition. Individuals, private associations, citizens' gatherings established by law, communal and departmental administrations, and any individual or collection of individuals can petition on matters of public safety and alleged abuses suffered because of the law or because of the actions of a public official.[198]

Against the atomizing tendency of a certain revolutionary faction—that Gauchet, Habermas, and, in a lesser degree, Rosanvallon seem to treat as the final word on the political subjects of that time—there is an ample array of actors that, besides individual variations, reaffirm and defend the right of collective subjects to take part in the establishment of government and of the revolutionary solutions. And this not only as insurrected people—as will be discussed later on this chapter—but as political subjects making use of institutional means.

Apart from the right to petition, the same issue can be seen in the debate over popular societies. In the final text, the topic only appears in one article, as part of the chapter on the guarantee of rights, which provides for the right of all French people to organize themselves in popular societies. This rule merely repeats the Committee of Public Safety draft and it is not the object of any speech when this chapter is discussed on June 18, 1793.[199]

The absence of a public debate does not mean an absence of controversy. The proposal by the Constitution Committee did not mention

direct translation of the original French *prières*. The problem is that the latter can be used outside a strictly religious context to denote a strong-willed request or solicitation. As these last two do not carry the weight intended by Robespierre's use of *prières*, I have opted for a direct, but somewhat misleading, translation.

[196] AP, t. XXV, 690.

[197] Comité de Analyse, *Projet du Comité, Droits politiques*, Article 15. Kersaint also states the primary assemblies' right to address the Legislative body (Armand-Guy-Simon Coetnempren Kersaint (Comte), *De la Constitution et du Gouvernement Qui Pourraient Convenir a la République Française* (AP, t. LXII (April 17, 1793)), 424).

[198] Debry, *Projet de Constitution*, Articles 44–45.

[199] Respectively, *Constitution*, Article 22; Comité de Salut Public, *Projet de Constitution*, XXVI, Article 1; and AP, t. LXVI, 677.

popular societies at all. If we examine how the issue was regulated before 1793, we find another dispute between Le Chapelier and Robespierre, now over what was to become the decree of September 29, 1792, that tried to eradicate popular societies from the revolutionary movement, as its preamble indicates:

> no society, club, citizens' association may have a political existence under any form, nor act in any way towards acts of the constituted powers and legal authorities; they cannot, under any pretext, appear under a collective name, either to present petitions or [propose] depurations.[200]

Le Chapelier claims that popular societies necessarily establish "a kind of exclusive privilege of patriotism,"[201] and instigates hatred against non-affiliated societies. In other words, they promote factionalism and thus represent an attack on public order. According to Le Chapelier, only societies focused on education and the enlightenment of its members may be allowed to exist. Their internal activities should not become public or present any collective character in regard to public opinion.

Robespierre's rebuttal is straightforward. Le Chapelier's proposal and justification "speak the language of freedom and of the Constitution to annihilate them both," while popular societies are precisely "those in charge of defending the rights of the nation against the artifices of deceiving men who talk about freedom with praise, only to oppress it with impunity."[202]

Le Chapelier's proposal is repeated in at least three drafts from 1793: Lanthenas, Beffroy de Reigny, and Anonymous H. The first revolutionary, for instance, authorized the creation of citizens' societies only for educational purposes. Anonymous H claimed that societies were important to beat despotism, but entrenching them in the Constitution may transform them into a power able to subjugate any established authorities, and presented an attack on public freedom.[203]

[200] Baudouin, *Collection Générale des Décrets*, v. 19, 832.

[201] AP, XXXI: 617.

[202] AP, XXXI: 619. It is a long debate, but there is no need to go into further detail in order to connect it to the 1793 drafts. The complete version of the discussion can be found in *Archives Parlementaires*, XXXI:616–624.

[203] Respectively, Lantenhas, *Motifs*, 17–18; and Anonymous H, *Vœu d'un Citoyen sur la Nouvelle Constitution*, Article 122. For Beffroy de Reigny, if the corporations were abolished, it would make no sense to allow for the continuation of others. That would not hinder

Goudelin adopts an intermediary position. The constitutional text should guarantee the right of meeting to the primary assemblies, but only tolerate the popular societies—he calls them *tyrans*—without giving them any constitutional basis. He justifies his proposals by referring to the February–March 1793 uprisings.[204]

This restrictive approach is not endorsed by the Convention. As mentioned above, this topic is ratified without much controversy and some drafts expressly stress the importance of popular societies. Bacon-Tacon defines them as "an essential element in our political organization."[205]

The most interesting treatment of the popular societies is that of Boissel. The revolutionary states that "the first law of a revolutionary people is to arm itself, organize itself, act and constantly keep watch."[206] To that end, Boissel proposes a network of popular societies spread all over the Republic. They are to be responsible for keeping watch, receiving complaints, and deliberating in public. They are to replace both the primary and electoral assemblies as the guardians of the sovereignty of the people:

> The popular societies shall debate, communicate and correspond among themselves over the means to preserve, enlighten and perfect the rights of the man and of the citizen, freedom, equality, fraternity, union, peace, also over the means to prevent and fight against evil.[207]

the freedom of assembly, as long as there were no public deliberative sessions since it cannot be allowed that a group of citizens "rival the legitimate authorities in any way" (Beffroy de Reigny, *La Constitution de la Lune*, 195–196). Lambert also seems to adopt a similar stance by claiming that all men have the imprescriptible right to form private societies to talk about public matters, but not to form political groups (Lambert, *Plan de Constitution Républicaine*, VII.II, Articles 6 and 7).

[204] Guillaume-Julien-Pierre Goudelin, *Observations sur Trois Dispositions du Plan de Constitution Présenté par le* Comité de Salut Public (AP, t. LXVII (June 24, 1793)), 318. The February uprisings were an expression of the popular movement against rising prices. Thousands of men and women forced Paris merchants to sell their products at a price set by the insurgents. Rudé explains the incident in detail (George Rudé, "Les Émeutes des 25, 26 Février à Paris: D'après les Procès-Verbaux des Commissaires de Police des Sections Parisiennes," *Annales Historiques de la Révolution Française*, 25, n. 130 (January–March 1953)) and a more general account can be found in Albert Mathiez, *La Vie Chère et le Mouvement Social sous la Terreur* (Paris: Payot, 1973).

[205] Bacon-Tacon, *Examen Impartial des Bases de la Nouvelle Constitution*, 604.

[206] Boissel, *Les Entretiens du Père Gérard*, III.I, Article 1.

[207] Boissel, *Les Entretiens du Père Gérard*, III.I, Article 14. See also, in the same section, Articles 5 and 17.

This is not a mere change of name, from primary assembly to popular society. Whereas the regulation of the former always included some kind of limitation on who could participate or how it could deliberate—even if we recognize that, in practice, these barriers were relative[208]—Boissel establishes no *a priori* limitation. The popular societies would then regulate themselves.

His proposal can be read as the radicalization of the defense of the freedom and autonomy of the primary assemblies without implying a partition of sovereignty. Only the people as a whole is sovereign and responsible for exercising the inseparable, inviolable, and inalienable national republican power.[209]

All oversight of government is done by the popular societies. If the Convention, the Legislative body, or one of its committees go beyond their attributions, the popular societies that were closer to the issue are responsible for starting an investigation.[210]

Boissel's popular societies are the means *par excellence* through which the people's sovereignty is guaranteed and where resistance to oppression occurs. A speech by Mathieu on June 14 on the subject of the primary assemblies illustrates this point. He talks about spontaneous primary assemblies in contrast to the legally predetermined ones:

> it is of the essence of national sovereignty, it is the only way available to the people to resist oppression, and as the committee thought that it should be freed from any kind of hindrance, it did not prescribe it any form.[211]

Both are manifestations of this chapter's epigraph: "a permanent state of public deliberation." Or, in Sade's words, insurrection is "the permanent state of a republic."[212]

Besides insurrection as a permanent state, there is also insurrection as the uprising of the people against immediate oppression. My starting

[208] See Godineau's text on female participation (Godineau, 'Privées par notre sexe').

[209] Boissel, *Les Entretiens du Père Gérard*, IV.I, Articles 3–4.

[210] Boissel, *Les Entretiens du Père Gérard*, IV.I, Article 25. Boissel divides the Legislature into thematic committees, such as Subsistence, Commerce, and Justice (Boissel, *Les Entretiens du Père Gérard*, IV.I, Article 11).

[211] AP, t. LXVI, 529.

[212] Respectively, Merry, *Réflexions Politiques*, 7, and Donatien Alphonse François de Sade, *Français, encore un effort si vous voulez être Républicains* (Paris : *s.l.*, 1796): 216. http://gallica.bnf.fr/ark:/12148/bpt6k42720t.r.

point is the conventional debates over the articles proposed by the Constitution Committee on this subject. The original article read: "Men united in society shall have legal means to resist oppression."[213] The subsequent article stated that these means were to be regulated by the constitution.

The debate over the right to resist oppression is directly linked to how the revolutionaries conceived of natural rights. In 1793, Garnier opened up the debate in the following terms:

> This right is in nature and you eliminate it the day you give it a legal form. I believe that there must be legal paths to resisting the violence exercised against a man, but resistance to oppression exercised by a people is a right that no law can confine. That is what we call the right of insurrection [...] the right of insurrection can never be legal since the law can never modify what is in nature.[214]

The first response to Garnier's speech comes from Salle. The latter affirms that precisely because it is a right originating from nature, legal channels must be established for its exercise. Salle distinguishes between oppression by constituted authorities against the nation and oppression by partial authorities against a citizen. For the latter case, a legal mechanism would always be necessary. The distinction is explained in simpler terms by an unnamed member, who dismisses the relevance of the source of oppression and reframes the distinction as the difference between the oppression against the people as a whole and individual oppression.[215]

The underlying reasoning is expressed by Vergniaud. Resistance to oppression occurs only by "the uprising of all the people against the tyrannical power which desires to oppress it."[216]

A more restrictive alternative is presented by Rabaut-Pomier. People's resistance should be a subsidiary option to a legally prescribed mechanism that showed itself worthless.[217] Regulating—that is, limiting—the right to

[213] Comité de Constitution, *Projet de Constitution* (AP, t. LVIII (February 15, 1793)), Article 31.

[214] AP, t. LXIII, 113.

[215] AP, t. LXIII, 113. The Constitution Committee's original draft did not make such a distinction, since it required legal means to oppose any kind of oppression (Comité de Constitution, *Projet de Constitution*, Article 32, *in fine*).

[216] AP, t. LXIII, 115.

[217] More precisely, a legal expedient "*qui fournira aux citoyens, sans troubler l'ordre de la société, la faculté de conserver la libre jouissance de tous leurs droits*" (AP, t. LXIII, 114).

resist oppression was necessary to secure the social order. In the words of Anonymous J, treating insurrection as a right is to "constitutionalize anarchy and perpetuate disorder."[218]

This restrictive approach is also present in a considerable portion of the drafts. Among the texts which raise this issue directly, the restrictive provision outnumbers the opposite approach, albeit by a slight margin.[219] Some authors are not explicit about the restrictions. For instance, Cusset simply states that the law is to indicate the means of resistance and Anonymous C that opposing tyranny is a right of the society.[220] If we consider that part of the justification for the restrictive view was precisely to recognize the people as a whole as the sole political subject that can legitimately resist, reasonings such as the one presented by the anonymous author fall within the restrictive group.[221]

[218] Anonymous J, *Dernier Crime de J D Lanjuinais. aux Assemblées Primaires, Sur la Constitution Proposée en 1793*, Archives Nationales, Series Lb41, n. 723, 20.

[219] List of restrictive proposals: Anonymous C, Anonymous H, Bancal, Barailon, Barère, Beaulieu, Boissy d'Anglas, Chevret, Cusset, Dupont, Durand-Maillane, Isnard, Robert, and Thorillon. The latter makes use of ambiguous language, as we will see later on, and it would not be implausible to argue for his exclusion from this list. If we include the already mentioned case of the Constitution Committee and Anonymous J, we reach a total of 16 restrictive proposals. Fourteen texts defend the non-regulation of the topic: Bacon-Tacon, Bonnemain, Mont-Réal, Coupé, Daunou, Momoro, Montgilbert, Pepin, Robespierre, Romme, Ruault, Varlet, Analysis Committee, and Committee of Public Safety. I did not include those that simply enunciated the right to insurrection without explicitly dealing with the question of regulation, such as Saint-Just. Even if we consider that this silence could be interpreted as an implicit recognition of the more expansive view—a supposition that seems appropriate in Saint-Just's case—I have opted to provide a more conservative count.

[220] Respectively, Joseph-Marie Cusset, *Projet Relatif aux Droits de l'Homme* (AP, t. LXII (April 17, 1793)), Article 24, and Anonymous C, *Plan d'une Constitution*, II, Article 1.

[221] Chevret, who declares that the resistance against oppression is grounded in national sovereignty, and therefore it belongs to the people as a whole (Chevret, *Principes de Sociabilité*, Article 19). This limitation shows up in other restrictive proposals, such as Barailon (Barailon, *Projet de Constitution*, II, Article 14), whose text requires individuals to complain first through the legal procedures. This limitation that conceives of insurrection as a subsidiary right is common. Anonymous H restricts insurrection to when the recourse to law has proven ineffective (Anonymous H, *Vœu d'un Citoyen sur la Nouvelle Constitution*, Article 35); Barère says resistance is a duty only if the legally available means are feeble (Barère, Bertrand (Barére De Vieuzac), *Déclaration du* Comité de Salut Public (AP, t. LXV (May 29, 1793)), Article 29). Isnard proposes the notion of an insufficient legal guarantee (Isnard, *Déclaration des Droits de l'Homme [et] Projet de Pacte Social*, Article 18) and Robert dispenses with insurrection altogether by stating it would be enough to create a legal institution allowing the people to oppose any action or inaction by the established powers (Robert, *Discours*, 231). In other texts, the language is ambiguous, and the reader is not able to pin-

But we also find two intermediary approaches to the matter: Dupont and Chabot. The former states that people as a whole exercises its sovereignty in a general insurrection (i.e., only the totality of the people is the insurrectional political subject) and that a non-general insurrection should be considered a crime.[222] Chabot defends a similar opinion:

> each citizen has the right to call for an insurrection against the government [...] the section of the people that is closer to those who govern, thus of the oppressors, has the right to seize the opportunity and even to oppose force with force; but it responds for the legitimacy of the insurrection before the majority of the sections and before the representatives of the nation.[223]

This opinion is, at the same time, more or less restrictive. On one hand, it supports the individual call for insurrection. On the other, it submits its legitimacy to the majority of sections (in other words, the whole of the citizens with political rights) or even the members of the Legislature (in a complete inversion of the logic of insurrection, as it is conditioned to the ratification of the constituted powers).

To understand the other side of this debate, we need to go back to the debate of April 22, 1793, at the National Convention. The first answer to the restrictive approach comes from Robespierre. According to the revolutionary, those *conventionnels* were confusing the right to resist oppression with the right to complain. The latter was related to protests against laws deemed worthless. It did not encompass oppression. For these cases, some kind of legal regulation was needed, as already discussed in regard to the right to petition and the role of people in the legislative procedure. When it comes to oppression, it would be ridiculous and impossible to define its convenience.[224]

In his draft of the Declaration, Robespierre is even more emphatic. Robespierre presents five articles on resistance to oppression. The first three are included in the final version of the Declaration of 1793 with no changes:[225]

point the author's intention. Thorillon states that the use of insurrection is not anarchy, and proposes an annual procedure for ratifying the reforms (Thorilon, *Idées ou Bases d'un Nouvelle Déclaration*, 590), which seems to imply that such a procedure would be enough to answer any legitimate popular desires.

[222] See Dupont, *Bases de la Constitution Française*, I, Article 11 and Dupont, *Bases de la Constitution Française*, II, Article 1.

[223] Chabot, *Projet d'Acte Constitutif*, III, Article 1.

[224] AP, t. LXIII, 114.

[225] The only alteration was changing *Lorsque* to *Quand* in Article 35.

Article 33. Resistance to oppression is the consequence of the other rights of man.

Article 34. There is oppression against the social body when a single one of its members is oppressed: there is oppression against each member when the social body is oppressed.

Article 35. When the government violates the rights of the people, insurrection is for the people and for each portion of the people the most sacred of rights and the most indispensable of duties.

As mentioned above, this is the only duty from natural law that is explicitly mentioned in the Declaration of 1793. This attests to the centrality of the right to insurrection in the philosophy of modern natural law of the Year 3 revolutionaries.

Robespierre's draft had two other articles that did not make it to the final text. The first stated that a citizen may revert to his natural right to defend himself when the social guarantees failed.[226] Resistance to oppression and insurrection, therefore, also had an individual dimension—contrary to what Salle, Verginaud, and others defended. The second article was a direct response to those who defended the need to regulate the right of insurrection. In a provision encompassing the individual and collective dimensions of resistance, Robespierre affirmed: "In one case or the other, to subject the resistance to oppression to legal forms is the last refinement of tyranny."[227]

Robespierre's stance is exemplified in the Simoneau case, mentioned above in this chapter. Commenting on the occurrence, he says: "Tranquility is public order, it is social harmony. Can it exist without justice, without freedom, without happiness? Who are those who disturb it? It is the tyrants who violate the rights of the peoples, or the peoples who demand them?"[228]

A few months later, when discussing the connection between commercial freedom and the natural right to insurrection, Robespierre goes back to the same issue:

the people is naturally righteous and peaceful; it is always guided by pure intentions; the malicious cannot provoke it if they do not present it with a reason that is powerful and legitimate in its eyes. They profit from the people's discontent but they did not create it; and when they bring inconsider-

[226] Robespierre, *Déclaration*, Article 30.

[227] Robespierre, *Déclaration*, Article 31.

[228] Maximilien de Robespierre, *Œuvres de Maximilien Robespierre*, 2. V. (Paris : A. Carrel, 1840), 416.

ate change under the pretext of subsistence, it is because the people is inclined to receive this impression because of oppression and misery.[229]

Both passages lead us back to the previously quoted article 30 of Robespierre's Declaration of Rights. Against the abuse of property by some, the people is in the full exercise of its natural right when it responds to this oppression by the use of force.[230]

The right to insurrection is described as a natural right also by Daunou, to whom it is also manifested through the individual right that every man has to resist, and by Pepin: "it is a natural right [...] Such a movement cannot be regulated by law [...] Any legal regulation to insurrection would be, therefore, in my view, an obstacle against its manifestation." The only law of resistance to oppression is that of necessity.[231] The only arbiters, according to Romme, are the oppressed themselves:

> Insurrection is, therefore, a sacred and imprescriptible right that is superior to the law, and such right, in its exercise, knows no other regulator than the virtues of the oppressed themselves, and their generous and sublime devotion to the conservation of public freedom.[232]

Appendix

Historical References for the 1792–1793 Debates

Explanatory Notes

1. Whenever possible, the drafts are cited by article or chapter and article, not by page.

[229] Robespierre in Philippe-Jospeh-Benjamin Buchet and Pierre-Célestin Roux-Lavergne, *Histoire Parlementaire de la Révolution Française*, v. 22 (Paris: Paulin, 1835), 182.

[230] Coupé defends a similar opinion. This draft declares that, as the social economy degenerates the government into violence and oppression, "it is dissolved *de facto* and the insurrection reestablishes the first conventions" (Coupé, *Idée Simples de Constitution*, *Droits de l'homme*, Article 11).

[231] Respectively, Daunou, *Essai sur la Constitution*.1, Article 5; Sylvain Pepin, *Observations sur le Projet Présenté par le* Comité de Constitution (AP, t. LXIII (April 24, 1793)), Article 31; and Varlet, Jean-Françoș, *Projet d'un Mandat Spécial et Impératif aux Mandataires du Peuple à la Convention Nationale* (AP, t. LIIV (December 9, 1792)), Article 22.

[232] Charles-Gilbert Romme, *Exposé des Différents Projets de Déclaration des Droits de l'Homme* (AP, t. LXII (April 17, 1793)), 266.

2. I reference the anonymous texts' authors as "Anonymous A" to "Anonymous U" to more easily reference them in the main text of this book.
3. Since this is an abridged version of the original thesis, not all of the texts listed below are mentioned throughout the main text. I chose to include them in the references for fellow researchers interested in the topic.
4. The final and approved text of the Declaration and Constitution of Year 1 of the Republic are cited as *Declaration* and *Constitution*. The other primary texts are listed below.

Parliamentary Notes, Newspapers, and Legal Texts

Archives parlementaires de 1787 à 1869 (First series). Paris: Paul Dupont, 1867–2021. [cited as "AP," followed by tome number, page, and the document's date, when available].

Baudouin, François-Jean (ed.). *Collection Générale des Décrets Rendus par l'Assemblée Nationale*. Paris: Baudouin, 1789–1795, 67 v. [A digital version is available through: https://collection-baudouin.univ-paris1.fr].

Drafts

Anonymous A. *Cit. ***. Réflexions sur les Bases D'une Constitution…Présentées par Bresson*. Archives Nationales, Series AD/XVIIIC/257, n° 20.

Anonymous C. *Plan d'une Constitution Libre et Heureuse selon Justice, Raison et Sagesse, Trouvé Chez M. Laporte*. Archives Nationales, Series AD/XVIIIC/219, n. 14.

Anonymous E. *Quelques Idées sur une Constitution Populaire pour un Grand État*. AP, t. LXIII (April 24, 1793), 296–302.

Anonymous F. la *France Déchirée par Ses Enfants, Sa Plainte Au Tribunal du Genre Humain et Autres Textes [Imprimé a Londres]*. Archives Nationales, Series AD/XVIIIC/262, n. 19.

Anonymous H. *Vœu d'un Citoyen sur la Nouvelle Constitution Présentée par la Convention [Chez Frouillé, Imprimeur-Librarie, 1793]*. Archives Nationales, Series Lb41, n. 702.

Anonymous J. *Dernier Crime de J D Lanjuinais. aux Assemblées Primaires, sur la Constitution Proposée en 1793.* Archives Nationales, Series Lb41, n. 723.
Anonymous L. le *Vétéran, en Civisme comme en Service Militaire, a ses Concitoyens: Observations Politico-Morales, sur l'Étymologie & la Définition des Mots Patrie, République, Citoyen, Liberté, Égalité, Etc. – par un Propriétaire-Agriculteur, Appellé Philosophe, Philantrope.* Archives Nationales, Series Lb41, n. 2388.
Anonymous M. le *Dix Commandemens du Vrai Républicain.* Archives Nationales, Series Lb41, n. 2393.
Anonymous N. *Déclaration des Droits et des Devoirs de l'Homme [1792–3 ?].* Archives Nationales, Series Lb41, n. 2395.
Anonymous O [Par Cosmopolite]. *Discours Fraternel et Instructions a mês Citoyens pour les Mettre a la Hateur des Républicains: Ouvragre Nouveau sur les Droits de l'Homme et du Citoyen, d'Après des Principes Physiques et Moraux.* Archives Nationales, Series Lb41, n. 2982.
Anonymous U. *Lettre sur la Prétendue République Française, a un Membre de la Prétendue Convention Nationale.* Archives Nationales, Series Lb41, n. 698.
Bacon-Tacon, Pierre Jean Jacques (Comte de). *Plan Patriotique, ou Idée d'une Bonne Constitution Républicaine, en France.* Archives Nationales, Series AD/XVIIIC/262, n. 4.
Bancal, Jean Henri (Bancal des Issarts). *Du Nouvel Ordre Social.* AP, t. LV (December 24, 1792), 409–423.
Barailon, Jean-François. *Projet de Constitution Présenté a la Convetion Nationale.* AP, t. LXVII (June 24, 1793):187–220.
Barère, Bertrand (Barére de Vieuzac). *Déclaration du Comité de Salut Public.* AP, t. LXV (May 29, 1793), 579–580.
Beaulieu, Claude François. *Nouvelle Rédaction de la Déclaration ses Droits et des Deux Premier Titres de la Constitution.* Archives Nationales, Series Lb41, n. 80.
Barlow, Joël. *Lettre a la Convention Nationale sur les Vices de la Constitution de 1791 et sur l'Étendue des Amendements a y Porter, pour Lesquelles cette Convention a Eté Convoquée.* AP, t. LIII (November 7, 1792), 286–297.
Beffroy de Reigny, Louis-Abel. *La Constitution de la Lune, Rêve Politique et Moral, par le Cousin-Jacques.* Archives Nationales, Series Lb41, n. 706.
Billaud-Varenne, Jacques-Nicolas. *Élements du Républicanisme.* AP, t. LXVII (June 24, 1793), 220–246.
Blaviel, Antoine-Innocent. *Opinion.* AP, t. LXII (April 17, 1793), 286–287.

Boissel, François. *Les Entretiens du Père Gérard.* AP, t. LXVI (June 17, 1793), 613–642.

Boissy d'Anglas, François-Antoine (Comte de). *Constitution.* AP, t. LXII (April 17, 1793), 291–315.

Boissy d'Anglas, François-Antoine (Comte de). *Déclaration des Droits de l'Homme et des Principes de Toute Organisation Sociale.* AP, t. LXII (April 17, 1793), 289–291.

Bonguoyd, Marc-François. *Essai d'un Catéchisme sur les Devoirs et les Droits de l'Homme.* Archives Nationales, Series AD/XVIIIC/259, n. 11.

Bonnemain, Antoine-Jean-Thomas. *Instituts Républicains, ou Développement Analytique des Facultés Naturelles, Civiles et Politiques de L'homme.* Archives Nationales, Series Lb41, n. 2385.

Borel, Hyacinthe-Marcelin (du Bez). *Opinion sur la Régénération des Mœurs.* Archives Nationales, Series Le38, n. 689.

Bourgois, Nicolas. *Plan de Constitution Proposée a la République Française.* AP, t. LXIII (April 24, 1793) 259–279.

Calés, Jean-Marie. *Suite des Notes.* AP, t. LXII (April 17, 1793) 325–333.

Cappin [or Capin], Joseph. *Projet de Constitution.* AP, t. LXIV (May 6, 1793) 235–243.

Carnot, Lazare-Nicolas-Marguerite. *Déclaration des Droits de l'Homme.* AP, t. LXII (April 17, 1793) 335–337.

Chabot, François. *Projet d'Acte Constitutif des Français.* AP, t. LXVII (June 24, 1793) 261–266.

Chevret, Jean. *Principes de Sociabilité, ou Nouvel Exposé des Droits et des Devoirs de l'Homme et du Citoyen, Suivies d'Observations Importantes, Relatives aux Propriétés, a la Liberté du Commerce & a la Proportion du Prix des Subsistances avec les Facultés des Citoyens.* Archives Nationales, Series Lb41, n. 2883.

Cloots, Anacharsis. *Bases Constitutionnelles de la République du Genre Humain.* AP, t. LXIII (April 26, 1793) 389–403.

Comité de Analyse. *Projet du Comité de l'Analyse ou Commission des Six.* AP, t. LXII (April 17, 1793) 267–269.

Comité de Constitution. *Projet de Déclaration.* AP, t. LVIII (February 15, 1793) 601.

Comité de Constitution. *Projet de Constitution.* AP, t. LVIII (February 15, 1793) 602–609.

Comité de Salut Public. *Déclaration des Droits de l'Homme.* AP, t. LXVI (June 10, 1793) 259–260.

Comité de Salut Public. *Exposition des Motifs.* AP, t. LXVI (June 10, 1793) 256–259.

Comité de Salut Public. *Projet de Constitution du Peuple Français.* AP, t. LXVI (June 10, 1793) 260–264.

Coupé, Jacques-Marie (Abbé). *Idée Simples de Constitution.* AP, t. LXVII (June 24, 1793) 266–279.

Cusset, Joseph-Marie. *Projet de Décret sur la Constitution.* AP, t. LXIII (April 29, 1793) 599–601.

Daunou, Pierre-Claude-François. *Essai sur la Constitution.* AP, t. LXII (April 17, 1793) 350–370.[233]

Daunou, Pierre-Claude-François. *Vues Rapides sur L'organisation de la République Française.* AP, t. LXII (April 17, 1793) 343–350.

Debry, Jean-Antoine (Baron). *Projet de Déclaration des Droits de l'Homme et de Constitution Française.* AP, t. LXIII (April 24, 1793) 236–238.

Ducastellier, M. *Le Drapeau de l'Indépendance sous lequel les Français Doivent se Réunir à l'Assemblée Conventionnelle.* AP, t. LXIII (April 24, 1793) 241–259.

Dupont [de Bigorre], Pierre Charles François. *Bases de la Constitution Française.* AP, t. LXVII (June 24, 1793) 310–315.

Durand-Maillane, Pierre-Toussaint. *Examen Critique du Projet de Constitution, Présenté a la Convention par son Comité, avec un Ordre Nouveau dans le Plan.* AP, t. LXII (April 17, 1793) 374–388.[234]

Edwards, George. *Idées Pour Former une Nouvelle Constitution, et Pour Assurer la Prospérité et le Bonheur de la France et d'autres Nations* AP, t. LIX (February 28, 1793) 482–498.

Faure, Pierre-Joseph-Denis-Gauillaume. *Observations sur le Gouvernement de France, Relativement Au Plan du Comité de Constitution.* AP, t. LXIII (April 24, 1793) 279–292.

Goudelin, Guillaume-Julien-Pierre. *Observations sur Trois Dispositions du Plan de Constitution Présenté par le Comité de Salut Public.* AP, t. LXVII (June 24, 1793) 317–320.

Guyomar, Pierre-Marie-Augustin. *Le Partisan de L'égalité Politique entre les Individus ou Problème Très Important de l'Égalité en Droits et de l'Inégalité en Fait.* AP, t. LXIII (April 29, 1793) 591–599.

Harmand, Jean-Baptiste. *Préliminaire et Ordre de la Discussion sur la Constitution.* AP, t. LXVII (June 24, 1793) 320.

[233] The document is subdivided as follows: *Projet de Déclaration, Bases de l'Établissement en France, Constitution ou Définition et Distribution des Pouvoirs dans la République Française,* and *Principes de la Législation en France.*

[234] Includes: *Projet de Déclaration*, 379–384; and *Projet de Constitution*, 384–388.

Isnard, Henri-Maximin. *Discours et Présentation.* AP, t. LXIV (May 10, 1793) 417–421.

Jollivet, Jean-Baptiste-Moïse. *Principes Fondamentaux du Régime Social Comparés avec le Plan de Constitution.* AP, t. LXI (April 12, 1793) 644–666.

Joubert, Louis. *Essai sur la Force Publique Ou Recherches sur les Bases d'une Recensement Conforme aux Principe de la Justice, de la Liberté, de l'Égalité, de l'Humanité. Rapport Fait à l'Assemblé Permanente de la Section de Beaupaire Ci-Devant des Thermes de Julien.* Portiez de l'Oise Collection, t. 547, n. 7.

Kersaint, Armand Guy Simon Coetnempren (Comte). *De la Constitution et du Gouvernement Qui Pourraient Convenir a la République Française.* AP, t. LXII (April 17, 1793) 420–429.

Lagrange et Dupin. *Projet de Constitution.* AP, t, LXIV (May 6, 1793) 248–252.

Lambert, Charles. *Plan de Constitution Républicaine, Précédé de Quelques Observations sur Celui que le Comité de Constitution a Présenté a la Convetion les 15 et 16 Février.* AP, t. LXII (April 17, 1793) 434–466.

Lanthenas, François-Xavier. *...Sur la Constitution. Prononcé dans la Séance du Vendredi 10 Mai 1793.* Archives Nationales, Series AD/XVIIIC/258, n. 3.

Lanthenas, François-Xavier. *Déclaration des Devoirs de l'Homme, des Principes et Maximes de la Morale Universelle.* Archives Nationales, Series Le38, n. 320.

Lanthenas, François-Xavier. *Motifs de Fair de 10 Août un Jubile Fraternel, une Epoque Solennele de Reconciliation Génerale entre tous les Républicains, en Consacrant une Déclaration des Devoirs de l'Homme, des Principes & Maximes de la Morale Universelle. 1793.* Archives Nationales, Series Le38, n. 404.

Masuyer, Claude-Laurent-Louis. *Sur les Conditions Nécessaires Pour Acquérir la Qualité de Citoyen Français.* AP, t. LXVI (June 11, 1793) 429–433.

Merry, Robert. *Réflexions Politiques sur la Nouvelle Constitution qui se Prépare en France.* Archives Nationales, Series Lb41, n. 125.

Momoro, Antoine-François. *Déclaration des Droits.* Archives Nationales, Series Lb41, n. 2978.

Mont-Réal, Louis-François. *Projet de Constitution.* AP, t. LX (March 2, 1793) 615–620.

Montgilbert, François-Agnes. *Avis au Peuple sur la Liberté et L'exercice des Droits, Contenu dans un Projet de Constitution Républicaine*. AP, t. LXVII (June 24, 1793) 328–339.

Montgilbert, François-Agnes. *Projet des Lois Constitutionnel*. AP, t. LXVII (June 24, 1793) 352–362.

Montgilbert, François-Agnes. *Suite de l'Avis au Peuple sur la Liberté et L'exercice des Droits, Contenu dans un Projet de Constitution Républicaine*. AP, t. LXVII (June 24, 1793) 339–362.

Oswald, John. *The Government of the People; or, a Sketch of a Constitution For the Univesal Common-Wealth*. Archives Nationales, Series Lb41, n. 2983.

Palloy, Pierre François. *Serment Républicain*. Archives Nationales, Series Lb41, n. 292.A

Pénières, Jean-Agustin. *Plan et Projet de Constitution Pour la République Française*. AP, t. LXII (April 17, 1793) 477–482.

Pepin, Sylvain. *Observations sur le Projet Présenté par le Comité de Constitution*. AP, t. LXIII (April 24, 1793) 292–294.

Poultier, François-Martin [Poultier d'Elmotte]. *Constitution Populaire*. AP, t. LXII (April 17, 1793) 482–492.

Ragonneau. *Plan d'une Nouvelle Constitution*. AP, t. LXIV (May 6, 1793) 252–259.

Robert, Pierre-François-Joseph. *Discours*. AM, t. 16 (April 27, 1793) 230–231.

Robespierre, Maximilien Marie Isidore de. *Déclaration*. AP, t. LXIII (April 24, 1793) 198–200.

Robespierre, Maximilien Marie Isidore de. *Discours sur la Nécessité de Commencer la Discussion du Projet de Constitution Présenté par le Comité des Six, par une Discussion Générale sur les Droits de l'Homme et du Citoyen*. AP, t. LXII (April 15, 1793)157–161.

Robespierre, Maximilien Marie Isidore de. *Discours sur le Gouvernement Représentatif par Maximilien Robespierre Prononcé à la Tribune de l'Assemblée Nationale*. Archives Nationales, Series Le38, n. 245.

Romme, Charles-Gilbert. *Exposé des Différents Projets de Déclaration des Droits de L'homme*. AP, t. LXII (April 17, 1793) 263–266.

Rouzet, Jacques-Marie. *Projet de Constitution Française*. AP, t. LXII (April 17, 1793) 496–513.

Ruault, Alexandre-Jean, *Projet de Constitution de la République Française*. Portiez de l'Oise Collection, t. 176, n. 15.

Rudel, Claude-Antoine. *Discours sur l'Éducation Publique Précédé de Notions Préliminaires sur la Constitution de la République Française.* Archives Nationales, Series AD/XVIIIC/240, n. 15.
Salle, Jean-Baptiste. *Examen Critique de la Constitution.* AP, t. LXVII (June 24, 1793) 391–400.
Saint-Just, Antoine-Louis-Léon de. *Projet de Constitution.* AP, t. LXIII (April 24, 1793) 200–215.
Seconds, Jean-Louis. *De l'Art Social ou des Vrais Principes de la Société Politique.* AP, t. LVI (January 7, 1793) 577–583.
Schreiber, Jacques. *Exposé des Principes sur l'Instruction Publique de la Jeunesse pour Consolider leurs Amês a l'Amour de Dieu, a la Vertu et aux Bonnes Mœurs, et de Former au bon Citoyen de la République du Genre Humain.* Archives Nationales, F/17/1001, n. 83bis.
Thirion, Didier. *La Pierre Angulaire de l'Édifice Constitutionnel.* AP, t. LXVII (June 24, 1793) 403–409.
Thorillon, Antoine-Joseph. *Idées ou Bases d'une Nouvelle Déclaration des Droits de l'Homme, de cette de ses Devoirs et d'une Nouvelle Constitution pour la République Française, où l'on Traite, entre Autres Choses, de la Liberté, de l'Égalité, des Insurrections, de l'éducation Nationale, du Code Civil, et Notamment des Enfants Naturels, de l'Adoption, d'une Seule Substitution Officieuse, de l'Organisation d'un Nouvel Ordre Judiciaire, etc.* AP, t. LXII (April 17, 1793) 582–598.
Varlet, Jean-François. *Déclaration Solennelle des Droits de l'Homme dans l'État Social* http://gallica.bnf.fr/ark:/12148/bpt6k6699x
Wandelaincourt, Antoine-Hubert. *Élements de Morale ou Devoirs de l'Homme et du Citoyen, d'après les Seuls Principes de la Raison & de la Conscience.* Archives Nationales, Series AD/XVIIIC/261, n. 20.
Williams, David. *Observations sur la Dernière Constitution de la France avec des Vues pour la Formation de la Nouvelle Constitution.* AP, t. LXIII (April 29, 1793) 583–591.
Wlriot (de Tours). *Hommage a la Convention d'un Projet de Gouvernement Républicain a Donner a la France.* AP, t. LXII (April 17, 1793) 574–582.

References

Bosc, Yannick. "Robespierre et l'Amour des Lois." *Jus Politicum* 10 (2013).
Bosc, Yannick. "Sur le Principe de Fraternité." Révolution Française.net. Published January 19, 2010. https://revolution-francaise.net/2010/01/19/359-sur-le-principe-de-fraternite.

Buchet, Philippe-Jospeh-Benjamin and Pierre-Célestin Roux-Lavergne. *Histoire Parlementaire de la Révolution Française*, v. 22. Paris: Paulin, 1835.

Durelle-Marc, Yann-Arzel. "Nature et Origines du Droit de Pétition." *Revue Administrative* (November 2008): 47–60.

Fage, Anita. "La Révolution Française et la Population." *Population* 8, n. 2 (1953): 311–338.

Gauchet, Marcel. *La Révolution des Droits de l'Homme*. Paris: Éditions Gallimard, 1989.

Gauthier, Florence. *L'Aristocratie de l'Épiderme: Le Combat de la Société des Citoyens de Couleur, 1789–1791*. Paris: CNRS, 2007.

Gauthier, Florence. *Triomphe et Mort de la Révolution des Droits de l'Homme et du Citoyen*. Paris: Éditions Syllepse, 2014.

Godineau, Dominique. "Privées par Notre Sexe du Droit Honorable de Donner Notre Suffrage" Révolution Française.net. Published March 12, 2008. https://revolution-francaise.net/2008/03/12/215-privees-notre-sexe-droit-honorable-donner-suffrage.

Gouges, Olympe. *Les Droits de la Femme. [Dédies] a la Reine*. Paris : [*N.p.*], 1791. http://gallica.bnf.fr/ark:/12148/bpt6k426138.

Jaume, Lucien. *Les Déclarations des Droits de l'Homme*. Paris: Gm Flammarion, 1989.

Mathiez, Albert. *La Vie Chère et le Mouvement Social Sous la Terreur*, v. 1. Paris: Payot, 1973.

Naudin-Patriat, Françoise (coord.). *La Constitution du 24 Juin 1793: L'Utopie dans le Droit Public Français? (Actes du Colloque de Dijon, 16 et 17 Septembre 1993)*. Dijon: Editions del'Universite de Dijon, 1997.

Ollivier, Nathalie. "Les Projets Constitutionnels de 1793." PhD Diss. Université Panthéon-Assas, 2002.

Pastorello, Thierry. "La Sodomie Masculine dans les Pamphlets Révolutionnaires." *Annales Historiques de la Révolution Française* 361 (July/September 2010): 91–130.

Robespierre, Maximillien de. *Œuvres de Maxililien Robespierre*, v. 2. Paris: A. Carrel, 1840.

Rosanvallon, Pierre. *Le Sacre du Citoyen: Histoire du Suffrage Universel En France*. Paris: Gallimard, 1992.

Rudé, George. "Les Émeutes des 25, 26 Février à Paris: D'après les Procès-Verbaux des Commissaires de Police des Sections Parisiennes." *Annales Historiques de la Révolution Française* 25, n. 130 (January–March 1953): 33–57.

Sade, Donatien Alphonse François (Marquis de). *Français, Encore Un Effort Si Vous Voulez Etre Républicains*. Paris: [*s.l.*], 1796. http://gallica.bnf.fr/ark:/12148/bpt6k42720t.r.

Wahnich, Sophie. "Une Religion Civile des Droits de l'Homme et du Citoyen en 1792." *Républicanismes et Droit Naturel: Des Humanistes aux Révolutions des Droits de l'Homme et du Citoyen*, edited by Marc Belissa,, Yannick Bosc and Florence Gauthier, 71–86. Paris: Kimé, 2009.

CHAPTER 8

Final Remarks

In this book's first chapter, I posed a set of questions and problems regarding how legal scholars and political theorists interpreted and made use of the legal framework of the French Revolution. By analyzing authors from a wide range of political and ideological backgrounds, I have shown how the historiographical references were not that dissimilar, leading to the repetition of a limited number of approaches and conclusions. I can finally reframe those issues through seven main themes: a monolithic interpretation of the French Revolution *versus* the radical popular historiography; Revolution against History; the Revolution's (alleged) abstractionism; atomization and individualism; nationalism and the Nation-State; sovereignty; and the relation between law, right, and legiscentrism. My study of the 1793 proposals and drafts allows us to go back to those questions, now in a new light.

The first issue is reading the short but intense French revolutionary period. Almost all of the interpreters presented here (excluding the school of modern natural law philosophy) looked at the French Revolution as a single block to be interpreted as a whole. In some cases, the interpretation was secondary to the author's main discussion. For example, Rawls claimed that the Declaration of 1789 was pure form deprived of any content, and that it favored libertarianism. But even authors concerned with the place of the French Revolution in a larger context, as in Moyn and Douzinas, seem to adhere to this monolithic approach.

E. Baker, *Human Rights and Humanity's Rights During Year Three of the French Revolution*,
https://doi.org/10.1007/978-3-030-99508-9_8

Following their point of view, the Revolution had a single truth to be extracted from the historical experience. There was a uniform or at least a dominant lesson to be learned. A stabilizing lesson, in sum—be it positive (as in Habermas' idea of an unfinished project of modernity) or negative (partially or as a whole, as expressed respectively by Rawls and Furet).

Even if we could reduce the French Revolution to a sole common denominator, this operation appears to tell us more about the interpreters than about the revolutionary phenomenon. In most cases, the forms of interpretation are connected to the kind of use each author makes of the French Revolution. For instance, Moyn reads the Revolution as a nationalist endeavor that created the Nation-State, as he aims to guard the cosmopolitan aspect of the rights discourse to the human rights movement rising during the 1970s. However, we have seen a clear and strong cosmopolitical trend during the French Revolution—especially in the writings and speeches of Robespierre and Grégoire.

The traditional opposition to the unity of the Revolution was inaugurated by Staël and reframed by Furet through the notion of *dérapage*. The French Revolution had then two stages: a good and positive first period, which was interrupted by popular intrusion leading to the Terror. The hypothesis is not that far removed from the monolithic reading and reduces the Revolution to two separate historical blocks, each one with its own single enunciable truth.

Nevertheless, a reading of the drafts and speeches has shown us that few issues were met with actual unanimity. In fact, the interpretations we have seen in the first chapter fixated on specific documents or moments and extrapolated a totalizing interpretation, such as Habermas' claim that the Declaration and the *Code Napoléon* were part of a continuum favoring freedom against prior laws.

However, instead of simply trying to erase the past, the revolutionaries—or at least a significant part of those analyzed in this book—were concerned precisely with how to guarantee old freedoms against new attempts to restrict them. This was exemplified by the debate between Robespierre and Le Chapelier over popular societies and the collective right to petition. The Prince-Bishopric of Basel's defense of its independence also was expressed as, even if partially, restoring a prior status.

The Napoleonic Code and the Declaration could not have been more opposed to one another. While the former rejects any recourse to natural law,[1] the Declaration—be it the 1789 or 1793 version—created a permanent opening to modern natural law (in itself already a bridge and reappropriation of the past). The past itself was polysemic. We have seen some, albeit few, defenses of a return to monarchical rule as the sole legitimate governmental regime for France. These variations only reinforce a refusal to adhere to a monolithic interpretation while, at the same time, they reiterate the importance of the past and of memory in the constitution and comprehension of revolutionary thought.

Instead of a simple erasure of the past, as mentioned by Konder, or a mere confusion between the old and the new, as defined by Rosanvallon, we have a plethora of different ways of using the past that opens up to a multiplicity of different ways of building that present. Much in the same way the revolutionaries looked at their past, we can look at the French Revolution as a field of significations to be disputed.

Our following topic is that of abstraction as the alleged hallmark of revolutionary thought. We have seen how Douzinas, leaning heavily on Furetian historiography, expounded this thesis. We have also seen how this reading can be traced back to Burke and his opposition between the British and the French experience. The former built their institutions through their own moral and political history. The latter made use of the empty category of the rights of men. This hypothesis was also refined by Gauchet, and he explains how the use of an abstract lexicon serves to concentrate power.

Through the readings presented in this book, we can identify at least two related questions: to what extent we can call the revolutionaries' legal thought abstract; and what role this abstraction has played and how was it used?

In the first chapter, we saw how Konder Comparato had allegedly identified an abstract and generalizing style in the French revolutionary language. This claim was already in Burke, to whom the rights of men constituted the main motor behind revolutionary thought. However, even if we accept the abstraction of the right of men hypothesis, the drafts and proposals we have seen here show the revolutionaries' concerns going beyond the enunciation of general maxims.

[1] In its original text, Article 9 of the *Code* listed equity and natural rights as a recourse to be applied if the law lacked a clear response. This possibility was removed, and it was reiterated that the law was to be the sole available means to solve disputes.

Their objective was not to write down a declaration of rights but to alter social organization and government. The discussions at the Convention were not metaphysical debates but attempts to find the best practical solutions to immediate problems while considering the constitution of something never before seen in French soil: the creation of a Republic.

The challenge tackled by the projects was precisely how to give an institutional and social form to the rights of man. We have seen the diversity of proposals put forward in relation to many and varied problems. One of them was how to organize a justice system that did not favor despotism, in which the debate over civil juries was not over abstract principles of justice but concerned with the possible practical consequences of the different positions. Also, the option for a secret or open ballot was not considered in light of an ideal scenario but given the vicissitudes of the concrete reality of the time.

The sheer volume of drafts is a monument to the revolutionaries' concern with realizing and practicing the principles of law that the declarations and the revolutionary practice presented. The issue of war is an example. We have seen the controversy over who was authorized to declare war and what was its status. The French people's sovereignty and other peoples' sovereignty were the abstract principles at play, but these were not sufficient to provide an answer in a manner that could better regulate warfare. The risk of excessively strengthening the Executive and the use of war to consolidate its power are examples of matters taken into consideration, as well as guaranteeing that people were not to be forced to fight in a conflict they did not agree with. These were not abstract or generalizing concerns.

This reading does not imply that every appeal to concreteness is necessarily positive. During the discussions over female suffrage, Dufriche-Valazé, responsible for writing the report on the topic in the debate over the Constitution Committee's draft, recognized that women's right to vote was in accordance with natural law, but claimed that customs and practices of then-contemporary France prevented its implementation at the time.

If concreteness can lead to restrictive uses of natural rights, so can abstraction. On the second point raised above, Gauchet claims that abstract categories employed by the revolutionaries submitted individual rights to the law, as abstraction strengthened the concentration of power. On the one hand, efforts toward concreteness are already a resistance against this tendency. The revolutionaries' concern with creating a system of oversight and control of governmental activity is a testimony to this preoccupation. The roles and powers assigned to governmental bodies, especially within the justice system and the Executive, were tailored to prevent the risk of malfeasance and abuse of authority.

Even if Gauchet is right in claiming that notions such as "public necessity" provide greater discretionary latitude to the government, the governmental spheres of action are strictly limited under the law. Furthermore, we must not forget that such relative indeterminate notions are common even in contemporary legal documents, and not a relic of old jurisprudence.

The Declaration and its abstract notions were not mere instruments to govern action, but guidelines through which the citizens could read to understand and conceptualize their rights. Abstraction and indetermination were tools to protect rights and not a pretense to enable governmental authoritarianism. Even if we concede that such use did happen in the years following the time frame examined in this book, we should keep in mind that, during the 1793 debates, the role of the apparently purely abstract notion of rights of man was to limit governmental power and legitimize the mobilization of the people.

The case of Basel has also shown us how people can employ apparently abstract French revolutionary principles to affirm their concrete independence. Furthermore, this episode refers to the issue of the revolutionaries' relationship to their past. Instead of trying to erase it, they refer to it precisely as a way to assert their present natural rights through allegedly abstract notions of sovereignty and freedom of the peoples.

This emphasis on abstractionism is a way to reduce the revolutionary experience to a declaration of rights—as Gaucher, Burke, and Douzinas' argument seems to be restricted to the 1789 text—instead of examining the multiplicity of voices and events connected to the discussed issues, even if we only focus on Year 3. At the same time, declaring abstractionism to be the final truth of the French Revolution—thus equating the Declaration of 1789 and the Napoleonic Code, as did Habermas—is to reduce the vastness of the revolutionary experiences to an arbitrarily initial or late event. In both cases, the only way to adhere to such hypotheses is to forget multiplicities and tone down differences.

The abstractionism claim is directly related to my next point: atomization and individualism. In the first chapter, we have examined Habermas' claim that the principle of popular sovereignty was mobilized during the

French Revolution to promote the atomization of society. Rosanvallon, in a similar vein, claimed that, mainly through voting, a de-substantialization took place transforming individuals into mere quantities. The formal legal principle that was implemented to constitute a collectivity led to an individualized version of the citizen and of citizenship in general. Jaume and Douzinas explicitly say that modern natural law is individualistic.

Already in the first chapters, we saw how a direct analysis of the drafts from Year 3 problematized these readings. The notions of sovereignty and independence of the peoples were based on a conception of natural rights marked by reciprocity. Instead of atomization and individualism, Gauthier teaches us how central reciprocity was to the philosophy of modern natural law during the French Revolution. Freedom, equality, and sovereignty can only be thought through these lenses, and not as incommunicable rights of individual beings.

Besides the international sphere, reciprocity also appears during the debate over primary assemblies and popular societies. The assemblies were places for collective debate and construction. We have seen that a movement in favor of limiting their freedom to discuss and act was present, but it did not represent a majoritarian or even an expressive portion of the proposals sent to the Convention. Instead of promoting atomization, the primary assemblies and popular societies were places where collectivities and the collectivity of the nation acted and constituted themselves. The defense of the collective right to petition went along the same lines. Any individualistic tendency was, at least, countered by an equally strong tendency to assert the importance of the collective experience in guiding the Revolution. The uprising of August 1792 that led to the constitution of the National Convention is proof of the importance of collective action in shaping revolutionary politics.

At the same time, reciprocity prevented natural rights from being simply absorbed by a *raison d'état*. An individual dimension and a collective dimension are necessarily intertwined in the philosophy of modern natural law. If the importance of the individual and individual natural rights was recognized, then equally strong recognition of the interdependency of such agents was present. This created a social and political collective fabric that brings everything together (the notions of human family or humankind espoused by Cloots, Robespierre, and Grégoire are examples of this) without preventing the individual from fighting for their individual or collective natural rights.

This double dimension leads us to the question of, in Habermas' words, ethnonationalism and its alleged subordination of popular sovereignty. This was also presented in the first chapters, as expressed by many interpreters, albeit in a variety of forms, such as Habermas, Meister, Baxi, Barreto, Moyn, Douzinas, Burke, Furet, Gauchet, and Edelstein.

Moyn and Douzinas speak of the implementation of an excluding national sovereignty which justified the protection of citizenship but not of humanity. A universalizing discourse that was territorially restricted by the delimitation of an individualized French nation. One consequence of this notion is highlighted by Baxi and Barreto: it justified colonialism and domination as part of the revolutionary endeavor.

Going back to the analyzed drafts, it is hard to find consistent grounds for Habermas' claim that ethnonationalism subordinated popular sovereignty. Firstly, ethnic identification is virtually non-existent. Citizenship criteria (which, in practice, were mixed with the notion of nationality) are open and inclusive. In most cases, when compared to the Constitution of 1791, we have more encompassing criteria. There are some restrictive proposals, but, even considering the identification of foreigners as potential enemies (after all, France was at war with a vast portion of the European continent during the conventional debates), the revolutionaries' stance is one of openness and inclusion.

Protecting citizenship is not the same as protecting the "ethnically" French citizen. Neither is it the protection of the French citizen as a whole. The French revolutionary discourse was cosmopolitical and universal. The discussions on external relations and the sovereignty of the peoples manifested the concern for expanding the guarantees of natural rights beyond the French soil. This may take not exactly democratic forms—as in a war of expansion—but even this cannot be read as a nationalistic restriction to the protection of rights. Cloots' position, as presented in a previous chapter, for instance, shows us a bellicose yet cosmopolitan stance.

In the debates on war and external relations, we have seen a generalized rejection of offensive warfare and the recognition of each people's sovereignty. In this case, the speeches are ambiguous and do not always carry the principles proposed to their ultimate consequences. Even so, we have seen that a good number of drafts asserted the independence and their self-determination of the colonies.

We have seen Robespierre's denunciation of war as a subterfuge employed by the Executive to concentrate power. Against the strengthening of the state apparatus and the emphasis on the State, the idea was to strengthen society and limit governmental power. During the debates, this issue appeared in the mistrust of the role of the Executive in negotiating treaties and declaring war, leading to the idea that the people should have the last word on French external politics.

In Grégoire, we have seen one of the best-articulated stances against exclusionary nationalism. The human race was part of natural law, and so was the recognition of each people's sovereignty. At the same time, we had natural principles and a declaration of universal rights, applicable regardless of time and space. This, however, did not imply the need to impose or to directly transpose the French institutional design, as some revolutionaries proposed. According to Grégoire, universal natural law did not erase differences and local circumstances. The latter would impose changes in the actualization of natural law within each territory.

As in the case of Savoy, the notion of reciprocal sovereignty and liberty among the peoples favored an appropriation of the revolutionary language by other peoples in order to claim their own autonomy. Instead of promoting an exclusionary view of the coming nation, this perspective strengthened the solidarity between the peoples. We have seen how, between the expropriation of neighboring peoples and the discourse on sovereignty, an ambiguous field of meanings was appropriated by different sides of the debate in order to propel particular notions of law and the world, especially in the European context.

On the question of sovereignty, the straightforward approach of Rosanvallon and Eldestein was highlighted. The latter, as discussed in the first chapter, spoke of a physiocratic natural republic or Jacobin natural republicanism, allegedly characterized by a tutelary authority responsible for guaranteeing property rights. According to the author, the state of nature and civil society would be equal and no social contract existed. Again, this position had already been articulated by Burke, to whom the despotism of the monarch was simply replaced by the despotism of the multitude. Furet and Gauchet posed fundamentally the same criticism, albeit in different words. Furet speaks of totalitarianism and Gauchet speaks of the nation taking the place previously occupied by the king.

This first criticism is directly linked to the abstractionism hypothesis. The operation described by Burke, Furet, and Gauchet depends on an abstract notion of Nation and people as disconnected from the concrete citizens. On the contrary, we have seen a nation embodied in sovereignty. The tutelary authority supposed by Eldestein did not exist inside the revolutionary discourse—at least not consistently and coherently. If some discourses favored a concentration of power (Brissot, for example, opposed the convocation of the assemblies after the king's betrayal and proposed to simply maintain the Constitution of 1791), during the Year 3 the prevalent notion is the recognition and expansion of popular freedom. Sade and the idea of insurrection as a natural and everyday corrective to politics is a testimony to this conception of politics.

Some other examples presented in the previous chapters reinforce the inadequacy of Eldestein's thesis. One example is that of the female participation of Olympe de Gouges, for example. According to her, the principle of sovereignty necessarily implied the participation of all, both men and women, in the formation of the political society. Men had no tutelary authority over women. All members of the social and political body should take part in its constitution and concrete fulfillment.

The lack of tutelage repeats itself in other spheres. In the international context, the relationship among peoples was one of reciprocity, as defended by Grégoire, Saint-Just, Robespierre, and Bonnemain. The natural right to sovereignty also applied to the colonies, as preached by Demun, Ruault, Barlow, and Edwards. These proposals not only reinforce the inadequacy of the notion of the Nation-State or nationalism as bases to understand the revolutionary discourse, but they also propose a conception of the sovereignty of the people that is completely different from that presented by Edelstein.

In the first chapter, we have also seen Rosanvallon's more subtle hypothesis. According to the author, 1792 marked a break from the previous period by establishing permanent and direct sovereignty by the people, in which representatives were mere mandataries and the primary assemblies were the real source of legitimacy. Rosanvallon translates this into a dichotomy between the savage sovereignty of the people and sovereignty as organized and made operable through elections. In accordance with his atomization hypothesis, the outcome of the French Revolution was the domestication of popular sovereignty by individualized suffrage.

If we contrast these claims with the source material analyzed in this book, that is, the actual proposals presented to the Convention and the debates over the constitutional text, they do not seem to fit. As we have seen, no defense of any sort of absolute democracy—the revolutionaries' term to what we today would call direct democracy—was found. The primary assemblies' importance is acknowledged and their freedom of assembly and deliberation reiterated, but this did not imply (at least not in the words of those defending such positions) that the Legislature, the

Executive, and the sub-administrations were dispensable. The very idea of representatives as mere mandataries was minoritarian and subject to controversy. An imperative mandate appears in only two drafts, and even the idea of recall is not widely supported.

Even those who defended some of these policies—as Robespierre's speech against the use of the term *representatives* to designate the deputies—do not do so to reject the role and centrality of the Legislative body. This idea of the people as the unique source of legitimacy was actually present in most texts and it coincides with the scheme proposed by Rosanvallon.

If we do see some propositions calling for some kind of intermediary between what the author calls the people's savage sovereignty and the organized sovereignty of the elections, there is also a clear trend that tries to jointly embrace both manifestations as one, albeit under multiple forms. Voting is seen as an act of sovereignty, but those who take the parliamentary mandate do not become embodiments of this sovereignty. To a well-defined group of revolutionaries, sovereignty remains and rests solely with the people. This is the "savage" sovereignty. But the people are no bestial mass. According to Robespierre, the people are wise and the government and its public officials, including the members of the Legislature, are those that are potentially corruptible.

This tension between representation and democracy, as stated in Hérault de Séchelles' introduction to the project for the Committee of Public Safety, was no actual tension. Be it because representation did not occur (the minoritarian position of Robespierre), or because sovereignty stayed in the hands of the people. If representation was faulty, the people had a series of tools available to correct its course.

Among these, we have seen proposals for censorship, grand national juries, guarantors of the constitution, and many other analogous instruments proposed to keep representation, or its effects, in check. The shortening of mandates and the innumerous variations of the law's ratification by the people are other examples seen in the previous chapters that point to the insufficiency of Rosanvallon's dichotomy hypothesis.

We now reach our final point: law, natural rights, and the alleged problem of legiscentrism. I must caution the reader that my analysis still leaves much room for further research, as the precise contours of the natural rights of freedom, equality, and property during the constituent debates of the Year 3 were not discussed as comprehensively as the other topics.

Even considering that a more detailed approach would shed new light on some of these issues, I believe that the path traveled so far gives us enough reason to reject the hypothesis shared by most of the interpreters presented in the first chapter.

This thesis was presented under different guises. Griffin and Baxi spoke of the secularization of natural law, which was replaced by human rights. Natural law was relegated to the position of moral precepts that are independent of law or convention. Rosanvallon seems to, at least partially, subscribe to such a reading. Meister has said something similar when he claims that the (allegedly) political approach of the French Revolution to human rights stood in opposition to the (allegedly) moral stance taken after 1989.

My reading of the proposals and discussions showed, on the contrary, the centrality of natural law to revolutionary thinking. There was no overcoming or mere secularization of natural rights. They are not morphed or reduced to the rights of men. Natural law and natural rights remain operative and central to the revolutionaries' notions of the republic, government, and society. Some do propose the overcoming of natural law with the constitution of civil law, and we have seen the defense of such a position, but the revolutionary *épopée* cannot be reduced to these revolutionaries. This is especially true in regard to Year 3, where the constitution of the rising French Republic cannot be understood without appealing to the revolutionaries' notion or notions of natural law.

Neither does the hypothesis of natural rights purged from morality holds up. On the contrary, we have seen how the revolutionaries' view on natural law had a profoundly moral connotation. This was evident in the idea of the virtue of the republican citizen, in the recognition of the people's natural correctness (in Robespierre), and in the general notion of reciprocity as an intrinsic component to every natural right. Reciprocity necessarily adds a moral dimension to legal reasoning, as the debates over external relations have demonstrated.

Robespierre explicitly connects law and morality, to the point of subordinating the former to the latter. However, this morality is not an abstract value or even a previously well-defined given content, it is rather natural law as practiced by the people. Morality and natural law are inseparable because both are guided by reciprocity. It is important to point out that, from this standpoint, the State or legislators are not the keepers of the one and true morality to be imposed on the people. Sovereignty belongs to the people alone.

That is why the legiscentrism thesis fails. For its proponents, the problem of the political philosophy of law during the French Revolution was about reducing a legal phenomenon to posited law. Only enacted laws would be legitimate to solve conflicts and that would lead to the concentration of power and state authority.

The Year 3 drafts and discussions show us the plethora of opinions on law and rights that are ignored in these readings. If some revolutionaries try to identify in law the whole scope of human action—as Sinety's proposals seemed to do—another stronger trend supports the power of the people and the freedom of each male or female citizen to assert their natural rights.

Law can be seen as the center around which the revolutionary experience revolves. This law, however, is not the enacted legislation, even after being ratified by the people. There is a constant concern in ensuring that the final outcome of legislative activity matches the will of the people. The majority of the propositions on how to institutionalize the Executive, local and regional administrations, the Justice system, and the Legislative body showed similar concerns. They took into consideration how to best guarantee the people's sovereignty and the people and its citizens' freedom of action. There were few direct opponents to an expansive view on the people's sovereignty, such as those who proposed the return of monarchical rule, but even in these cases, a more restrictive view is somewhat attenuated—even if this was due to the social *milieu* more than to personal convictions.

Going beyond the preoccupation with an institutional design that guaranteed and reflected the will of the people, our last chapter has shown that the final word and final act was under the responsibility of the people in action. The Republic as conceived by the revolutionaries was not a republic of representatives and administrators managing an atomized mass, but a living and pulsating experiment in popular engagement.

Index[1]

[1] Note: Page numbers followed by 'n' refer to notes.

E. Baker, *Human Rights and Humanity's Rights During Year Three of the French Revolution*,
https://doi.org/10.1007/978-3-030-99508-9

FSC
www.fsc.org
MIX
Papier | Fördert gute Waldnutzung
FSC® C083411

Kolibri 360 GmbH
Ferdinand-Jühlke-Straße 7
99095 Erfurt, Deutschland
produktsicherheit@kolibri360.de